AGRICULTURAL
FOREIGN
DIRECT INVESTMENT

IN

ZAMBIA

OPPORTUNITIES AND CHALLENGES FOR
POVERTY REDUCTION AND
DEVELOPMENT

刘海方　刘均　主编

赞比亚农业
外国直接投资

（中英双语版）

减贫和发展的机会与挑战

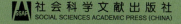

社会科学文献出版社
SOCIAL SCIENCES ACADEMIC PRESS (CHINA)

目 录

前言 ……………………………………………… 梅家永　1

导言　四国学者在赞比亚实验非洲中心主义的调查研究

　　　 ……………………………………………… 刘海方　1

报告一　赞比亚农业外国直接投资：减贫和发展的机会与挑战

　　　 ——趋势与政策概述 …………………………… 朱倩文　1

报告纲要 ……………………………………………… 1

1　介绍 ……………………………………………… 4

2　研究方法 ………………………………………… 6

　2.1　数据 …………………………………………… 6

　2.2　制约 …………………………………………… 8

3　赞比亚的发展和农业环境 ……………………… 10

　3.1　赞比亚与发展 ………………………………… 10

　3.2　赞比亚农业概述 ……………………………… 12

4　赞比亚的投资环境 ……………………………… 17

　4.1　赞比亚近期投资趋势 ………………………… 17

　4.2　贸易和援助 …………………………………… 19

　4.3　投资政策和赞比亚发展署的作用 …………… 22

5　赞比亚农业投资概述 …………………………… 25

5.1 农业承诺投资概述（1998~2012 年） ⋯⋯⋯⋯⋯ 25

5.2 赞比亚农业投资的特点 ⋯⋯⋯⋯⋯⋯⋯⋯⋯ 28

5.3 描述新老农业投资者 ⋯⋯⋯⋯⋯⋯⋯⋯⋯⋯ 31

6 评估赞比亚在农业投资上的努力 ⋯⋯⋯⋯⋯⋯⋯ 39

6.1 农业投资政策 ⋯⋯⋯⋯⋯⋯⋯⋯⋯⋯⋯⋯ 39

6.2 农业投资的监管环境 ⋯⋯⋯⋯⋯⋯⋯⋯⋯⋯ 41

6.3 获取土地的过程 ⋯⋯⋯⋯⋯⋯⋯⋯⋯⋯⋯ 42

6.4 农业与生计 ⋯⋯⋯⋯⋯⋯⋯⋯⋯⋯⋯⋯⋯ 47

7 结论和建议 ⋯⋯⋯⋯⋯⋯⋯⋯⋯⋯⋯⋯⋯⋯ 50

缩略语表 ⋯⋯⋯⋯⋯⋯⋯⋯⋯⋯⋯⋯⋯⋯⋯⋯ 52

附录 ⋯⋯⋯⋯⋯⋯⋯⋯⋯⋯⋯⋯⋯⋯⋯⋯⋯⋯ 54

附录1 赞比亚发展署提供的综合所得税和增值税优惠政策 ⋯⋯ 54

附录2 据赞比亚发展署收到的排名前50名农业投资承诺

（1998~2012 年） ⋯⋯⋯⋯⋯⋯⋯⋯⋯⋯⋯⋯ 55

报告二 印度在赞比亚农业部门的私人投资
      ——案例研究

⋯⋯⋯⋯⋯⋯〔印度〕奥博拉吉多·比斯瓦斯 阿贾伊·杜贝 59

1 研究介绍 ⋯⋯⋯⋯⋯⋯⋯⋯⋯⋯⋯⋯⋯⋯⋯ 59

2 总况 ⋯⋯⋯⋯⋯⋯⋯⋯⋯⋯⋯⋯⋯⋯⋯⋯⋯ 61

2.1 印非关系 ⋯⋯⋯⋯⋯⋯⋯⋯⋯⋯⋯⋯⋯⋯ 61

2.2 印度海外直接投资政策 ⋯⋯⋯⋯⋯⋯⋯⋯⋯ 62

3 印度在非洲农业部门中的存在 ⋯⋯⋯⋯⋯⋯⋯⋯ 70

3.1 发展合作与农业 ⋯⋯⋯⋯⋯⋯⋯⋯⋯⋯⋯ 70

3.2 印度对非农业投资 ⋯⋯⋯⋯⋯⋯⋯⋯⋯⋯ 75

4 印度与赞比亚的互动 ⋯⋯⋯⋯⋯⋯⋯⋯⋯⋯⋯ 81

4.1 赞比亚的农业政策 ⋯⋯⋯⋯⋯⋯⋯⋯⋯⋯ 81

4.2 印度在赞比亚的农业投资 ⋯⋯⋯⋯⋯⋯⋯⋯ 86

4.3 赞比亚实地考察 ⋯⋯⋯⋯⋯⋯⋯⋯⋯⋯⋯ 87

5 印度团队研究成果概述 ……………………………… 90

　5.1 研究方法 …………………………………………… 90

　5.2 赞比亚发展署（ZDA） ……………………………… 94

　5.3 赞比亚土地协会 …………………………………… 96

　5.4 赞比亚实地调研中的观察和发现 ………………… 96

6 在德里的访谈 ……………………………………… 97

　6.1 推动印非经济合作 ………………………………… 97

　6.2 粮食安全之外的事项 ……………………………… 99

　6.3 印度对赞比亚农业的投资 ………………………… 100

　6.4 双边交往的背面 …………………………………… 101

　6.5 印度——关键伙伴 ………………………………… 102

附录 …………………………………………………… 103

　附录1 已有研究及其方法 …………………………… 103

　附录2 受访者列表 …………………………………… 104

　附录3 在德里联系的专家列表 ……………………… 106

　附录4 未联系到的机构 ……………………………… 108

Report One　Agricultural Foreign Direct Investment in Zambia:
Opportunities and Challenges for Poverty Reduction
and Development

An Overview of Trends and Policies ……… *Jessica M. Chu* 109

Executive Summary …………………………………………… 109

1）Introduction ………………………………………… 114

2）Methodology ………………………………………… 116

　A. The Data ……………………………………………… 116

　B. Limitations ………………………………………… 119

3）Zambia's Development and Agricultural Context ……………… 122

　A. Zambia and Development ………………………… 122

B. Profile of Agriculture in Zambia 124

4) Zambia's Investment Environment 131

A. Recent Investment Trends in Zambia 131

B. Trade and Aid 133

C. Investment Policy and the Role of the Zambia Development Agency 137

5) Overview of Agricultural Investments in Zambia 141

A. Overview of Agricultural Investment Pledges (1998–2012) 141

B. Characteristics of Agricultural Investments in Zambia 145

C. Mapping New and Old Agricultural Investors 149

6) Evaluating Agricultural Investment Efforts in Zambia 160

A. Agricultural Investment Policy 160

B. Regulatory Environment for Agricultural Investments 163

C. Processes of Land Acquisitions 165

D. Agriculture and Livelihoods 172

7) Conclusions and Recommendations 177

References 180

A. Data Sets Consulted 180

B. Interviews Conducted 180

C. Investment Policy Documents Analysed 181

D. Works Cited 182

Appendices 188

Abbreviations and Acronyms 194

Report Two   Indian Private Agro-Investments in Zambia

a case study .... *Aparajita Biswas & Ajay Dubey* 196

1   Introduction to the Study 196

Section 2   Overview 199

2.1   India – Africa relations 199

2. 2　Indian FDI Policies ································· 200

Section 3　India in Africa's Agriculture Sector ··············· 210

3. 1　Development Cooperation and Agriculture ··············· 210

3. 2　India's Investment in Agriculture in Africa ··············· 215

Section 4　India – Zambia Engagement ··············· 222

4. 1　Zambian Agriculture policies ··············· 222

4. 2　Indian Agricultural Investments in Zambia ··············· 227

4. 3　Field visit in Zambia ··············· 229

Section 5　Outline of India Team Research Findings ··············· 233

5. 1　Methodology ··············· 233

5. 2　Zambia Development Agency ··············· 237

5. 3　Zambia Land Alliance ··············· 239

5. 4　Observations and Findings from the Field Visit ··············· 240

Section 6　Interviews in Delhi ··············· 241

6. 1　Promoting India – Africa Economic Cooperation ··············· 241

6. 2　Beyond Food Security ··············· 244

6. 3　Indian Investment in Zambian Agriculture ··············· 244

6. 4　The Other Side of the Engagement ··············· 246

6. 5　India, a crucial player ··············· 247

References ··············· 248

Annexure ··············· 255

Annexe 1　What research was done and how ··············· 255

Annexe 2　Log of those who responded ··············· 256

Annexe 3　List of experts contacted in Delhi ··············· 259

Annexe 4　Agencies unreachable ··············· 261

前　言

　　在许多发展中国家,大多数最贫困的人群生活在农村地区,并以务农来维持生计。在这些国家的农业领域进行投资,可以提供显著的发展和消除贫困的机会。因此,在发展中国家和地区的政策制定者的议题中,农业投资与减贫是一个普遍性的话题。

　　不可否认,在全球的外商投资中,对农业领域的投资不到各行业总投资的百分之一。大多数农业国际投资的流向是发展中国家。此外,一些人认为,针对发展中国家的农业领域的外商投资将会增加,推动这一趋势的力量包括新兴经济体不断增长的粮食和肉类消费需求,生物燃料使用的增长,实现能源安全的努力,其他国家对自然资源的消耗(尤其是土地和水资源),浮动的食品价格以及农产品投机。

　　作为一个致力于消除贫困的组织,乐施会关注那些依赖农业为生的人们的生活状况与生计水平,并特别关注投资对此带来的潜在变革性影响。通过我们的合作伙伴的努力,我们已经看到,外来投资能够对农业发展与减贫发挥积极作用,并且为贫困的农民和当地社区带来一系列好处,包括收入增加、技术转让、生产力提高、市场准入权利和就业机会的增加。然而,经验也证明了这样的投资裹挟着风险,包括强制拆迁、夺取当地社区的土地、加剧基于土地和水资源的冲突、扭曲常规的土地所有权制度、加剧当地治理问题的复杂程度、缩小以小农为本的农业政策制定空间,以及迫使市场趋向于追逐集中式一体化的农业企业的利益和交易。

　　为了更好地了解农业领域的外来投资对贫困的影响,2012 年,香港乐施会决定与其他乐施会分支机构和驻地办公室通力协作,支持一系列针对在许多亚非发展中国家的投资的研究。本书包括该系列的两个关于赞比亚的研究报告，赞比亚有超过一半的人口以农业为生。

在本书的第一部分，伦敦大学亚非学院的 Jessica Chu 博士对赞比亚的农业外来直接投资的主要趋势和政策进行了概述。在第二部分，孟买大学的 Aparajita Biswas 教授以印度在赞比亚的农业投资为重点，研究了其性质和可持续性。研究过程中，两位作者都进行了广泛的文献综述、利益相关者分析和权力分析。他们还进行了实地考察，在非洲研究专家，如北京大学的刘海方教授和贾瓦哈拉尔·尼赫鲁大学的 Ajay Dubey 教授，以及来自印度、南非、英国和赞比亚的乐施会工作人员的支持下，采访了广泛的利益相关者，包括政府官员、投资公司、学者和非政府组织。

我们希望本书提出的分析和建议能够促进对关于农业外来投资是不是赞比亚等发展中国家消除贫困和经济发展的动力的深入思考和讨论，并促成有力的政策改善和持续行动，使这些投资成为使人们摆脱贫困的有效动力。

乐施会感谢所有为在赞比亚的研究贡献专业知识的合作伙伴和工作人员。我们特别感谢刘海方教授的支持，是她使这本书的中英文版得以在中国出版。

梅家永

项目和研究经理

乐施会，北京

2016 年 12 月

FOREWORD

In many developing countries, the majority of the poorest people live in rural areas, and depend on agriculture for their livelihoods. In this regard, investment in the agricultural sector of these countries can present significant opportunities for development and poverty eradication. As such, it is a common element in the discussions and discourse of policy makers in the developing world.

Admittedly, the global foreign investment which goes to the sector of agriculture is less than one percent of the total investment in all sectors. Most of this international investment in agriculture, however, is going to developing countries. Additionally, some contend that such foreign investment in developing countries' agricultural sector will increase, with the forces driving that trend including a growing demand for food and meat from emerging economies, increases in bio – fuel initiatives, efforts to meet energy security needs, depletion of natural resources (especially land and water) in other countries, volatile food prices, and agricultural commodity speculation.

As an organisation dedicated to combating poverty, Oxfam Hong Kong is particularly concerned about the potentially transformative impacts of investment on the lives and livelihoods of people tied to and dependent upon the agricultural sector. Through the work of our partner organisations, we have seen that foreign investment could play a positive role in agricultural development and poverty reduction and bring a range of benefits to poor farmers and local communities, including earnings increases, technology transfer, higher productivity, market access and job creation. However, experience has also shown that such investment carries the risk of forced evictions, depriving local communities of their land, increasing conflicts over land and water, distorting customary land tenure systems, compounding local governance issues, reducing the policy space for peasant – oriented agricultural policies and distorting markets towards increasingly concentrated agribusiness interests and trade.

To better understand the poverty impacts of foreign investment in agriculture, Oxfam Hong Kong decided to support a series of research on the investment in a number of developing countries both in Asia and Africa in 2012, in collaboration with other Oxfam affiliates and country teams. This book contains the two research reports of the series about Zambia, where its agricultural sector provides livelihoods to more than half of the population.

In the first part of the book, Dr. Jessica Chu of the School of Oriental and African Studies of the University of London provides an overview of the key trends and policies in the agricultural foreign direct investment in Zambia. In the second part, Professor Aparajita Biswas of the University of Mumbai focuses on the Indian agricultural investment in Zambia and examines its nature and sustainability. To undertake the research, both authors conducted extensive literature review, stakeholders mapping and power analysis. They also made field visits, interviewing a wide range of stakeholders including government officials, investing companies, academics and NGOs, with the support of Africa's experts such as Professor Haifang Liu of the Peking University, and Professor Ajay Dubey of the Jawaharlal Nehru University, as well as Oxfam staff from India, South Africa, the United Kingdom and Zambia.

We hope that the analysis and recommendations presented here will foster thoughtful debate and discussion about the role of agricultural foreign investment as a vehicle for poverty eradication and economic development in developing countries, especially in Zambia, and also lead to strong policies and sustained actions which make the investment an effective force in lifting people out of poverty and deprivation.

Oxfam Hong Kong thanks all partners and staff who contributed their expertise to the research in Zambia. We also extend very special thanks to the support of Professor Haifang Liu, who made possible the publication of the book in China and also in both English and Chinese.

Kevin May

Programme and Research Manager

Oxfam Hong Kong, Beijing

December 2016

导言

四国学者在赞比亚实验非洲中心主义的调查研究

2006 年初《中国对非政策白皮书》的发表、当年 11 月中非峰会以空前的规格和热情氛围隆重举行,让中非关系瞬间成为当代国际关系中最为热门的话题。然而随着中非合作在各个领域的风生水起,种种明显带有偏见、臆测成分的说法开始甚嚣尘上,比如有关中国公司利用双边良好政治关系在非洲进行大规模圈地的说法。与此同时,随着印度紧跟中国,大量增加了在非洲的合作实践,关于印度的圈地传言在国际舆论界也增加起来,只是远没有针对中国的那么剧烈。

向来以扶危救困、匡扶社会公平正义为己任的香港乐施会,在此前后也开始关注中非关系的话题,而且秉承从民众中来的传统,积极在社会大众层面探讨中非关系的影响,并且以“发现优秀实践案例并积极推广”为弧旳。这与北大非洲研究中心所秉承的坚持客观研究并积极进入一线以寻找可以用于启发、引导的正能量来逐渐克服中非关系中的粗糙性的宗旨不谋而合。2012 年,笔者开始了第一次与香港乐施会在非洲问题上的合作,第一个任务是与学生一起,翻译出版了在赞比亚的乐施会支持的调研报告《赞比亚农业发展及其对小农生计的影响》(社会科学文献出版社,2013)。借由报告中翔实的关于赞比亚农业管理框架的分析,很多即将或者已经开启了在赞比亚投资的中国企业获益,它们反馈说,这本书非常及时地为它们的决策提供了指南。中国援助赞比亚农业示范中心的包主任也发来信件,诚恳地肯定我们的工作并且认为报告有利于他们思考下一步示范中心的走向。

受到鼓舞,加上考虑到赞比亚吸引的包括中国投资者在内的各国投资者已经数目可观,由梅家永协调的来自乐施会国际联会多个成员的同事和北大的团队开始探讨把赞比亚作为非洲国家的一个典型案例,详细研究中国农业合作者与以往合作者的异同之处,特别是从非洲人受益的这个角度,从而回应国际上有关中国在非洲大量"圈地"等的舆论,试图通过实证性的研究,来证实或者证伪这些论调。经过多轮方法论研讨和周密的文案准备工作,由梅家永先生、我和研究生宛如组成的调研小组于 2013 年 8 月末出发去赞比亚。之前,家永通过乐施会国际联会其他成员已经协商组成了南非调研小组、印度调研小组和英国小组,此时也都分别到达。整个"多国部队"的组成既有来自各国的多年从事非洲研究的同行,也有乐施会国际联会成员驻这些国家的代表。更难得的是,乐施会在赞比亚的团队提供了办公室,联系了赞比亚方面的种种机构供我们采访调研。

研究非洲的各国同行,本来就有格外的共同的"非洲情结",将非洲的减贫和可持续发展作为衡量的标准,是不言自明的共识。这是典型的非洲中心(Afro – centrism)的视角,即无论哪个国家来合作,都不要自说自话、自我宣传,而是从长时段的非洲发展的历史纵深来看非洲的特殊性,理解其结构性制约、当下的需要和面临的挑战;从方法论上,我们希望通过将纵向的非洲发展和横向的各国以援助、贸易和投资方式与非洲合作的种种实践作为时代大背景,将受到争议的包括中国在内的新兴经济体的对非合作放置在这个大背景上来分析其成败得失,既给予更开阔视角的理解,同时力图客观公允地进行分析,用更加开放的眼光看待在新兴经济体的带动下新一轮对非合作的国际竞争与热潮。

两个多星期的时间里,十几个人共同住在一个小客栈,每天早饭时间交流各自前一天的发现心得,然后各自去调研自己国家的农业投资者;部分时间是大部队集体去赞比亚发展署等部门访谈,大家就在车上继续交流。跟这么多同行一起做实地调查,这在我近二十年的非洲研究中尚属首次,收获大,发现多,且因为要与其他团队不断交流调研方法在实操层面的可行性,探讨出来可能的新路径,非要进行"深入肌理"的交流切磋不可——对于大多数习惯于孤独个体式工作方式的研究者来说绝对是一次打破常规的新鲜经历。相信对每一个队员,这次考察从方法论和工作方式上的创新都是前所未有的;此后是否还有幸因为梅家永带领的乐施会团队的创新精神而促成、凝聚成类似的团队进行集体调研还未可知。我相信,这次经历会让我们中的每个人都会在若干年的时光里慢慢品味那个开着金合欢和蓝樱花的院落,那晚风中的散步,那一个又一个正式和非正式的工作坊,那些工作坊里面说出来和没说出来的许许多多设想和尝试。

伦敦大学亚非学院的朱倩文博士候选人原本就在赞比亚调研,她成为英国团队的主要调研者,而且她也愿意承担整体上将赞比亚的团队调研成果写成一个总报告的任务。中方团队的宛如女士(现在已经毕业,在迪拜从事国际金融工作)承担了报告的翻译工作;印度团队中孟买大学的 Aparajita Biswas 教授和贾瓦哈拉尔·尼赫鲁大学的 Ajay Dubey 教授共同完成了印度在赞比亚农业投资的分报告,硕士生马婕同学完成了该报告的中文翻译工作。我的博士生刘均和我分别承担了中英文报告的编辑、文字加工及校对工作。不能不提的是,香港乐施会的梅家永先生、贾丽杰女士、李梦瑶女士和蔡睿女士先后在推动调研小组的报告撰写和沟通方面发挥了巨大的作用。没有乐施会的同事,没有他们的执着理念和接地气的工作方式的感召,这次调研和调研的成果,都是很难想象的。最后也要特别感谢社科文献出版社高明秀女士的持续督促和对我们的宽容,让这本书得见天日。

中国在赞比亚投资的案例,我们收录在随后的一本论文集里,也即将付梓,欢迎读者继续关注北大非洲研究中心陆续推出的农业研究相关成果。

刘海方

北京大学非洲研究中心

2016 年 12 月

Introduction: Four countries' scholars trying Afro – centric Methodology in Zambia together

The publication of the Whitepaper of China's African Policy in January 2006, and the successful convention of the first China – Africa Summit in Beijing in November with the unprecedented scale in term of the participation and its special enthusiastic atmosphere, have stimulated the close watch to China – Africa relation since then, and it probably have become one of the most popular topics in the whole International relation arena. However, while the cooperation unfolding in more and more directions, lots of misunderstandings and misperceptions also have emerged towards China's intentions in Africa, such as the speculations on China's land grab in Africa. Likewise, as India also geared her diplomacy towards Africa since 2003, and myths on India's presence in Africa also have ascended.

Oxfam Hong Kong(OHK), with its consistent vision of empowering people to create a future that is secure, just, and free from poverty, started to pay attention to the emerging markets' new cooperation with Africa at this point, especially China's engagement; and what makes it different has been the "bottom – up" approach as usual to look at the positive impacts on the disadvantaged people, and to disseminate among the policy level these "good practices" collected from the grass – root level. This approach obviously is very much shared by Peking University Centre for African Studies (PKUCAS), as we also have been insisting on reflecting current China – African Relations based on our first – hand resource collected on the ground and solid objective findings with concrete inspirations and guidance on how to push China – African cooperationfurther while conquering the roughness in the beginning. The collaboration between OHK and PKUCAS started in 2012 from a small project to translate a report already commissioned by Oxfam in Zambia, namely *Assessment of the Status of the Zambia's Agriculture SectorDevelopment Framework and Its Impacts and Contribution to Improvement of Small Scale Producers' Livelihoods*. After publishing both the English and Chinese versions into a book's form in 2014, we received lots of very positive feedbacks from different stakeholders, such as Chinese farms that are planning or have done investment in Zambia, or Mr. Bao, the Director of Chinese Agricultural Demonstration Centre in Lusaka about the utility for him to understand better the way forward of the centre.

With all these encouragement, Oxfam colleagues, coordinated by Mr. Kevin Mei (Jiayong), and my team decided that we should push things further by carrying on deep research on both China and other Emerging powers' involvement in African agriculture sector given the importance of it for African long – term development. Due to what we had known about Zambia's good conditions of carrying on Agriculturaldevelopment and its attractiveness to foreign direct investment, we decided to take Zambia as a pilot country. On one hand, we all as Chinese nationals had a pressure to respond to the discourse of China's land grad in the international media; on the other hand, we hope this empirical research could serve for a thorough understanding of the differences of players from China (and other emerging powers) and those from traditional powers.

After many rounds of discussions of methodologies within and without, our team, composed by Kevin, me myself and my MA student Wan Ru, started our field journey to Zambia in September of 2013. Thanks to Kevin's Oxfam colleagues based in different countries, scholars from India, UK, South Africa also arrived to join us. And Oxfam country team in Zambia had been kindly arranging our accommodations, meetings with relevant organizations, etc. Africanists coming from different countries normally feel close as we all share an "Africa Complex" which may not be understood by experts of other geo – areas. To take poverty alleviation and sustainable development as benchmark is easily a common ground for us and it always goes without saying. This is an obvious Afro—centrism and we agreed among our team members that instead of looking at any particular country's intervention in Zambia's agriculture which might end up in trapping ourselves in boasting this or that country's modality, we would like to look in depth at a group of countries in comparative perspective, and at Zambia's own long—term development to understand its structural problems, its own needs as well as the challenges ahead. Methodologically, this is to provide both a horizontal axis of African own development and a vertical axis of external involvements to understand the three—dimensioned space that Chinese and other emerging players are entering. With this panorama picture we will be able to reach a reasonable evaluation of these new players' approach as well as their contribution, and also a balanced understanding on the new international competition on Africa stimulated by new Emerging markets.

In two weeks' time, members of this "multinational force" lived together in a cozy guesthouse in beautiful Lusaka, using breakfast time to recap the previous day's job and discuss and provoke one another. After this gathering together time, we would take our wheels again to visit more farms from our respective four countries. Otherwise, we would all join Oxfam colleagues to visit stakeholders of Zambia, such as Zambia Development Agency; then it would be time for us to share beautiful scenery as well as the time of chatting together. Personally, I never ever had experience like this to conduct field work with a group of colleagues in Africa, and neither thereafter. It is so unique not only because of the collective but also separate investigation experience, but also the way we carried the job together in a shared temporal as well as geographic space, and methodologically we developed this common approach which requested dialogue "as deep as skin texture" among us and constant reflections on possibilities or impossibilities. For any scholar used to the normal "individually solitary approach", this made a very different experience, which might be not possible if it was not supported by Oxfam with staff members locating different parts of the world and its members helped to identify a group of international colleagues to work together, which was so innovative in term of methods and manners of working. It is also hard to imagine the possibility without Kevin, as coordinator of all different staff members of Oxfam bringing people from four countries and worked so harmoniously and complementarily for two weeks. I also believe for certain that in future all of us would always remember the yard of the guesthouse brimming with fragrance of blue jacaranda and silk trees, together with the beautiful memories of those many formal and informal workshops we had inside and spoken and unspoken ideas and imaginations for African development purpose......

Jessica Chu, candidate of SOAS, London University, back to the time of this research kindly took the job to write the general report on behalf of all the team members; Ms. Wan Ru, helped to translate the English version into Chinese. Prof. Aparajitao Biswas and her colleague Prof. Ajay Dubey from India offered the country case report based on field work carried, and Ms. Ma Jie helped with this part to be translated into Chinese. I, assisted by Mr. Liu Jun, took the liberty to compile the two great reports into one book's form with all the editing, proof-reading and refining work. I have to properly mention some great names that have contributed to the publication of this book finally, Ms. Jia Lijie, Ms. Li Mengyao, Ms. Cai Rui, Kevin from OHK. Without all of your generous help, this is not possible, and specifically, it is your idealist working manner that has constantly pushed us forward to work for people on the ground. Last but not the least, Ms. Gao Mingxiu, from the Social Sciences Academic Press, has been so encouraging and so tolerant to our delay and finally make this book come out.

We decide that we put our findings on China's investment in Zambia in another book that we are editing and hopefully it will also come out soon. Thank you in advance for your critical feedback.

Liu Haifang

报告一

赞比亚农业外国直接投资：减贫和发展的机会与挑战

——趋势与政策概述[*]

朱倩文 著，宛如 译[**]

报告纲要

在撒哈拉以南的非洲地区，外国恢复了对农业的投资兴趣。对农业进行更多投资的需求也许为改善农村贫困人口的生活提供了直接的解决途径，但如果这些投资未能恰当实施，则会造成农村社区无法获得自然资源，从而愈加贫困。

本报告试图考察这种趋势在赞比亚是如何形成的。近年来赞比亚经济发展迅速，其主要原因在于外国投资的增加和当前高企的铜价。然而，这些投资并没有带来贫困的相应减少。因此，本报告首先概述赞比亚农业方面外国直接投资（FDI）的趋势和政策，以此作为理解农业外国直接投资与减贫之间

[*] 本报告受乐施会委托、由朱倩文写作。本文内容纯属本人观点，不代表乐施会立场。感谢乐施会的研究员和同事们对投资者进行的案例研究，尤其感谢刘海方教授和宛如（北京大学）、Aparajita Biswas 教授（孟买大学）、Ajay Dubey 教授（尼赫鲁大学）的帮助，以及他们对中非关系和印非关系提供的见解；同时也感谢乐施会的同事 Mthandazo Ndlovu、Supriya Roychoudhury、Kevin May 和 Robert Nash。很多受访者花时间回答了研究团队的问题，包括问卷调查的对象和赞比亚发展署的代表，在此一并表示感谢。笔者还要感谢乐施会各成员组织对本报告初稿提出的批评和建设性意见，也感谢乐施会对本次研究的支持。

[**] 朱倩文：伦敦大学亚非学院人类学社会学博士，现在是评估和研究咨询师。主要研究撒哈拉以南非洲大规模兴起的土地征用问题，关注其对于农业发展的影响和意义。在赞比亚进行过大规模的实地调研。其他研究志趣还包括农业发展和粮食安全、土地所有权以及发展人类学。宛如：北京大学国际关系学院硕士毕业。

潜在关系的第一步。随着农业投资趋势的不断上升，还有必要对它们带来的后果和如何发展演变进行更详细的研究。

本报告使用了大量文献、对关键利益相关方的采访，以及对赞比亚发展署（ZDA）提供的农业承诺投资额数据的描述性分析。虽然该数据在很多方面还不完整、不确切，但它仍是关于农业投资趋势最全面的信息来源。正因为数据存在一些明显缺陷，因而可以就此对赞比亚发展署提些建议。

虽然农业部门在赞比亚政府的总体经济增长战略中影响越来越大，但农业增长政策与农村减贫战略脱节。提高农业生产率的政策集中于农业的集约化，而其他研究表明：尽管小农看起来拥有大量土地，但实际上在获取土地上面临限制，这就制约了他们收入的增长。然而，虽然农业生活与贫困之间的联系非常清晰，但目前尚未有研究强调农村地区农业商业化与减贫之间的联系。

赞比亚发展署是负责为各个领域吸引国内外投资的主要部门。农业方面，它帮助投资者申请执照和许可证，获取土地；它也是通过投资承诺记录对投资方式进行监督的主体。虽然到目前为止就吸引投资而言，赞比亚的投资政策获得了成功，但它仍存在一些不足之处，尤其是关于调整机制的政策。这些机制确保赞比亚能适应需求的变化，包括更好的监管和数据搜集机制，以及更好的制度运行和咨询机制，以便提供反馈、促进变化。

对赞比亚发展署提供的承诺投资数据进行分析表明，农业投资的确处于上升态势，近些年来承诺投资总额不断增加，还出现了一些相当大型的投资。虽然发展署鼓励优先投资的是高附加值农产品，但仍有很多农业承诺投资进入种植业。然而，这些数据无法为鼓励农业投资促进加工和制造业增长的方式提供深刻作证。最后，虽然编拟了一份初步清单，但发展署对有多少土地通过农业投资进行了转让并不能提供相关信息。

赞比亚发展署的数据为更全面理解赞比亚的农业投资提供了条件。数据表明：投资既吸引大型企业，也吸引中小型企业；既来自传统投资国如英国、津巴布韦和南非等，它们仍主宰着农业投资，也包括新兴经济体（如中国和印度）的新角色参与其中；这些投资沿着复杂的金融链，通过知名的金融渠道国家进行，从而使投资更容易。然而，这些数据也有局限，如缺少关于投资实现率的数据、预计中小型投资也被低估。但是，无论农业投资来自哪里，它们都同样受赞比亚政策的管理和约束。

本报告指出了促进农业投资的政策还存在很多不足。信息的透明度仍是关注的重点，这不仅指政府部门和公司参与研究的意愿，更重要的是信息的可获得性。即使有合作关系，笔者也经常无法获得对投资进行监管和评估的重要信息，例如承诺投资的实现率。环境影响评价始终是投资最重要的公共信息来源，但投资环评尽管是公共档案，实际上仍很难通过公开途径获得。赞比亚发展署和赞比亚环境管理署的能力都必须加强，以便有效监管进入农业领域的投资，包括数据搜集能力及创设了解投资及其影响的管理机制。这些机制应当将新的国际准则，如《国家粮食安全范围内土地、渔业及森林权属责任治理资源准则》，作为参考范本。

至此，对于农业投资带来的影响，笔者可以得出一些初步结论。虽然赞比亚发展署试图建立土地银行和农垦区，吸引农业投资，但投资者们更愿意从自愿的卖家手中购买已有的法定土地。赞比亚土地法为法定土地提供了更多保护，而殖民历史又使适宜农业的商业土地数量众多。虽然到目前为止，获取法定土地也许会减少流离失所的现象，但仍应该对农业投资如何进一步鼓励传统土地转化为法定土地的过程报以同等关注。对农地的需求可能一直持续，但保护小农传统土地产权的机制却非常少。

在雇用和劳工、农业市场和粮食安全等重要领域，投资的作用既可能是积极的，也可能是消极的。然而，却没有一个可以确定农业投资影响的机制，只能通过农业投资模式大致了解其影响。截至目前，通过赞比亚发展署进行的许多农业投资承诺似乎更青睐大规模商业和种植园模式：雇用人数少、融入当地社区程度低。尽管有政策意愿，但到目前为止，在使农业投资模式倾向于穷人方面，发展署作用甚微。为更有效地推动农业投资模式，使之能将小农和农村社区融入其价值链中，农业投资政策必须重新考量。虽然量化评估这些变化还为时尚早，但农村贫困的痼疾和获得工资收入的渴望（经常化为绝望）为更多农村地区的农业投资提供了廉价劳动力。

此外，还应鼓励加工业和制造业等部门在农村的扩展，而不是将其局限于城市。最后，对这些农业投资企业雇用当地居民和妇女的情况也应有更深入的了解。无论是通过工人培训项目还是针对经济上能承受的技术开放市场，农业投资都必须转移技能技术，农业产量低和多元化不足仍是粮食安全的重重障碍。也有必要关注农业投资对家庭生产的小农带来影响，包括作物选择、家庭消费、当地食物价格和家庭收入支出等方面。

本报告希望研究农业外国直接投资对赞比亚的最贫困、最脆弱的人群有哪些正面和负面的影响。赞比亚还有土地未充分用于农业，在鼓励开发土地更好地用于农业的同时，也应加深对小农为何及如何面临着土地获取限制问题的理解。

为让外国农业投资能够对小农的减贫有所裨益，必须考虑以下问题：

— 投资会恶化土地权属压力吗？

— 投资会为当地社区带来持续和有意义的就业机会吗？

— 投资对于农业价值链的上下游发展有帮助吗？

要回答以上问题，赞比亚政府必须采取措施改善对农业投资的监督和管理。

1 介绍

人们日益关注外国对撒哈拉以南非洲的农业和土地收购投资的上升，这些关注大部分集中于农业投资对东道国潜在的不利影响上。这些投资常被称为"抢地"，被认为是外国公司和政府以损害农村贫民利益为代价攫取利益。然而，越来越多的人也意识到农业投资这种趋势的复杂性和多样性，农业领域的外国直接投资（FDI）能为经济发展提供所需的资本和增长，能促进减贫吗？

为着手处理这个问题，必须先研究农业领域的外国直接投资牵涉哪些方面，本报告以赞比亚为例进行研究。赞比亚位于撒哈拉以南非洲的"几内亚大草原"，近年来因高收益"钱景"①、丰富的土地资源、稳定的政府和支持

---

① 收益差额（yield gap）指农业潜在收益和已实现收益之间的差额。Deininger and Byerlee（2011）。此处译为收益"钱景"。——译者注

投资的政策环境，不断吸引着全世界投资者的关注。的确，赞比亚农业领域出现了一股投资"狂热"。为了解农业外国直接投资在赞比亚的影响，本文试图回答两个问题：投资者是谁，指导投资的程序是什么。农业投资对发展经济的贡献与减少贫困的贡献之间有一个微妙界限，它往往源于管理过程和监管机制。因此，能否发挥农业投资的潜力，使之既促进经济发展又减少贫困，取决于赞比亚处理对其农业部门和土地日渐增长的兴趣的能力。

两个重要趋势构成本研究的动因：其一，尤其相比采矿业，农业在赞比亚 GDP 和 FDI 中的份额虽然很小，但它正发挥着日益重要的作用；其二，尽管英国和南非等传统投资国在农业投资中仍发挥很大的作用，但诸如中国、印度等新兴经济体的作用正日渐突出，显示了新角色在赞比亚农业中发挥的额外作用，因此有必要进行深入的研究。

表 1　农业承诺投资总额前十名国家排名（1998～2012 年）

单位：美元

国　　家	承诺投资数	承诺投资总额	平均承诺投资额
英　　国	64	596249513	9316399
南　　非	50	273639189	5472784
马　拉　维	2	113319000	56659500
印　　度	21	112061375	5336256
赞　比　亚	32	107188553	3349643
津巴布韦	70	99445907	1420656
毛里求斯	5	43427000	8685400
新　加　坡	1	35000000	35000000
中　　国	34	33301378	979452
爱　尔　兰	3	26761392	8920464

资料来源：赞比亚发展署（2013）。

其他对赞比亚农业投资增长的研究要么是研究特定案例[①]，要么是追踪投

---

① 例如：行动援助（2013）；世界粮农组织（2013a）；Mujenja and Wonani（2013）。

资的全过程。① 这些问题虽在文中也有所涉及，但本报告致力于对赞比亚主要的投资服务部门——赞比亚发展署所提供数据显示的趋势进行更深入的观察，集中从农业投资政策的功能和效率的角度对这些过程进行探索。尽管此方法也有局限性（将在后文方法论部分进行详细阐述），但笔者希望通过对投资者兴趣和行为趋势的研究，对研究赞比亚农业外国投资的文献有所贡献。此外，对发展署提供的数据所进行的评估也为衡量其行为和政策提供了方法上的借鉴。

希望本文中的信息有助于更好地推动农业投资趋势的政策导向，文中的研究成果有助于公民社会更好地参与到赞比亚政府对农业投资的推动中去，并借此寻找理解农业投资影响、评估农业投资能否促进减贫的方法。

2 研究方法

2.1 数据

本文回顾了大量的文献，采访了许多关键利益相关者，而讨论的主体仍有赖于对赞比亚发展署所提供农业承诺投资者数据的描述性分析。根据研究需要，农业投资指来自外国、在农业生产部门的直接投资②。然而，对"投资者"本文主要使用发展署的界定。作为促进投资的主要机构（包括内外资），发展署签发投资许可证，因此可以了解投资的动机（将在第四部分进行详细介绍）。发展署维持着一个数据库，投资许可证按部门存放在其中，它为本文的承诺投资者列表提供了基础。因此，文中的农业投资者，指发展署农业生产部门数据库中列出的承诺投资者。

本文回顾的文献不仅有赞比亚外国直接投资的二手资料，而且有赞比亚涉及投资的政策性文件。同时，还有对关键知情人的访谈作为补充。③ 在2012年7月、2013年7月和9月进行了实地调研和采访，对一些关键利益相

---

① 例如：世界粮农组织（2013b）；German et al.（2013）；Nolte（2014）。
② 对于外国直接投资的定义，可参见联合国工业发展组织（UNIDO）对其的定义"一国居民实体获得另一国企业长时间的投资"，或者更加明确的定义，即外来投资者拥有普通股的至少10%或者等值的资产（UNIDO, 2008：3）。
③ 具体访谈人名单和记录参见附录。

关者进行了半结构化的访谈，包括赞比亚发展署、环境管理署、公民社会组织和非政府组织的代表，以及专家学者。采访在被访者的办公室进行，每次大约1个小时。半结构化访谈涉及对农业外国投资范围的了解，尤其是关键投资者的信息，以及投资引起的顾虑和影响。笔者注意到：无论是政府机关还是其他公民社会组织，对农业外国直接投资进行的基层研究都非常少。

获取外国直接投资和投资者的数据仍是本研究最大的瓶颈。赞比亚虽号称14个可获得全国土地投资清单的国家之一，但以往研究表明，资料的可靠性有待商榷。[①] 由于外国直接投资的数据既不容易获得，有时又不可靠，因此本文结合文献回顾和采访所得，主要对数据所显示的趋势进行描述性分析。

赞比亚不断变化的研究环境是本报告的另一个制约因素。随着时间的推移，政府机关与研究人员接触并分享信息的限制有了显著变化，原因在于政府机关努力对众多雇员提供的信息进行更好的引导和掌控。政府努力确保信息可以被权威机关获得和引导，从而降低不专业和腐败的风险，这是它努力的一部分。然而，该措施的结果是使研究必然被官僚机制严重阻碍，主要是等待官方批准时经常遇到拖延。但总体来说，政府机构尤其是赞比亚发展署，表现出了乐意帮助研究的态度。

用于分析农业外国直接投资的数据由赞比亚发展署研究部提供，记录了获得发展署颁发农业投资许可证的承诺投资的层次。该数据包括注册公司名称（如非注册公司则记录个人姓名）、承诺投资的年份、投资者申报的国籍和承诺投资的规模（以美元计）。公司的情况（如私有还是公有）及其他注册或附属公司的信息均不得而知。[②] 但是如果条件允许，笔者会将公司的信息同专利与公司登记署（PACRA）和赞比亚环境管理署提供的信息进行比对，并与公司公布的信息进行核实。

研究集中于1998～2012年的15年间，因为本研究希望重点关注近期农业投资的变化。重要的是，该时段包括2006～2008年，此间全球发生了许多重

---

① Deininger and Byerlee (2011).

② 虽然投资的细节，如农场的大小和公司的情况，无法从赞比亚发展署的数据集中获得，但是偶尔专利与公司登记署（PACRA）的记录中会有使用与发展署登记名称相同的公司的数据。

大事件，如粮食危机、全球金融危机和能源危机，以及赞比亚发展署2006年合并后投资政策的调整。[①]

文中其他数据来自联合国相关机构（联合国粮农组织以及联合国贸发会议）的公开数据。虽然要确保外国直接投资数据保持前后一致很难，但笔者在数据使用时力求做到这一点。数据的前后不一致表明它在可获得性和透明度方面都存在着很大问题，这也是FDI所涉及的明显问题，但已超过本文讨论范围。

2.2 制约

本文存在一些制约，包括前文提及的外国直接投资数据的获取。使用赞比亚发展署的数据是为帮助更好地理解农业外国直接投资，但这些数据本身也有着其他问题，后文将进行讨论。虽然公众可通过申请获得农业承诺投资的数据，但是这些数据存在前后不一致、更新慢和更正不及时等问题。发展署收集的数据来自投资者自己上报的调查问卷，但迄今为止它对数据的可靠性进行监督和评估的能力很有限。因此，可能因上报错误或计算方式的变化，数据常有错误。

另外，通过赞比亚发展署进行投资的投资者比例和已知承诺投资项目的实现率均不得而知。发展署相信，通过它的激励计划，许多投资者的确会通过发展署进行投资，虽然他们获得投资许可证后不一定继续和它保持联系。因此，发展署提供的数字应作为一种趋势指标，而非精确的量化指标使用。

表2 FDI 流入与农业承诺投资总额对比（1998～2012年）

单位：美元

年　份	FDI 流入	ZDA 公布的承诺投资总额
1998	238000000	—
1999	86000000	—
2000	121700000	82095718

---

① 该行为对 FDI 投资额度的影响将在后文中进行讨论。

续表

年　份	FDI 流入	ZDA 公布的承诺投资总额
2001	145300000	115108990
2002	298400000	82935945
2003	347000000	119797798
2004	364000000	124994483
2005	356900000	252645995
2006	615800000	737512040
2007	1323900000	1986144108
2008	938600000	10883998005
2009	694800000	2010202370
2010	1729300000	4809365296
2011	1108000000	5464446729
2012	1066000000	6287305537

资料来源：ZDA（2013）；联合国贸发会议统计数据（2013）。

对外国直接投资的流入和赞比亚发展署提供的数据进行简单比较，就可看出两者在大多数年份都存在一定的差异，它既体现在承诺投资额小于 FDI 的额度（尤其是 2000~2005 年）上，也体现在近几年超出 FDI 的额度上。其产生有许多因素，包括很难维持数据记录，但是后几年的变化表明许多投机的投资并没实现，或在承诺投资和外国直接投资的上报之间存在滞后。但重要的是，这些数据表明了相似的上升趋势，特别是 2006~2007 年变化明显。

对许多细节，如投资者来源、投资部门和次级部门，赞比亚发展署的数据过于简单。来自多国的投资者或是身为跨国公司的投资者、在不同产业投资的公司（如采矿、交通和建筑等非农产业）或在多个次级部门投资的公司（如种植业、园艺业和畜牧业，或初级产品生产、二次加工及增值等部门）等信息，都并不能在数据中得到准确反映。

赞比亚发展署内部也承认数据存在缺陷，[①] 认为数据的收集机制需要改进。近期，发展署调整了研究机构，使它有更强的能力去记录承诺投资的相

---

① 国际消费者团结与信赖协会（CUTS International，2003）。

关信息和数据，以便为投资者创立更好的"后续服务"、与每个投资者保持更长时期的交往、吸引投资向可持续投资转变，这也是政府努力的一部分。为实现这一目标，发展署已开始对每个承诺投资的状况和进展搜集更系统全面综合的信息。可以预知，未来这些信息将会为理解外国直接投资的后果，尤其是对像农业这种投资后果和成功需要更长时间才能显现的部门，提供更多的帮助。[①]

3 赞比亚的发展和农业环境

3.1 赞比亚与发展

为理解农业外国投资对赞比亚经济增长和减贫战略的重要性，本章将对赞比亚现有发展轨迹及农业的重要作用进行详细描述。最近几年，以成功成为"中等偏下收入国家"（LMIC）为标志，赞比亚的经济格局有了显著变化。变化源于赞比亚近年来的经济增长，通过 GDP 的上升和持续的经济增长来体现。2007～2008 年西方国家经济增长率下降，毫无疑问影响了外国直接投资流入，但赞比亚的经济依然保持增长。这些变化确保赞比亚实现了"六五计划"（2011～2015 年）中第一年的宏观经济目标。

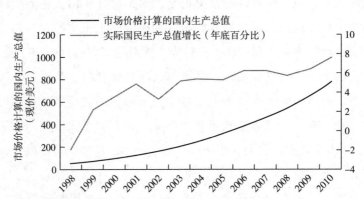

图 1 赞比亚 GDP 总额和实际 GDP 增长（1998～2012 年）（ZMW）
资料来源：中央统计办公室（2013）。

---

① 访谈赞比亚发展署代表（2013）。

　　然而，尽管宏观经济很成功，但社会发展指标并没有同步改善。2011年 "六五计划" 年度进展报告纲要提到，政府在改善刑事司法体系、减少感染 HIV/艾滋病人数、降低性别暴力、解决森林滥伐和环境退化，以及关注残疾人和无障碍设施建设等问题上，或是存在倒退，或是停滞不前。[①] 赞比亚的社会发展指标进展缓慢也可从联合国开发计划署（UNDP）的人类发展指数（HDI）排名得到印证，它在 187 个国家中排第 163 位，属于人类发展低水平。虽然自 1980 年以来赞比亚的分数有一定提高（同比提高 11%，年均增长 0.3%），但仍落后于几个邻国和大陆其他相应的经济体。[②]

表 3　赞比亚人类发展指数的变化（1980～2012 年）

年份	出生时预期寿命	预期受教育年限	平均受教育年限	人均国民收入（2005 年购买力平价 $）	人类发展指数数值
1980	52	7.7	3.3	1424	0.405
1985	51.2	7.7	4	1185	0.405
1990	47.5	7.9	4.7	1135	0.398
1995	43.5	7.9	6.1	959	0.385
2000	42	7.9	5.9	981	0.376
2005	44.4	7.9	6.4	1060	0.399
2010	48.5	8.5	6.7	1234	0.438
2011	49	7.9	6.5	1307	0.43
2012	49.4	8.5	6.7	1358	0.448

　　资料来源：UNDP（2013a）。

　　赞比亚在千年发展目标（MDGs）方面取得了缓慢的进步。具体来说，在第二项目标（实现普及初等教育）、第三项目标（促进两性平等）和第六项目标（与艾滋病、疟疾和其他疾病抗争）方面有所成就，同时在第八项目标（制订促进发展的全球伙伴关系）上保持良好状态。尽管经济强势增长，其他

---

① 赞比亚共和国政府（2012）。
② UNDP（2013a）.

目标的实现却非常欠缺。举例来说，以基尼系数计，赞比亚在极端贫困人口减半和重视日渐增加的不平等问题上无所作为。[1]

3.2 赞比亚农业概述

虽然赞比亚经济增长强劲，但多项社会发展指标进展缓慢，这表明经济增长并未改善大部分最贫穷人口的生活。[2] 这说明：尽管经济很成功，但很有必要更深入研究经济增长的领域，以及让增长如何惠及更广泛的赞比亚民众。

办法之一是重点关注赞比亚的农业部门。虽然农业在赞比亚经济中的份量相对较轻，但仍是大多数赞比亚人和政府最关心的事项之一。农业是大多数赞比亚人的主业，2010年66.7%的人口从事农业。虽然自2006年以来从事农业人口的比例有所下降（2006年为71%），但从事农业的家庭从2006年的1551952户增加到2009年的1631000户，明确表明农业仍是重要的就业渠道。

同时，农业为大多数居住在农村的人口提供了就业。这对于减贫意义重大，因为大多数生活在贫困线以下的人口（占赞比亚人口的60.5%）住在农村。2010年，农村贫困率是77.9%，而城市只有27.5%。[3]

因此，农业仍然是赞比亚减贫和农村发展最重要的行业。这不仅因为有很多家庭与农业息息相关，还因为农业生活与其他关键的农业发展指标如粮食安全等，有密切的联系。农业也有重要的政治意义，因为它构成了一个庞大的选民基础；也使经济从采矿业中独立出来，更加多元化，因此还有重要的经济意义。本章将详述赞比亚当前农业政策的方向，然后就农业部门的一些关键趋势和问题进行简要分析。

历史上，农业在赞比亚一直被认为是矿业的补充。它最初是为支持城市和矿业工人而存在，因此农业经济的增长有双重目标，即除了大范围农村小

---

[1] 以最近一次2010年发布的数据看，赞比亚的基尼系数是0.65；2015年的目标是0.34，但是不太可能达到（UNDP, 2013c）。
[2] Resnick and Thurlow (2014).
[3] 赞比亚共和国政府 (2010)。

农经济以外，还有集中的商业化农业部门。独立之后，虽然赞比亚系列发展计划都把农业增长放在优先地位，以便使矿业为主的经济多样化，但实际上对农业政策的关注却很少。[①] 20 世纪 70 年代中期铜价和大部分矿业经济的崩溃，以及随后 80～90 年代结构调整政策（SAP）的实施，推动了一波经济自由化浪潮，其焦点集中在玉米生产上。

因此，在创造全面经济增长和减贫方面，赞比亚农业政策的作用一直很有限。农业对于 GDP 的贡献主要来自高附加值的经济作物，它们又集中产自大型商业农场。虽然在实行结构调整政策和农业自由化之初，农业生产有所下降，但 2000 年以来又缓慢恢复。如今，农业再次被视为经济多元化和减贫的方式。

赞比亚目前的农业政策受国家农业政策（NAP）（2004～2015 年）指导。后者的目标是"推动农业部门的有效竞争和可持续发展，以保证粮食安全、提高收入"，强调增加产量和部门自由化、商业化，促进公司部门之间的合作以及提供更有效的服务。[②] 在推动大规模出口导向商品农业发展的同时，国家农业政策还想推动小农的增长。这些政策与其他指导性原则，如全国的 2030 年远景规划（2006）和当前的全国发展计划——"六五计划"（2011～2015 年），紧密呼应。

2030 年远景规划为农业制定的目标是"2030 年实现一个有效、竞争、可持续、出口导向的农业部门，保证粮食安全、提高收入"。规划中将有助于实现这些目标的农民分为三类：个体农户[③]、商业个体农户[④]、大型商业农场主。规划中认为提高农业尤其是小农的生产率，将对农业发展有显著的贡献；增加土地灌溉面积、农业机械化、增加牲畜和鱼类数量等目标似乎都是针对

---

① Wood (1990).
② GRZ MACO (2004).
③ 虽然 2030 年远景规划中使用了"个体农民"这一称呼，但是一般更常用的对农民最小的分类是"小农"，本报告也将使用这一称谓。典型的小农定义是拥有少于 20 公顷土地的农户，而赞比亚政府进一步将范围缩小到少于 5 公顷（Sitko and Jayne, 2012）。
④ 也被称为"新兴农民"（emergent farmer），他们主要耕作 5～20 公顷土地，但也有一些其他特征，如有商业技能、可获得资本、有创新和活力等（Sitko and Jayne, 2012）。

小农而制定的。虽然性别并不在小农的分类范围内，但规划承认：无论依据习俗还是法律，女性在获取土地时都面临更大的困难。①

2030 年远景规划和国家农业投资政策（NAIP，2014～2018 年）都制定了路线图，以实现"非洲农业综合开发项目"（CAADP）规定的目标，该项目由非盟和"非洲发展新伙伴计划"于 2003 年联合发起。作为非洲农业综合开发项目的签约国，赞比亚希望通过将国家预算的至少 10% 划归农业，以实现农业部门年均 6% 的增长率。②

在赞比亚政府最近发布的农业政策文件（如国家农业政策、2030 年远景规划和国家农业投资政策）中，可以清楚地发现政府不仅强调增加农业产量，还关注发展出口导向型、增值型的农业生产，以减轻作为经济增长支柱的粮食和铜矿价格波动带来的冲击。这些举措都是为了将经济从对采矿业的依赖中解脱出来，使之多样化。然而，虽然农业生活和农村贫困之间的联系非常清晰，但是农村农业商业化和减贫之间的联系尚未被强调。

过去 12 年里，农业稳定地为赞比亚 GDP 贡献了大约 20%。从更长时间段看，1965～2001 年农业是增长最快的行业，年均增长率为 3.1%，但增长集中于 1992 年开始的后市场化改革阶段。③ 图 2 展示了不同部门在 GDP 中所占的比重。第一产业包括矿业、采石业，及农业、林业和渔业，在 GDP 构成中后者的比重最大，2011 年达 18.4%，预期将会略有下降；然而，GDP 总量增长最多的还是第二产业。

第二产业中，建筑业一直是增长最快的部门，食品、饮料和烟草业紧随其后，近几年有显著增长（参见图 3）。图 4 显示第一产业的主要组成部分农林渔业中，虽然农业和林业的增长率普遍较高，但近年来都略有下降，渔业则稍有起色。同时也要注意，近些年的增长并不稳定，波动很大。

---

① GRZ (2006：23).
② NAIP (2013).
③ GRZ (2006).

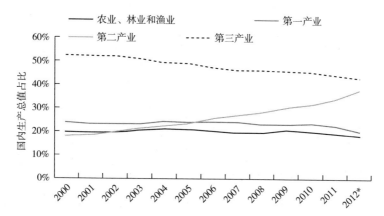

图2 经济部门和农业在 GDP 中所占百分比（2000～2012 年）

*表示预测值。

资料来源：CSO（2013）。

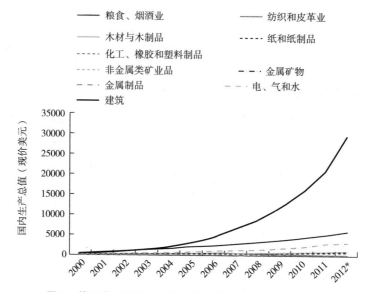

图3 第二产业部门贡献的 GDP 数额（2000～2012 年）

*表示预测值。

资料来源：CSO（2013）。

也许农业增长率的波动可以解释：为何农业增长并不必然相应大幅减轻小农的贫困。赞比亚国家农业投资政策将生产力低下和种植单一作为赞比亚

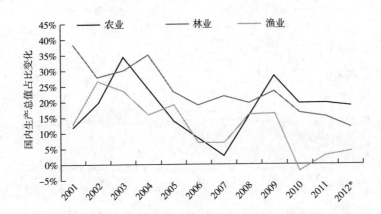

图 4 农业部门增长率以现价格为准的百分比变化（2001~2012 年）
资料来源：CSO（2013）。

农业，尤其是小农面对的两大主要挑战。杂交玉米的主导地位人尽皆知，2010 年 82% 的小农户种植玉米。[①] 一方面是因为文化需求（将玉米作为主食），另一方面也有各届政府对进出口市场经济的考虑。除了种植玉米，小农还种植木薯、花生和甘薯，而棉花和烟草是小农出口的重要经济作物。

　　土地规模受限经常被单独作为制约小农生产力的一个原因。根据赞比亚中央统计办公室（CSO）的数据，72.7% 的小农在不到 2 公顷的土地上进行耕作。[②] 缺乏获取劳动力和资本的途径，而不是缺乏可耕地，经常被看作导致耕地受限的原因。但是越来越多的证据表明，土地受限是因为缺乏获得土地的渠道，而并非没有可耕地。[③] 传统农耕区域的小农很难在其村子附近获取更多的土地，而一个对农民进行的调查显示，他们认为自己的社区并没有额外无主地可供分配。重要的是，另外的调查显示，如果为这些最小的小农增加耕地，则将显著提高农业销售额。对于底层 50% 的小农来说，如果增加 1 公顷土地，他们的农业销售将提高 319%~788%。[④]

---

① 国家农业投资政策（2013）。
② 国家农业投资政策（2013）。
③ Sitko and Jayne（2012）.
④ Hichaambwa and Jayne（2012）.

农业增长政策和农村减贫政策之间仍然脱节。前者将关注重点放在农业生产的集约化上，而其他调查却显示：虽然人们认为小农会有足够的土地，但他们其实面临着获取土地的限制，制约了他们的收入增长。尽管非洲农业综合开发项目的战略针对的是小农，但模拟场景是大部分农业的公众投资仍然倾向于大型商业农场。[①] 强调出口型农作物增长而非通过适当针对小农的农作物来强调更广泛的农业增长，将使赞比亚农业增长计划只能获得有限的成功。

外国农业投资如何惠及小农和农村贫困人口仍是一个大问题，后者很难从近期的经济增长中获益。然而，依然有极大的合作空间，如赞比亚的制造业，尤其是食品和饮料加工业正蓬勃发展，这些产业很有可能在不受土地约束的同时还带来经济增长。

4 赞比亚的投资环境

4.1 赞比亚近期投资趋势

近年来赞比亚的经济增长归功于大量的外国直接投资，[②] 因此，要想了解农业投资趋势，就必须了解赞比亚投资的大趋势和投资政策在其总体经济战略中扮演的角色。外国直接投资不仅可以带来技能、技术和专业知识，还可以作为其他投资和增长的枢纽，将本国和全球市场联系起来。[③] 本节将简要介绍近些年的投资趋势及一些决定因素，如贸易、援助以及赞比亚的投资结构等。

自 1992 年开始私有化和 90 年代初实行贸易自由化以来，赞比亚吸引的外国投资不断增加。如果将 1980 ~ 2010 年流入几个发展中国家的外国直接投资进行比较，可以看出：相比其他国家，如乌干达、加纳、马里、坦桑尼亚和塞内加尔，赞比亚经济更依赖 FDI；这在很大程度上归因于赞比亚长期以来一直以铜矿业为主的经济格局。

---

① Thurlow et al.（2008）.
② NEPAD OECD（2011）.
③ FAO（2013）.

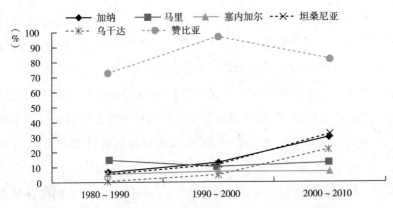

图5 一些非洲经济体外国直接投资存量对 GDP 的相对贡献

资料来源：FAO（2013）。

　　赞比亚发展署列出了赞比亚政治体系吸引投资者的几点优势（如政局稳定、亲投资者的投资环境等），也强调了赞比亚丰富的资源优势。如表4所示，所有流入的外国直接投资中，采矿业和采石业在制造业中仍然表现强势，占据主导地位；农业位居中游，2010年只占所有外国直接投资流入的1.8%。

表4 赞比亚各部门的 FDI 流入（2007～2010 年）

单位：美元

部　门	2007 年	2008 年	2009 年	2010 年
农业	3800000	2700000	−14100000	45600000
采矿及采石业	671600000	554360000	367000000	1652600000
制造业	108700000	77100000.00	285000000	423700000
建筑业	9200000	6530000	44200000	17400000
批发零售业	80400000	57030000	65000000	−2200000
旅游业	12700000	9010000	40900000	4300000
交通通信业	67800000	48090000	−10700000	204300000
金融机构	111500000	79080000	−83500000	−11200000
房地产	2900000	2060000	−400000	−4500000
其他	255300000	103060000	600000	166400000
总　额	1323900000	939020000	694000000	2496400000

资料来源：赞比亚发展署（2013）。

赞比亚不断落实政策，如协调投资和贸易监管、改造私营部门，希望将外国直接投资的增长趋势保持下去。

4.2　贸易和援助

贸易和援助在赞比亚经济中都发挥着重要作用。出口导向型的贸易促进了在赞比亚的投资，也展示了它在成长市场中的重要性，而这与农业投资密切相关。以前的农业出口集中于园艺和花卉等高附加值产品，然而市场一直有限。作为一个没有天然港口的国家，赞比亚政府开始将它打造为"陆联国家"（land - linked）——以强调赞比亚成为对周边新兴市场出口中心的潜力，而不是出口海外。

贸易协定构成了赞比亚吸引外资能力的另一个重要组成部分，也是使投资流入确保经济增长能力的一部分。作为一个内陆国家，赞比亚重视周边国家市场，依赖与它们的贸易；除南非外，刚果（金）和津巴布韦一直是赞比亚的重要贸易伙伴。国际上，欧盟和瑞士是赞比亚的主要出口市场。赞比亚是南部非洲发展共同体（SADC）① 和东南部非洲共同市场（COMESA）② 的成员，并在努力建立 SADC、COMESA 和东非共同体之间的三方自由贸易区。③ 同时，赞比亚还是美国非洲增长与机遇法案（AGOA）的成员之一，因此向美出口特定产品时享受零关税。迄今为止，AGOA 允许进口纺织品和服装、鲜切花、园艺、汽车和钢铁。④

赞比亚主要出口如电解铜、精炼铜等半成品，二者共占全国出口总额的86.3%，其他日用消费品、机器等生产资料和原材料仅占13.7%。⑤ 赞比亚政府目前正努力使出口商品多元化，不仅要降低矿产品的比重，而且还要降低

---

① 南部非洲发展共同体包括：安哥拉、博茨瓦纳、刚果民主共和国、莱索托、马达加斯加、马拉维、毛里求斯、莫桑比克、纳米比亚、南非、斯威士兰、坦桑尼亚、赞比亚和津巴布韦。
② 东南部非洲共同市场包括：布隆迪、科摩罗、刚果民主共和国、吉布提、埃及、厄立特里亚、埃塞俄比亚、肯尼亚、利比亚、马达加斯加、马拉维、毛里求斯、卢旺达、塞舌尔、索马里、斯威士兰、乌干达、赞比亚和津巴布韦。
③ OECD（2012）.
④ ZDA（2013）.
⑤ CSO（2013）.

与之相关产品的比重。① 2013 年，亚洲是赞比亚最大的出口市场，占出口总额的 30.2%；这主要得益于与中国的贸易（占其与亚洲贸易额的 78.4%），以及与阿联酋（16%）、新加坡（3.3%）、日本（1.2%）和印度（0.5%）等国的贸易。对南部非洲发展共同体的出口排名第二，占出口额的 23.8%，其中刚果（金）是赞比亚最大的出口对象国（占对南部非洲发展共同体出口额的 43.7%），其次是南非（34.6%）。进口方面，SADC 和 COMESA 中赞比亚邻国的作用十分重要，主要向赞比亚出口机械和建筑材料，以及矿产品。南非对赞比亚出口额占其进口总额的 32.2%，是赞比亚主要的进口来源国，而中国和印度一共才占 11.5%，分别排第四和第五。②

我们可以明确发现，尤其是从赞比亚试图将贸易从铜矿出口为主变得更多元化、增加农产品等非传统商品的出口这一举措中可以得知：它越来越将自己视为一个地区出口国。赞比亚还努力完善其贸易政策，改善其在奇龙杜（通往津巴布韦）、卡蒂玛姆利洛（通往纳米比亚）、卡宗古拉（通往博茨瓦纳）、纳孔德（通往坦桑尼亚）和卡素梅赖萨（通往刚果金）等地的边防哨所。

在援助方面，近些年赞比亚获得的政府开发援助（ODA），尤其是来自经济合作组织（OECD）下属机构——发展援助委员会（DAC）的援助正在下降。2010 年赞比亚获得的政府开发援助（8.52 亿美元）比 2000 年（15 亿美元）减少了近一半。③ 另外，通过重债穷国协议和多边减债计划，IMF 和世界银行减免了赞比亚大量外债。④ 援助国认为赞比亚发展资金来源多元化，最近又成为"中等偏下收入国家"（LMIC），使它们有信心降低赞比亚对 ODA 的依赖。随着 ODA 的减少，在赞比亚 GDP 中 FDI 将会比 ODA 占据更大比重。这些因素将很可能使赞比亚在制定政策时更倾向于继续吸引外国直接投资，以弥补 ODA 的减少。

---

① OECD（2012）.
② CSO（2013），原文 13.6% 。——译者注
③ Prizzon（2013）.
④ Prizzon（2013）；OECD（2012）.

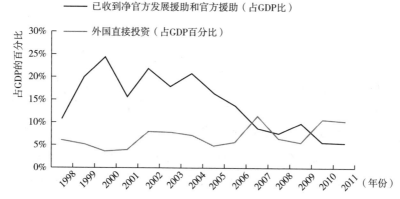

图 6　赞比亚 GDP 中官方发展援助和外国直接投资的比重对比（1998～2011 年）
资料来源：世界银行数据（2013）。

发展援助中，全球非传统发展援助（NTDA）日益增多。非传统发展援助是指"因公共或人道主义原因，提供给发展中国家的跨境金融资本，有一定的优惠，但并非传统的双边或多边官方发展援助"。[①] 非传统发展援助来源众多，既有如盖茨基金会和克林顿倡议等慈善组织，也有金砖国家等发展援助委员会成员国之外的国家。非传统发展援助仅占世界官方发展援助很小的一部分，而且主要是全球性的卫生保健基金；然而，中国已成为发展援助委员会成员国之外最大的捐助国，随着非传统发展援助的不断增多，中国的贡献也将越来越大。[②]

全球现在的趋势是减少援助，它促使政策越来越倾向于吸引和重视 FDI 流入。在金砖国家这样的新兴经济体中如此，在赞比亚这样的"中等偏下收入国家"也一样。这为金砖国家通过非传统发展援助，在发展中国家发挥更大作用提供了空间；也有助于投资者将赞比亚作为更加可行和稳定投资战略的一部分，但也增加了赞比亚对这些收入的依赖。它将使赞比亚的投资政策改革更有动力，以保证 FDI 惠及国家经济的方方面面，而投资也不会凌驾于赞比亚人民的生计之上。

---

① Prizzon（2013）.
② Prizzon（2013）.

4.3 投资政策和赞比亚发展署的作用

近些年，赞比亚自认为在吸引外资方面取得了成功，它在一些排名中的名次也有提升，如在世界银行的"营商环境"指数上现居第83位（撒哈拉以南地区排第7）。[1] 这些指标主要用于评估赞比亚吸引投资的能力，考察投资者创业、取得贷款和获得许可证的难易程度，以及税负压力大小。因此，虽然"营商环境"指数这样的指标将赞比亚排在其撒哈拉以南的许多邻国之前，但考察赞比亚投资政策如何影响它吸引农业投资以及吸引何种农业投资更有意义。

赞比亚的投资目标主要见于国家政策，如"六五计划"和2030年远景规划中。这些政策对赞比亚的经济重新定位，使之更多元（也更可持续）。[2]"六五计划"和2030年远景规划的目标在2006年颁布的发展法案中被确认。该法案不仅创立了发展署、明确其职责，还制定了投资优惠政策指导它工作。发展署一直是吸引外资最重要的部门，近年来在对外国投资和投资者进行维护和后期服务上的作用也越来越大。发展署是由赞比亚私有化机构、赞比亚投资中心、赞比亚出口局、赞比亚出口加工区管理局和赞比亚小型企业发展委员会等部门于2006年合并而成的半自治机构。其主要职能是"通过推进赞比亚的投资和出口，深化经济发展"，主要通过提供投资服务、发展市场和商业、对中小型企业提供支持来实现。[3] 除了为投资者服务、推动商业之外，发展署的另一项职能就是收集数据。通过与赞比亚银行和中央统计办公室协作，发展署成为外国投资和其他类似经济指标的主要来源。

虽然并非所有的外国投资都必须通过赞比亚发展署进行，但对投资者来说，通过它投资有很多好处，例如申请和成功获得投资许可证之后的税收优惠。发展署不仅提供系列普遍的激励政策（见附录1），还为某些行业的投资者提供特殊的激励政策。一般来说，主要措施是减免所得税和减免增值税，前者是鼓励投资者进入特定部门，而后者是为促进农业、矿业、制造业和旅游业的发展。

---

[1] World Bank（2013）.

[2] GRZ（2006）.

[3] ZDA（2012b）.

目前，赞比亚政府确定的农业优先部门为：

——初级农业：花卉（鲜花和干花）、园艺（新鲜和干燥蔬菜）、茶叶和茶叶制品、咖啡和咖啡制品、棉花和棉纱。

——次级农业：加工食品（小麦面粉及其他加工食品）、皮革制品、织物和服装、木材和木制品、棕榈油及其衍生品、纸浆、纸制品和纸板、纺织品。①

这些激励措施偏重于高附加值产品，也鼓励制造和加工业的进一步发展。

根据投资者承诺的投资额，赞比亚发展署对投资者还有其他的激励措施。例如，1000 万美元以上的投资可与赞比亚政府商讨额外的激励措施。在"经济特区"（MFEZ）投资 50 万美元以上，将获得如下优惠：

①首次分红后的 5 年内免征红利税；

②首次实现盈利后的 5 年内免征利润税，第 6 ~ 8 年内只对 50% 的利润征税，第 9 ~ 10 年内只对 75% 的利润征税；

③对原材料、资本货物、包括卡车和特种车辆在内的机械，5 年内免征进口关税；④对卡车和特种车辆在内的机械设备，延迟缴纳增值税。

总的来说，投资者必须在特定部门投入 50 万美元以上，才能享受普遍激励政策（见附录1），但"中小型企业"的投资有时也能免税。

在理解赞比亚税收方面还存在一些问题，已超出本报告的讨论范围。关于外国投资，税收政策一向存在争议，尤其是在矿业投资上，但在农业投资上的争议也越来越多。② 经合组织及其他机构也注意到赞比亚在协调稳定税收政策、强化税收管理上做出了不懈努力。③ 关于外国投资，如下问题值得我们继续思考：

①赞比亚政府能执行发展署制定的税收规定吗？遵守的人多吗？外国投资者是否能避开这些规定呢？

②激励措施会对税收收入造成什么损失？实行这些措施后，税收收入足

---

① 截至本报告完稿前，最新一版为 2013 年 2 月版。

② Action Aid（2013）.

③ OECD（2012）；NEPAD OECD（2011）.

以让农村贫困社区获益吗?

除激励措施外,赞比亚发展署还为投资提供便利,包括申请用地,获取水电、交通和通信等基础设施,取得某些执照,以及自我雇用和雇用外籍员工的许可证。作为世行多边贸易投资保证机构和非洲贸易保险机构的签署国,赞比亚还提供系列保证:利润和红利汇回投资者母国不受限制,政府不强制征用企业,不受非商业风险影响等。

为协调对传统土地的收购,赞比亚发展署创立了"土地银行"。[①] 通过土地银行发展官员,发展署与酋长就买卖传统地块进行商谈,以吸引投资。这意味着政府控制了土地交易,确保土地用于指定目的,还能使投资者的土地申请过程更加快捷。然而,这将土地分配权放到了政府手中,而根据《土地获取法案》(1975 年),政府有权强制征收土地,特别是农村土地。土地银行计划包括农垦区项目(见表5)、"经济特区"项目,还创设了农业产业"集群"。这是发展署 2012 年为推动初级农业与制造业和加工业协同发展而设立的新项目。[②] 之前推行过棉花(主要在东部省)和生物燃料项目,现在的项目以它们为基础。

表5 赞比亚发展署的农场区计划

单位:公顷

农业区名称	地点	预计面积
楠桑加	中央省塞伦杰	155000
卡鲁姆万格	西部省卡欧玛	100000
卢埃纳	卢阿普拉省卡万布瓦	100000
曼史亚	穆钦加省姆皮卡	147000
卢马/米克楞格	西北省索卢韦齐	100000
穆萨卡西(SADA)	铜带省穆富利拉	100000
穆库	卢萨卡省卡富埃	100000
西芒戈	南部省利文斯顿	100000
木瓦斯－庞维	东部省伦达孜	100000

资料来源:NEPAD OECD,2011。

---

① AfDB (2011);Oakland Institute (2011).
② 来自对赞比亚发展署代表的采访 (2013)。

虽然迄今为止赞比亚的不同部门能继续吸引外资，显示了发展署的成功；但是，是否大部分投资都通过发展署进行？倾向于通过开发署的投资者类型（例如：国内还是国际公司，公司的大小等）有哪些？以及何种激励措施最能吸引投资？这些问题却无人问津。激励措施能够带来长期的、可持续的业务以及创造就业吗？下一章将探究这些问题。

5　赞比亚农业投资概述

5.1　农业承诺投资概述（1998～2012年）

虽然赞比亚希望用农业投资带动经济多元化和减少贫困，但是采矿业仍然占据了赞比亚外国直接投资流入的主要地位（见表6）。然而，全球援助框架开始转而青睐一种 FDI 战略：既包括本国投资者，又包括塑造东道国的外资政策，如赞比亚。

表6　过去5年内各部门承诺投资总额（2008～2012年）

单位：美元

部　门	承诺投资总额
矿业	13824878263
制造业	5417330197
能源业	3314843645
房地产业	2466840101
旅游业	1491984249
农业	1139480207
服务业	584158168
建筑业	269976744
教育	242278633
电子信息产业	197562050
交通业	189899326
金融业*	180183954
健康业	135902400

*金融部门的数据并不完整，2008年和2010年的数据无法获得，并没有加到总额里。

资料来源：ZDA（2013）。

因此，本章将通过研究赞比亚发展署提供的农业承诺投资，对赞比亚的农业投资进行概述分析。这可以更好地洞察赞比亚推动农业投资的方式和过程，包括赞比亚目前正吸引投资进入农业政策存在的优缺点。

为评估赞比亚的投资政策，笔者先概述已完成的农业投资。之后，按国别进行分类讨论，展示新投资国发挥的独特作用。

本章将对发展署1998～2012年农业承诺投资数据所推断出的趋势进行更深入的分析。如前所述，虽然这些数据并不等于已实现的农业投资数据，但它们提供了农业投资最全面的信息，因此是研究农业投资更广泛趋势和特征的有用指标。

虽然农业投资享有系列政策优惠并获得了国际关注，但在承诺投资的部门中排名依然靠后。矿业是最主要的投资部门，接下来是制造业、能源业、房地产业和旅游业。

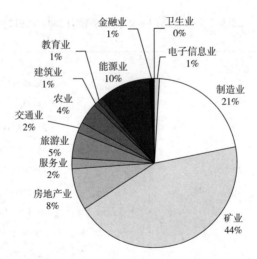

图 7　各部门承诺的总投资百分比（1998～2012 年）

资料来源：ZDA（2013）。

表6和图7都强调了矿业无论在外国直接投资流入还是承诺投资中都占据主要地位，而制造业追随其后，排名第二。然而，图8展示了2008～2012年承诺投资的百分比变化。

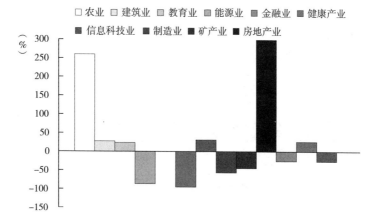

图 8　各部门承诺的投资百分比变化（2008～2012 年）

注：房地产的数字达到了 945%。

资料来源：ZDA（2013）。

农业和房地产业增长明显，建筑、旅游、教育和电子信息业也略有增长。图 8 中也出现了负增长，但与其说是负增长，还不如说是承诺投资的波动性大和投机活跃。

虽然从总额看，农业投资似乎在赞比亚的 FDI 中并不占重要地位，但很明显其作用正日益突出，外国对农业投资的兴趣也的确有所提升。图 9 显示：2009 年农业承诺投资有较大增长，虽然 2010 年下降不少，但 2011 年再次大幅增加，并保持到 2012 年。这个趋势也与农业投资文献所描述的一致，它们预测在 2007～2008 年全球粮食危机，即全球几种主要粮食作物的价格都达到顶峰之后，农业投资将会上升。断言全球粮价波动与实际投资会产生联动机制也许为时过早，但受一些大型关键项目影响，承诺投资也确实有些波动。

一个重要的趋势是：投资流向了初级农业，而非下游部门（如农业加工、饮料业及其他相似的部门）。下一部分将具体研究这些近期农业投资去向何方。

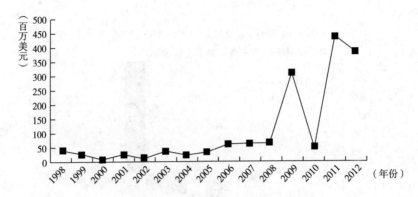

图 9　农业承诺投资的总额（1998～2012 年）

资料来源：ZDA（2013）。

5.2　赞比亚农业投资的特点

　　赞比亚发展署提供的农业承诺投资数据还可按投资来源国和投资项目进行分类排名，表 1 提供了 1998～2012 年排名前 10 位的国家，附录 2 提供了 1998～2012 年排名前 50 名的项目。表 7 是按投资总额和项目平均投资规模对数据重新整理后的排名，再次显示：排名靠前国家的投资趋势相似。

表 7　农业承诺投资前 20 名国家（2008～2012 年）

排名	国家	以总额计（美元）	国家	以平均投资规模计（美元）
1	英　国	596249513	马拉维	56659500
2	南　非	273639189	新加坡	35000000
3	马拉维	113319000	塞舌尔	14520000
4	印　度	112061375	德　国	9395000
5	赞比亚	107188553	英　国	9316399
6	津巴布韦	99445900	爱尔兰	8920464
7	毛里求斯	43427000	毛里求斯	8685400
8	新加坡	35000000	尼日利亚	7878000
9	中　国	33301378	开曼群岛	6640000
10	爱尔兰	26761392	南　非	5472784
11	丹　麦	18014920	印　度	5336256

续表

排名	国家	以总额计（美元）	国家	以平均投资规模计（美元）
12	尼日利亚	15756000	丹　麦	4503730
13	塞舌尔	14520000	塞浦路斯	3895970
14	澳大利亚	14172371	赞比亚	3349642
15	希　腊	11760301	加拿大	3000000
16	德　国	9395000	澳大利亚	2362062
17	塞浦路斯	7791940	希　腊	1960050
18	开曼群岛	6640000	津巴布韦	1420656
19	美　国	6548390	美　国	1091398
20	加拿大	6000000	中　国	979452

资料来源：ZDA（2013）。

以总额计，传统投资国（如英国、津巴布韦、南非和国内投资等）位居赞比亚的投资国前列，但名单中新增了一批投资国，比较突出的是印度和中国，还有一些单笔大额投资来自著名的金融渠道国家，如毛里求斯、新加坡、爱尔兰、塞舌尔和开曼群岛等。"项目平均投资规模"也显示：来自金融渠道国家的投资规模明显要比来自中、印等新兴市场国家的大得多。

然而我们必须注意到，因为金融渠道国家的出现，将投资按照来源国进行分类非常复杂，因为现实中这些钱和投资权益也许有其他来源。赞比亚发展署对于"投资者母国"的记录来自投资人提供的持股人名单，因此很难对投资按来源国进行划分。最后，许多投资都有多个来源国，使这一问题更加复杂。

排名前50位的企业投资总额达1341248169美元，约占1998～2012年承诺总额的85%（在记录的344个承诺投资中），但它们只占投资承诺雇用总数的39%；其中68%的企业（34家）投资于2008年或之后，只有少部分企业（16家）投资于2008年之前。这表明，2008年以来，随着许多大额投资主导了统计数据，农业投资规模的确越来越大。排名前5位的企业都投资于2007～2012年，占前50名企业承诺投资总额的64%。

如果我们更仔细地考察前50名投资者（见附录2），就会发现这些承诺投资中，虽然有些年份投资的行业无法知晓，但是大部分都投向了种植业，其他则投向混合种植业、养殖业和农业加工业，花卉园艺和渔业只占了很小部分。赞比亚发展署并没有对种植业所种植作物的种类进行进一步分类，但除传统作物如玉米、小麦和大豆外，糖类作物、烟草和大米虽然数量不多，却也有种植。值得注意的是，虽然普遍认为赞比亚对生物能源的兴趣浪潮早已平息，但对生物能源的投资仍有一定影响。[①]

仅从数据看，农业加工业似乎被低估了，但实际上它仍占重要的地位。赞比亚发展署把投资分为农业和制造业两类，并为它们设立了独立的名录，但是其分类标准却不明确，尤其是当一项投资横跨两大行业的时候。因此，虽然笔者应对这些名录进行初步审核，但仍主要致力于分析初级农业部门，这也是本文的局限之一。

重要的是，虽然一些数据有投资者列出的投资地点，但整个数据没有关于土地面积的信息。数据倒是提供了投资承诺雇用的人数，但它是投资者做投资承诺时自己申报的，缺乏可靠性和强制力；这也是发展署认定的、追踪投资进程和实现程度时需要重点监管的领域之一。在投资规模、投资类型（根据次级部门确定）和承诺雇用人数之间并没有相关关系，似乎也表明申报相当随意。

表 8　已知的土地征用情况整理

公司名称	征用土地的面积和途径	所在地	资料来源
乔贝农业前景有限公司	4155 公顷（法定）	中央省姆库希	Chobe Agrivision（2011a），（2011b），（2012）.
赞比亚阿玛西恩农业有限公司	14237 公顷（法定）	中央省蒙布瓦	Amatheon Agri（2012），（2013）.
ETC 生物能源有限公司（后被赞比亚牛肉公司收购）	46876 公顷（法定）	铜带省姆彭戈韦	Mujenja and Wonani（2012）.

---

① Locke and Henley（2013）.

续表

公司名称	征用土地的面积和途径	所在地	资料来源
索玛维房地产有限公司（后被乔贝农业前景公司收购）	12822 公顷（法定）	铜带省姆彭戈韦	Chobe Agrivision（2012）。
银地牧场	19090 公顷（法定）	南部省津巴	http：//www. miga. org/projects/index. cfm? pid = 1248
非洲农作物有限公司	25000 公顷（法定）	南部省乔马和卡洛莫	http：//www. africancropszambia. com
赞比亚 CBL 农业有限公司	438 公顷（法定）	南部省马扎布卡	对农场经理的采访（2013）。
赞比亚普阿利亚公司	2325 公顷（法定）	南部省卡宗古拉	http：//www. emvest. com/Emvest _ Livingstone. html

资料来源：作者编辑整理。

5.3 描述新老农业投资者

许多对非洲外国投资的研究都从宏观角度分析了 FDI 的趋势，[①] 并越来越关注中、印等新型投资者 FDI 的增长速度，[②] 它们主要关注贸易、政府间合作及援助等问题，并考察多个行业。同时，越来越多的文献专注于非洲的农业外国投资。[③] 这些报告对在多国选定的案例进行小规模个案研究，再做跨国比较，信息来源包括坊间传闻和媒体对特定投资案例的报道。最后，对中国（逐渐也包括印度）农业对外投资的关注也在不断提升，为研究更广泛的农业投资提供了一个不同的思路。它们和研究金砖国家的文章一样，更注重政府层面合作的空间，但对私人投资者没有给予同等重视。[④]

正如简介所述，在全球发展中国家尤其是撒哈拉以南非洲国家的外国直接投资中，新兴国家正扮演着越来越重要的角色。[⑤] 如金砖国家中，印度、中

[①] Bhinda et al. （1999）；UNIDO（2008）；McKinsey（2010）.

[②] O' Neill（2001）；OECD（2006）；Cheru and Obi（2010）；Mawdsley and McCann（2011）；Hofman and Ho（2012）；Carmody（2013）.

[③] World Bank（2007），（2009）；OECD（2010）；Deininger and Byerlee（2011）；Oakland Institute（2011）；FAO（2013b）.

[④] World Bank（2007），（2009）；OECD（2010）；Deininger and Byerlee（2011）；Oakland Institute（2011）；FAO（2013b）.

[⑤] Mlachila and Takebe（2011）.

国和南非都扮演着重要角色，虽然俄罗斯记录在案的投资只有两项（在同一农场），巴西则没有投资。①

俄罗斯在赞比亚的投资

俄罗斯在赞比亚记录在案的农业投资只有一项。虽然注册为两项投资（赞比卡和安比卡），但普遍认为二者在同一个农场。位于姆库希区的安比卡项目由俄罗斯商人米凯尔·奥尔洛夫先生投资，他创立了黑色地球农垦公司及后续的安比卡农业公司。② 前者曾在俄罗斯拥有 815450 公顷土地，2008 年奥尔洛夫放弃了它，然后在赞比亚创办了小麦种植和家畜养殖的新项目。③

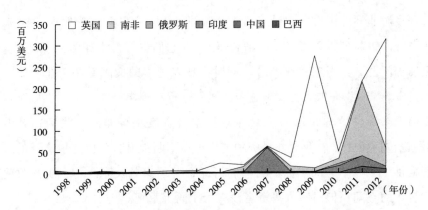

图 10　英国和金砖国家农业承诺投资数额（1998～2012 年）
资料来源：ZDA（2013）。

在对赞比亚的承诺投资中，英国和南非名列前茅（见表 1）。④ 此外，英国的投资占农业承诺投资总额的 38%，略高于 1/3，而金砖国家加起来只有 26%，其他国家占了 36%（见图 11）。有趣的是，如图 10 所示，所列出的国

---

① 投资数据截至 2012 年。俄罗斯的投资在 BOX1 中进行介绍，BOX2 中分析了巴西在赞比亚的利益。
② http://ambika–agro.com/index.html.
③ RBTH（2013）.
④ 排在这两个国家之前的只有津巴布韦。

家在2007年和2011年的投资都有相似的高峰。虽然英国通过与赞比亚的殖民联系和官方发展援助，一直在赞比亚农业投资中扮演重要角色，但另一种投资方式的兴起也许与英国日渐成为金融渠道国家相一致；与有大量投资的其他知名金融交易中心（如塞舌尔、毛里求斯等）一起，英国作为金融渠道国家的作用，也许证实了英国的统治地位不仅源自历史联系，更源自赞比亚农业投资中私募的不断增长。从某种程度上讲，从南非也能看到相同的趋势。①

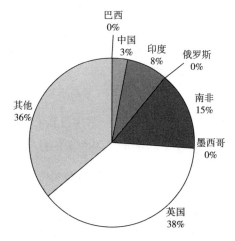

图11 金砖国家、英国和其他国家的农业承诺投资总额（1998~2012年）
资料来源：ZDA（2013）。

生物能源和金砖国家

虽然农业承诺投资的数据中没有显示，但金砖国家在生物能源相关项目上表现出很大兴趣。除在矿业和采矿设备部门大力投资外，中国还将投资指向了生物能源，而巴西则加入了一项生物能源领域能力建设和经验分享谅解备忘录。②

据记录，中国在制造业领域最大的承诺投资是凯迪生物赞比亚有限公司，一家由武汉阳光凯迪能源集团和赞比亚生物量开发公司（PLC）合作成

---

① Bhinda et al.（1999）.
② 《卢萨卡时报》（2010）。

立的公司。它在 2010 年承诺投资 4.5 亿美元，发展多种原料（包括麻风树）的生产和加工。最开始，该公司希望获得 200 万公顷的土地，但是只在纳孔德和伊索卡区获得约 7.8 万公顷的土地。[①] 然而，在此之后投资者就撤出了，[②] 声称撤出的原因是政府审批尤其是与土地分配相关的审批太慢。

虽然巴西目前还没有正式在农业领域进行投资，但是对能源领域的兴趣与日俱增。目前来看，巴西最大的投资在矿业领域（Vale），它在利用甘蔗和大豆做原料开发生物能方面也有丰富的专业知识。赞比亚的麻风树项目失败后，[③] 巴西已充分准备好向赞比亚提供专家、技术和设备，帮助它用农业中更常见的原料生产生物能源。

但与英国和南非相比，中国和印度在承诺投资趋势上的差别很明显。如果再次看表 1 的话，可以发现中印都承诺了大量的投资项目。

表 9　各国农业承诺投资额排名前十位的国家及其承诺
总额（1998~2012 年）（以承诺投资数量排名）

单位：美元

国　　家	承诺投资数量	承诺投资总额	平均承诺投资额
津巴布韦	70	99445907	1420656
英　　国	64	596249513	9316399
南　　非	50	273639189	5472784
中　　国	34	33301378	979452
赞 比 亚	32	107188553	3349642
印　　度	21	112061375	5336256
毛里求斯	5	43427000	8685400
爱 尔 兰	3	26761392	8920464
马 拉 维	2	113319000	56659500
新 加 坡	1	35000000	35000000

资料来源：ZDA（2013）。

---

① *The Post*（2012）.
② *Times of Zambia*（2013）.
③ Locke and Henley（2013）.

表 9 还显示，中国承诺投资的平均规模（以数额计）明显小于印度、南非和英国。有趣的是，印度和南非的平均承诺投资规模非常接近，也许意味着两国在投资类型上有相似之处，这可能又源自规模相似的农业扩张。这个发现强调了中国中小型企业（SMEs）的投资潜力，也强调了不同投资国的农业投资模式①的潜在区别。

接下来将以印度、中国、南非和英国为案例，简要介绍这些国家有哪些政策推动海外农业投资。投资者母国的政策必然对鼓励个体投资者向外投资的行为有影响；但是，这些政策本身并不专门针对赞比亚。相反，中国和印度政府运用特殊的话语，笼统地鼓励海外投资，而英国和南非的投资主要是通过自由的商业环境与赞比亚商品农业团体的历史联系进行。

印度

自 2000 年起，印度政府（GOI）将其与非洲的联系方式从历史上的善意接触，转向深化经济联系。印度政府试图将其非洲政策从依赖采掘工业转向可持续和有机的发展，因此开始涉足农业。印度企业家已将赞比亚作为农业投资沃土，这不仅因为当地市场相当不发达，还因为从印度本身的粮食安全考虑。印度政府已声明将考虑购买海外私有农地来保证国内的粮食安全。

印度政府在"聚焦非洲"计划中将赞比亚列为重要的对象国之一，大力宣传两国关系以鼓励印度企业家走出去。两国在各个层面上都有协定，包括系列贸易协定，与印度工业联合会的协作，以及赞比亚和印度的农业研究中心谅解备忘录。两国之间还有很多高层官员和商业代表交流。印非论坛高峰会就是这种政治联系的一个范例，它有助于促进印度向非洲贷款。在与非洲和赞比亚的战略交往中，印度最重视的是能源安全；其次把非洲作为印度商品和服务越来越重要的市场，以及作为印度制造业的原料来源地。作为交换，印度将向非洲提供合算的中等技术，尤其是为信息技术、农业、健康

---

① 操作模式指农业投资中可能采用的不同农业模式，这些不同的模式包括种植园模式、合约式和商品农业模式（Smalley，2013）。

和制药工业等领域提供技术。

虽然印度与赞比亚有历史联系，而且拥有日益增长和稳定的贸易关系，但是人们也逐渐关注它在撒哈拉以南非洲，尤其是在东非（特别是埃塞俄比亚）所获取土地不断增长的国际影响。[①] 然而，将其定义为"印度"在收购土地是错误的。事实上，许多领域中向撒哈拉以南国家扩张的主要是私人企业家。虽然对印度参与赞比亚农业的关注很多，但对它的实证研究却很少。

中国

关于中国与非洲，特别是与赞比亚关系的研究成果，日益成为一个明确的研究领域。赞比亚一直是中国对撒哈拉以南非洲的外国直接投资的重要目标之一，不仅投资农业，还有许多其他领域，如矿业、建筑业、通信业和制造业等。赞比亚城市里中国人的数量在不断增加，这也看出中国在赞比亚经济中扮演的角色越来越重要。2013 年 11 月，中国是赞比亚第二大出口目的国（占总出口额的 23.7%），出口产品主要是铜矿及其他矿石，但烟草是中国从赞比亚进口的第四大产品。[②]

虽然人们推测中国在农业投资方面的战略是保证农地以维护粮食安全（无论是通过直接进口还是通过提高整体产量），但系列研究表明，中国参与非洲农业的过程经历了几个不同的历史阶段。[③] 第一波介入非洲农业的浪潮可以被总结为"农业社会主义"，其特点是通过援助形成的多种合作方式，进行的农业示范项目规模也相对较小。20 世纪 90 年代以来，中国的农业投资被称为"农业资本主义"，它延续了农业合作项目，但更强调项目的赢利性以保证其在经济上可以自给自足。至于中国在非洲农业中的新形式——"农业帝国主义"，还未被观察到。迄今为止，中国的大部分投资分为

---

① Rahmato (2013) and Rowden (2013), both in Cheru and Modi, eds (2013).

② CSO (2013).

③ 例如参见 Brautigam and Tang (2009)；Sautman and Yan (2010), and Smaller, Qiu and Liu (2012)。其他讨论中国在赞比亚投资的重要文章包括 German et al. (2011)，而其他更广泛地研究中国在撒哈拉以南非洲的农业文章包括 Sun (2011), Brautigam (2012), Hofman and Ho (2012) 和 Brautigam and Zhang (2013)。

两种，一种是国有农业合作项目（例如中赞友谊农场、中垦农场[1]和中垦友谊农场[2]），另一种是在中国"走出去"战略的一部分，在激励下出现的个体私人企业家向外投资浪潮。"走出去"战略受到中非合作论坛（FOCAC）的支持，并由中国主要的银行机构，如中国开发银行和中国进出口银行提供金融支持。

南非

南非是赞比亚贸易往来的主要国家之一。两国交往的历史很长，有一系列贸易协定和双边合作。南非公司在零售业、矿业、安保行业和农业领域有重要的作用，最近又将关注重点放在了农业加工领域。南非的贸易与工业部负责管理贸易关系，随着出口营销和投资援助计划的发展，它计划在建设南非产品和服务的出口市场的同时，推动新的外国直接投资进入南非。

1990 年以前，南非与赞比亚的关系深受赞比亚支持南非国内反种族隔离运动的影响；赞比亚是前线领导国之一，甚至为非国大成员提供避风港，非国大还于 20 世纪 80 年代在卢萨卡建立总部。90 年代初，随着种族隔离制度的结束，南非和赞比亚恢复了外交往来，又进行了系列高层互访，借此实现了贸易关系正常化。现在，赞比亚已是南非在非洲的第二大贸易伙伴，南非一直是赞比亚机器等设备的主要进口来源国。2013 年 11 月，南非在赞比亚产品（主要是矿产）出口目的国中排第四位，在金砖国家中仅次于中国。[3]

南非向赞比亚投资的动因包括：对投资者灵活的税收和收入返国政策、低政治风险、低政治化的工党政权等政治因素，及肥沃的土壤和充足的水源等环境因素。南非向其他撒哈拉以南非洲地区，尤其是南部非洲地区的投资，主要是通过布尔人农民个体的迁移及南非农业综合企业的扩张进行。20 世纪 90 年代，南非进行的系列改革导致个体农场主开始退出南非农业，包括放松

---

① 英文文献中有时也称"Zhongken"，例如见 Sautman and Yan（2009）；Brautigam and Tang（2009）和 Brautigam（2012）。
② 见 Sautman and Yan（2009）和 Brautigam（2012）的描述。
③ CSO（2013）.

农业管制、大幅提高农用柴油和电力价格及其他政策变化——保障农业工人的基本劳动权利、延长雇用时间和以历史为由征收大片农田等。[①] 土地改革和转型一直是南非关注的重点，导致农民及农技知识转移到赞比亚等地区。虽然这股浪潮不一定持续下去，却为南非对外扩张的农业组织如"南非农业产业联合会"提供了先例。重要的是，赞比亚非常欢迎这些农技知识。[②] 除农场主外，南非农业综合企业如糖业巨头 Illovo 公司等，已在赞比亚开展了大量的业务。[③] 尽管这方面研究不多，但显而易见的是，大量南非农业综合企业进入赞比亚农业，以期投资多元化，寻求更高回报，这也得到南非新投资法的支持。

英国

英国与其前殖民地的历史联系显而易见，但它并没有针对赞比亚的特定战略。历史上许多商业农场是殖民地时期开垦、专供英国移民使用的。因此，与南非一样，英国对赞比亚商品农业的参与也最长久和最成熟。虽有上述联系，但很少有人关注英国公司在非洲获取农业用地中的特定角色。[④]

将英国投资者单独剥离出来观察并不简单，因为很多长期居住在赞比亚的英国裔仍持有英国护照，所以在发展署对投资来源进行分类时，他们常被认为是英国投资者。但是，很多这些更成熟的农场在整个赞比亚都相当知名。本报告集中分析近期的投资，因此许多更古老、更成熟的农场被排除在外。尽管如此，作为金融中心，英国在赞比亚开发署所提供的农业承诺投资表上依然举足轻重。当研究英国在整个撒哈拉以南非洲的参与时，这种倾向更为明显；虽然在英国想获取土地的目的国家中，赞比亚的份量有限；但在赞比亚农业外国直接投资中，英国公司却有相当的份量。[⑤]

投资于非洲农业的私募和风险资本的增加也越来越受到人们关注，虽然不是所有的英国投资都是私募投资，也不是所有的私募和风险资本都源自英

---

① Hall（2012）.
② Hall（2012）.
③ 见 Action Aid（2013）。
④ 例外可见 Action Aid（2013）。
⑤ Ottaviani（2013）.

国，但来自伦敦的资金在非洲农业中占有重要地位。[①] 非洲传统的商品农业投资者——英联邦发展公司（CDC），支持了几个新基金，在整个撒哈拉以南非洲寻求早期市场；[②] 然而，该公司以前的经历证明：长期来看，这些投资在经济上未必可持续，大规模的农业发展也不能带来如创造就业、为小农带来增长等实实在在的长期收益。[③]

6　评估赞比亚在农业投资上的努力

6.1　农业投资政策

本章旨在为赞比亚在农业投资方面的努力提供评估，包括两点。第一，很明显赞比亚发展署成功吸引了外资，很可能带来了当前经济的增长；然而，赞比亚到底吸引了何种农业承诺投资？这些投资如何证明它们就属于发展署所激励的那些投资种类？第二，审查完承诺投资的种类之后，农业投资趋势对赞比亚农村会有什么样的影响？

迄今为止，虽然在吸引投资方面，赞比亚的投资政策获得了成功，但是在一些领域中赞比亚的投资政策仍然存在缺陷或不足。特别是一些监管机制尤其存在不足，它们是为保证赞比亚能够适应投资者不断变化的要求和赞比亚民众的需求而建立的。可改善的空间包括更完善的监控机制、更齐备的数据收集、更良好的制度运作和咨询机制，以提供反馈，促进改变。如经合组织指出的几个关键领域：

—— 改善投资的管理框架，包括强有力的投资法、协调的投资规定及综合的投资政策；

—— 进一步改善赞比亚发展署的职能，强化它监管、评估和后期服务的能力，使其参与管理的能力最大化；

—— 强化与私营部门的咨询和对话，以及机构间协调的能力；

---

① OECD (2010).

② Silici and Locke (2013).

③ Mujenja and Wonani (2012).

—— 修订税收制度，提供优惠，尤其是矿业领域；

—— 关注投资模式的种类，包括推动公私合营，关注基础设施发展领域；

—— 推行"良好企业行为"管理，创造有竞争力的投资环境；

—— 适当关注教育和雇用需求，将投资转化为人力资源发展。①

虽然通过系列优惠政策，赞比亚政府列出了与农业相关的一些优先领域，但他们并不想评估这些领域所取得的增长成效。从赞比亚发展署的数据，尤其是排名前50的投资（见附录2）看，投资集中于种植业，但种植业本身不属于优先领域。没有证据显示这些投资是为了出口原材料；相反，这些投资可能通过垂直一体化的农业综合开发，促进了制造业的发展。两家最大的承诺投资——乔贝农业前景公司和阿玛西恩农业有限公司②也许是这种趋势最好的例子。③

在各种投资者中，英国投资者和欧洲公司无论从规模还是数量看，似乎仍然占据农业领域的主宰地位。但是来自印度、南非和中国不断增加的投资表明中小型企业领域（主要是中型企业）同样有增长。由于中小型企业更难被统计和监管，因此全面评估它们在农业领域投资的增长非常困难，④ 但正是大型投资项目才带来了传统投资趋势和新趋势之间的有趣区分。因此，大型项目的投资也许是一种不规律现象，是全球土地"热潮"的一部分。要想了解赞比亚开发署为了吸引农业投资而进行的努力能否提供更长久、更可持续的总体增长，必须对更小领域里的增长进行单独评估。

赞比亚发展署的优先领域未能强调农业增长和农村减贫之间的联系。这既包含对小农影响的理解（将在下一部分进行讨论），也包含对小农被纳入投资方式的理解。至于对农业投资的监管，重要的是了解投资趋势怎样才能支持小农和中小企业。通过对承诺投资类型的细分，将有助于我们理解：外国

---

① OECD（2012）.

② Big Concession 公司正式改名为阿玛西恩农业有限公司，后者更常被使用。

③ 两公司的更多信息可见 http：//www.chaytonafrica.com 和 http：//www.amatheon – agri.com/home.html.

④ Mlachile and Takebe（2011）.

直接投资的趋势是否支持更小产业的发展及其支持方式。

6.2　农业投资的监管环境

监督、评估和更广义的数据收集，对评价赞比亚发展署投资政策的效力非常重要。发展署开始强调监督和评估的能力问题，但也重视许多其他问题。虽然开发署提供的数据为研究农业承诺投资（并借此研究发展署在吸引投资兴趣方面的效力）提供了有价值的见解，但仍缺乏一些重要问题的数据：实现或流产的承诺投资所占比例、生产水平、纳税情况、创造就业情况、对其他行业的溢出效应等。如果赞比亚政府想要更多民众从全球对其农业不断增长的投资兴趣中获益，就必须继续提升发展署收集数据和监督投资的能力。

其他领域的农业项目

一些农业投资项目没被本报告收录。虽然赞比亚发展署的数据采集到了大部分农业领域的初级农业投资，但仍有许多农业生产项目被列在其他领域中，尤其是制造业。

生物能源、糖业和棉花产业特别突出，这些初级生产领域的投资与更完整的价值链紧密联系在一起。因此，对给定农业领域中的外国直接投资进行研究会有遗漏许多额外因素的风险，尤其是要想了解这些投资的总体影响时。赞比亚发展署对农业投资的主要激励措施为将经济从依赖矿业转向多元化、解决农村贫困问题提供了一种思路；在研究农业领域时，这两个目标都需要采用更广泛基础的方法。

因此，对该问题的延伸研究将会从更广泛的范围探索农业，包括与农业相关制造业的变化、农业市场的更大变化——通过产量、农村就业数量和粮价变化体现。

除对农业投资政策进行评估外，还应更加关注对它的监管；这有助于保证投资符合赞比亚的法律、认真服从法律管辖。不像其他重要的初级产业如

矿业和旅游业等，农业投资项目不需要额外的运营许可证。① 监管包括土地的
获取和变更，以及作物的种植种类。

目前，仅对农业项目开发初期进行管理，主要受环评（EIA）规定
（1997）条件的限制。该规定要求新建项目必须提交一份环境项目简报以供环
评，如果要改变已有项目，则要提交环境影响报告（EIS）。在农业领域的以
下行为必须进行环评：

①为大规模农业生产而进行的土地清理；

②新引进并在赞比亚使用的农用化学品；

③向赞比亚引进新的动植物，尤其是异国物种；

④50 公顷及以上农田的灌溉方案；

⑤鱼年产量在 100 吨及以上的养殖场；

⑥空中或地面喷洒②。

新建的商业农场项目，尤其是新投资经常需要提交环境影响报告，但是
褐地投资项目也常需要环境影响报告，因为它们往往涉及土地清理。③ 然而在
实践中，农业项目尤其是中小型项目，往往不要求提供环境影响报告。④ 此
外，不仅在 EIA 的申请上，而且在项目经批准后动工的环境和社会法规方面，
赞比亚环境管理署的监管和执行力饱受批评。作为仅有的几项农业项目管理
机制之一，EIA 在评价社会和环境影响上不可能实现有效的过程管理。

6.3 获取土地的过程

由于获得土地的途径仍然是小农和农村社区最大的障碍，土地的获取、
分配、拆迁，以及土地权利值得我们专门进行讨论。⑤ 农业投资者若取得大面

---

① 采矿许可证由部级机构颁发（矿产部、能源和水利开发部），而旅游业项目常常需要赞比亚野生
动物管理局（ZAWA）批准。

② GRZ（1997）.

③ 褐地投资（brownfield investment）项目包括对之前曾被使用或未被充分使用的土地进行再开发，
而绿地专指在未被开发的土地上进行的项目。

④ 赞比亚环境管理署公开了所有 2003～2011 年提交的 EIA 报告。虽然名单上有农业项目，但数量明
显不足。赞比亚环境管理署的员工称他们认为农业项目的 EIA 报告数量不足。

⑤ Hichaambwa and Jayne（2012）.

积的传统或国有土地，都可能对没有土地使用权保障的当地社区产生很大影响。下文将先对农业投资者获取土地的过程进行分析，然后讨论农业投资对土地所有权影响的一些趋势。

根据赞比亚1995年土地法，所有土地都由土地专员管辖，归于总统名下，这套土地管理系统从独立后卡翁达执政的共和国时期延续至今。土地法是分配土地所依据的主要法规，其中也包含对非赞比亚籍人士（暂住者）的土地分配规定。

独立之后，非赞比亚籍人士被剥夺了获取土地的权利；直到1995年的土地法出台，才允许外国人重新拥有土地。根据土地法，外国农业投资者可以通过多种渠道获取土地，包括是否为永久居民、是否有投资许可证、是否获得总统的同意、土地是否为注册在赞比亚的外国公司所有，或是否有5年以下的土地短期出租或租赁协议。[①] 因此，土地法为所有在发展署注册的投资者提供了获取土地的便捷方式。

想要获得有主土地，投资者有两种方法：通过地契转让租赁（国有）土地，或者通过将传统土地划归国有，获得地契。前者最长可租99年，同时需要向土地部缴纳地租。有时候，投资者（尤其是外国投资者）最长只能租14年，以便政府考核某片土地分配后的开发情况，但这让投资者感到不踏实，吸引力不强。[②] 如有意向，所有权可以转移（或转卖）给他人，但必须在土地部登记注册。

若想通过将传统土地划归国有取得土地，申请者必须采取一定的步骤才能获得批准。总体来说，包括以下几步。

—— 获得代表当地首长的村子头人同意，通过首长与社区进行磋商。[③]
—— 将首长的批准以书面形式提交给地方议会。

---

① 这些均可参见土地法（GRZ，1995）。
② Adams（2003）；ZLDC（2013）.
③ 虽然第1号行政通令（1985）中并没有要求进行磋商，但是土地法（1995）中进行了规定。然而，咨询的性质却无明确规定，因此很多环节都可以模糊解释，例如磋商的组成是什么。一般来说，与社区进行磋商需要在当地传统权威给予同意之前举行，但实践中往往并非如此。

——地方议会以向土地部申请开始所有权转移过程的形式表达同意。之后，需要对所涉及的土地进行进一步检查，并由注册测量员划分土地。

——收到调查结果后，土地部颁发地契。

——根据转化土地的面积大小，可能需要其他许可证。转化和分配250公顷以上的传统土地需要土地委员会的批准。[①]

若想保有地契，就必须每年支付地租，这个过程很耗时间，杂费众多，其中有些明确，有些含糊，如向酋长进献礼物等。此外，很多过程都高度集权，投资者需千里迢迢赶往首都卢萨卡，还得耐心等待。所有这些因素都是小农和农村家庭获得土地的障碍，而投资者却可以得到赞比亚发展署的帮助。

赞比亚国民可以通过其他方式获得农田。如向移民安置部副部长办公室提交报告，申请一项移民安置计划，涉及的土地被政府测量、调查后收归国有。从历史上来看，移民安置战略是为了控制大规模的土地投机，通过向商业农民指定土地而不是让他们去谈判获得传统土地。该政策最早由殖民政府执行，以限制和管理移民的农业活动，但导致今天农垦区项目和大面积"未被充分利用"的土地。虽然从涉及的土地面积看，新的移民安置计划与历史上类似的行为不在同一个层次，但历史上的安置过程与政府现行的农垦区开发战略很相像，包括塞伦杰地区的楠桑加农垦区。

与小农相比，外国投资者在竞争土地所有权时的优势在于充足的基金，以及在高度集权、烦琐而低效的土地注册过程中斡旋的能力。然而由于存在流离失所的风险，小农对自己土地的所有权感到不安。在赞比亚的双重所有权系统中，[②] 传统土地的拥有人（例如大部分小农）面临着土地产权风险的日益上升；而头人、酋长和政府，有权将土地再分配给投资者。

虽然政府的投资计划预计外国大型投资者将会通过发展署的农垦区项目获得土地，[③] 但对排名靠前的农业承诺投资的研究表明事实并非如此，因为农

---

① 参见第1号行政通令（1985）。

② 赞比亚的土地所有权系统为双重所有权，国家和传统首领都握有土地。

③ Oakland Institute（2011）；Nolte（2014）.

垦区项目一直很难操作。有迹象表明，农业投资者更愿意获取国有土地。[①] 这可能是因为历史上指定土地的大量存在——殖民带来的欧洲商业农垦人员已占了最适宜耕作的地区——紧靠主干道和电力等其他基础设施。另外，获得传统土地的过程耗时费力、费用不低，而且所有权还没保障，土地冲突的风险更大。简要分析几个知名的投资，就可知投资者的确因上述原因更偏好国有土地。传统的农垦区，如蒙布瓦区就有姆库希、大特许有限公司（Big Concession），铜带省和南部省的铁路沿线地区则吸引了乔贝农业前景公司和阿玛西恩农业有限公司。排名前 50 的农业投资项目中，至少 9 个是国有土地，[②]大量其他投资的地址也表明它们位于有大量国有土地的地区。[③]

如果当地酋长愿意将土地重新分配并转化，或者政府强行占有土地，生活在传统土地上人员的土地权益并没有保障。当然政府如要强制征收土地，就必须与当地社区进行洽谈，并支付赔偿金。[④] 如果农业投资仍然紧随当前获取国有土地的趋势的话，那么农村社区将会面临两方面的压力：居住在传统土地和国有土地边界的人没有意识到他们的"入侵"而被驱逐，或当农业投资者开始考虑获得与被分配国有土地相邻的传统土地时。

虽然投资者似乎并不热衷于获得传统土地，但传统土地向国有土地的迅速转化表明可能是农业投资造成了这样的后果。这样的事件一直在发生，尤其是通过影响当地精英、发生在矿业和旅游业领域。如果雄心勃勃的精英和酋长认为向投资者提供转化的土地有利于吸引投资，虽然投资者自身无责，

---

① 在这种情况下发生的重新安置，后果可能更严重。在几个案例中，由于地主不再存在，社区没有意识到他们生活在已被分配出去的国有土地上。当地契持有者过来索要土地时，生活在该片土地的人被认为是"斯夸特"（squatter），而由于赞比亚没有"斯夸特权利"法令，他们对土地的所有权利都被剥夺。在表面现象之下，是传统地区高密度的小农们面临的土地压力，及缺乏获得土地所有权状态信息的能力。赞比亚土地协会记录了一些类似案例。

② 这 9 个投资为：乔贝农业前景公司、阿玛西恩农业有限公司、ETC 生物能源有限公司、索玛维房地产有限公司、卡奥·阿玛齐有限公司、银地牧场、非洲农作物有限公司、赞比亚 CBL 农业有限公司和赞比亚普阿利亚公司。

③ 投资的地址详见附录 2。虽然有时列出的地址实际上是总部的地址，但总部常常就在农场上。因此，将地址申报为南省或铜带省地区的投资很有可能位于国有土地上。

④ 这点在土地收购法（1975）和土地法（1995）中都有体现。但是，通过当地传统权威的同意，将土地进行转化，私下获得土地的过程和上述两法的规定不同。

但土地仍然被从农村社区剥夺出去。

要理解农业投资者带来的影响，必须理解小农获取土地时最常面临的压力和问题。由于土地面积对农业增长和产能有直接影响，因此限制土地面积可能是制约小农收入增长的主要因素。然而，小农无法获取土地并不只是因为土地限制，还因为缺乏充分的信息，包括土地的所有权和获取土地的不同渠道等信息。现有压力会迫使小农迁移到边缘地区，使他们面临着土地产量低和权属不明确的双重危险。

像种植业和养殖业等农业模式常常需要大面积成片且有产权的土地。许多这样的投资都满足于获取殖民时期已划分好的农地，他们也许不能赶走那些有能力守护自己土地的社区，但却能轻易逼走那些生活在边缘地区的弱势社区。同时，订单农业项目也仅对有土地产权的农户开放，只有他们才有能力和手段对土地进一步开发。

很明显，在获取土地上，男性和女性面临着不同的问题。[1] 许多影响土地所有权的因素都指向了性别问题；即使能够获取土地，女性也常常无法获得和男性相同的土地安全保障，而且常常只拥有更边缘、更容易被占用的土地。因此，当土地的所有权遭到威胁时，她们就更处于劣势，解决冲突或建立安全网的办法也更少。

许多国际指南可以帮助政府、投资者、公民社会和社区团体解决土地征用问题。虽然赞比亚政府正努力解决搬迁和重新安置问题，但它目前还没制定"重新安置政策"。[2] 迄今为止，还没有一个明确的机制来保护农村社区使之免受拆迁之苦，也没有政策规定赔偿和重新安置的最低标准。

联合国粮农组织最近通过了《国家粮食安全范围内土地、渔业及森林权属负责任治理自愿准则》。[3] 它适用于政府、公民社会组织、私营部门和社区

---

① FAO (2013a).

② 赞比亚最初是将非洲联盟关于国内流离失所者的坎帕拉公约国内化。因此，流离失所和重新安置的问题都是在强制移民的框架下进行管理。该情况并没有很好地解决开发导致的流离失所问题，但如果使用大型农业投资者，如阿玛西恩农业有限公司和乔贝农业前景公司采用的世界银行经营政策4.12和国际金融公司的指导性说明第五条，却可以解决。

③ 以下简称"自愿准则"。

等，希望有助于对土地所有权的管理，强化不同行为体积极接受并尊重土地的使用权利。在赞比亚，尚未有将该准则引入国内的尝试，也没有评估农业投资对这些国际标准的反对意见。然而，投资来源国、投资对象国应该共同发起一场运动，号召国际投资者也坚持实施这些准则。

6.4　农业与生计

除土地压力外，农业投资者可以通过与市场的联系，对小农产生大的正面或负面影响。农业投资者既可以与小农竞争，也可以和他们合作。在对农业外国直接投资进行分析时，最受人关注的问题是它们对当地小农和贫困水平的必然影响。这些影响既可以是直接的（获取土地），也可以是间接的（如影响当地就业，或影响当地农业生计和市场等）。理解和量化农业投资对农村社区的影响需要大量的实地工作，超出了本报告的范围，本部分将关注现有农业投资信息与基层开发所影响两个领域之间的联系：农业模式和雇用、农业生计。

农业劳动力模式与雇用

随着农业投资被推崇为增加农村就业机会的驱动力，人们必须对不同模式怎样促进当地劳工市场的评估给予同等关注。历史上，农业可分为三种模式：种植园农业、契约农业和商品农业。[①] 典型的种植园种植单一作物，但需要大量劳力（当地人或外地人）进行生产。契约农业可以通过不同的方式组织：或是重要核心连接次要农户，或是通过合同将分散小农组织起来。最后，商品农业需要连片的土地，可种植多种作物，但一般都高度机械化，不需要太多劳动力；人数多少根据作物种类而定，但一般比种植园农业少。

对排名前 50 位投资的研究表明，其中 16 个投资是商品农业项目［12 家从事作物种植，4 家从事混合农业，包括乔贝农业前景公司（ChobeAgrivision）、德国阿曼松农业公司（AmatheonAgri）和 ETC 生物能源投资公司等］。

---

① Smalley（2013）。也有其他农业模型分类法，如 IIED 推行的分类法，包括：合约式农业、管理和租赁合同，佃农农业、合资公司、农民所有商业，和上游下游商业链接。然而，很多模型在赞比亚并不常见，包括管理和租赁合同式农业、佃农农业和合资公司（Vermeulen and Cotula, 2010）。

名单中也有种植园农业，它们主要是糖业、大米和烟草种植园（共 7 家，包括 CBL 投资公司和非洲农作物有限公司）。契约农业，如订单农业，在赞比亚发展署的分类中并没有明确体现。然而，家禽、家畜和鱼等养殖业在赞比亚有很多投资项目（11 家，包括银地牧场），但却没有被传统的农业投资分类包括进来。最后，有 3 项投资为生物能源投资，2 项为园艺业投资（园艺业与商品农业分开计算，因为园艺产品的价值比较高），8 项没有明确的投资内容。

名义上，需要劳动力较少的农业模式，如种植业、牲畜和渔业养殖都有投资项目。高价值农业和种植园农业都存在，并出现了更多劳动密集型模式。然而，看来被提出的农业模式和雇用承诺人数之间并没有一个清楚的趋势，因为一个重要的变量——投资的生产规模是未知的。

农业加工方面也有很多投资。如果加工设施建在农村地区，垂直整合趋势和对在国内进行加工和制造的强调，都将有助于为那些地区提供更多的就业机会。迄今，农业加工设施仍然集中在铜带省的多个城市或卢萨卡这样的中心城市。

虽然政策鼓励订单农业项目，以及几个前景很好的糖业投资案例也没被收录在附录 2 中，但投资者似乎并不喜欢这种模式。赞比亚最大的订单农业项目来自糖业和棉花领域，但像马扎布卡赞比亚糖业公司或伊洛沃（Illovo）糖业公司，及棉花方面的投资，在发展署提供的名单上明显缺失——它们被列入了制造业。

雇用情况也不能只关注投资创造了多少岗位，还要看当地社区受聘于这些岗位的能力。创造的岗位对当地社区有多大意义？在给当地社区提供就业和找到能满足农业生产需求的工作者之间存在一个平衡；当地技工市场并不总是存在。种植业和种植园农业这样的模式青睐低技能工人，有助于创造上岗快、工期短的职位。在姆彭戈韦 ETC 公司以前的农场，以及马扎布卡赞比亚糖业公司的种植园里，永久岗位一般雇用男性，女性能获得的工作多限于季节性、兼职、没有雇用合同的工作。① 在赞比亚，订单农业主要限于棉花生

---

① FAO (2013a).

产，虽然也在麻风树和大豆生产中采用。订单农业同时可以提供技能技术转移，但小农往往要承担更大的风险。

如上所述，如果农业投资的确能带来雇用机会，那么人们需要更关注对农村雇用情况的管理，以保证农村社区能切实获益。到目前，农业投资并没有带来大量的就业机会，主要原因是很多大型投资都采用了对劳力需求少的生产模式。

其他问题涉及农业投资应对低工资（或低于最低标准）等恶劣工作条件的能力、对安全条例和劳工法的遵守和社会保障的提供。此外，如在土地所有权无保障的例子中所表现的，女性往往在劳工市场处于劣势，面临着工作环境危险、职位没保障、工作技术含量低，以及相应的低工资等情况。如果女性能够获得土地和劳动力的话，订单农业的机会也能平等地为女性带来福音。①

虽然许多大型投资者推行的企业社会责任项目能为他们与当地社区的关系带来积极影响，但 IIED 认为农业商业模式可以给当地社区带来更大的帮助。投资者越愿意采用包容性的商业模式，当地社区和小农通过影响决策和商业模式对农业投资的参与越多，那么投资就越可能对周边社区带来正面影响。② 政府政策在影响和激励不同的农业模式上也能发挥重要作用，虽然通过发展署运作的赞比亚政府在这方面还没取得成功。

当地农业市场和粮食安全

农业产量低和多元化不足被视为小农经济增长的主要挑战。农业投资帮助小农提高产量的办法之一是转移技能技术：通过培训项目专门对农业工人进行培训，或者为当地创立或扩展简单可行的农业技术市场。

对整个赞比亚小农而言，杂交玉米占据主导地位。虽然目前对投资者选择种植的作物了解有限，但若产出的农产品在当地市场上和小农竞争，投资者选择的作物种类（如粮食或经济作物）会带来明显不同的后果。不像园艺

---

① FAO (2013a).
② Vermeulen and Cotula (2010).

产品和种植园作物这些以出口为导向的作物，商品粮种植业、畜牧业和渔业养殖的产品主要还是供应当地或赞比亚国内市场。然而畜牧业、渔业养殖和玉米之外的其他主食（如小麦和大豆）生产，主要是供应城市市场，而非当地农村市场。

如果农业投资不能很好地融入当地农业的上下游市场，那么它就会像一块飞地，只供应城市中心，而不会为当地社区带来积极影响。如果农业投资与当地社区密切合作，通过生产、加工和仓储，可以形成规模经济。诸如乔贝农业前景公司和阿玛西恩农业有限公司意欲推行的垂直整合模式，一旦被允许融入当地的价值链，将有潜力促进区域发展。

增加农业投资不仅有助于赞比亚全国，也有助于保障投资所在地区的粮食更加安全。粮食安全可以通过增产或引进某些作物，尤其是那些高营养价值的作物，或是通过增加收入（提高工资、增加市场准入机会等方式）来实现。要想全面评估农业投资对粮食安全的贡献，就必须获取投资之前的基础数据，以及对不断变化中的家庭收入和支出模式、当地市场和粮价进行分析，才能够进行。

7　结论和建议

本报告不仅调查了赞比亚农业外国直接投资的基本情况及动因，还通过研究农业生产的形式分析了农业外国直接投资是如何进行的，这为了解投资对当地甚至对赞比亚全国贫困状况的影响提供了重要基础。随着全世界对发展中国家农业投资兴趣的增长，赞比亚的农业投资也呈增长之势。虽然农业投资仍然只占赞比亚 FDI 流入总额和 GDP 很小的部分，农业增长依旧对经济多元化以及重要的减贫问题有很大影响，但值得关注的是，农业投资并不等于减贫，政府的任务在于确保所吸引的投资也能使小农获益。

这个任务在当前尤为重要，因为农业投资的数量自 2008 年以来便一直攀升。它们既包括中小型投资，也包括前所未有的大型投资。一系列投资政策得以改善，尤其是赞比亚发展署对众多投资优惠政策的整合，有助于投资的进行。以上因素外加稳定的政治环境，使得赞比亚成为投资的乐土。

　　赞比亚发展署提供的数据使我们对赞比亚的农业投资有一个更全面的了解。这些数据表明，大型和中小型投资都有人在开展；来自传统投资国如英国、津巴布韦和南非的投资仍然占据农业投资的主要部分，但是也有一些来自新兴经济体（如中国和印度）的投资；投资往往由已知的金融渠道国家帮助进行，金融链很复杂。这些数据也有不足之处，如：缺乏投资承诺实现率方面的数据，或许多中小型投资在数据中没体现出来。但是，无论这些农业投资来自哪里，都同样受到赞比亚政策的管理和约束。

　　本报告也注意到，政策与促进农业投资的实际需要之间还存在差距。信息的透明度依然是关注的关键领域，这不仅体现在政府机关和企业参与研究的意愿度上，更体现在信息的可获得性上。即使有合作关系，笔者也经常发现对投资进行监督和评估的重要数据，如承诺投资的实现率很难获得。环境影响评估仍然是投资信息的重要公众来源，但很多报告虽是公共档案，却很难为公众获得。为更有效地监管入境的农业投资，赞比亚发展署和赞比亚环境管理署的能力都必须得到加强，包括提高数据收集能力，创设了解投资及其影响的管理机制；这些机制应参考新的国际准则，如联合国粮农组织的自愿准则。

　　在研究目前农业投资带来的影响时，笔者可以得出一些初步结论。对农业用地的需求一直很大，如果这种需求继续攀升的话，少有机制能保证小农手中传统土地使用权的安全。在雇用与劳动力、农业市场和粮食安全这些关键领域，投资可能带来正面或是负面的影响。然而，没有一种让农业投资遵循的机制可以评估它带来的影响，很多时候只能依靠投资的农业模式进行分析。迄今为止，许多通过赞比亚发展署进行的承诺投资都青睐大规模商业和种植园农业模式，只提供很少的就业岗位，与当地社区的融合度也很低。至此，赞比亚发展署虽有政策意愿，但在推进支持穷人的投资模式上束手无策。赞比亚必须重新考虑其农业投资政策，以便有效推进将小农和农村社区纳入其投资价值链的农业投资模式。虽然量化评估这些变化还为时尚早，但农村贫困的痼疾和获得工资收入的渴望（经常化为绝望）为更多农村地区的农业投资提供了廉价劳动力。

下一步研究的方向将集中在系统地搜集基础数据，对当地和家庭层面发生的变化进行筛选和量化，以便综合评估大型商业农场和小而精的中小企业等投资新形式所带来的影响。该研究应集中关注农业投资影响的几个重要方面：

—— 土地所有权的获得、土地整合对土地市场影响、土地权利和使用权保障、土地收购与"事先和知情的同意"（FPIC）的作用、居民拆迁与重新安置、土地用途变化带来的环境影响等问题；

—— 劳动力与雇用——尤其对雇用劳动和工作条件、工资转化为家庭福利（特别是医疗卫生、粮食安全、教育等领域内的家庭福利）、劳动力构成以及其变化的性别影响等问题；

—— 农业市场变化——尤其是粮食价格、小农的竞争力和农业生计、获得上下游服务（如投入和加工）和进入市场能力的变化；

—— 粮食安全和营养变化——各种农产品的可获得性；粮食安全战略在家庭层面的变化。

缩略语表

AGOA　非洲增长与机遇法案

AU　非洲联盟

BRICS　金砖国家（巴西、俄罗斯、印度、中国和南非）

CAADP　非洲农业综合开发项目

CDC　英联邦发展公司

COMESA　东部和南部非洲共同市场

CSO　中央统计办公室（赞比亚共和国政府）

DAC　发展援助委员会

DRC　刚果民主共和国

EIA　环境影响评价

EIS　环境影响评介

FAO 联合国粮食及农业组织

FDI 外国直接投资

GDP 国内生产总值

GRZ 赞比亚共和国政府

HDI 人类发展指数（联合国开发计划署）

IFC 国际金融公司（世界银行）

LMIC 低中等收入国家

MDG 千年发展目标

MFEZ 多功能经济区（"经济特区"）

NAIP 国家农业投资政策

NAP 国家农业政策

NTDA 非传统发展援助

PACRA 专利与公司登记署

ODA 官方发展援助

OECD 经济合作与发展组织

SADC 南部非洲发展共同体

SME 中小型企业

SNDP 第六个全国发展计划（"六五计划"）

UK 英国（大不列颠联合王国）

UNCTAD 联合国贸易暨发展会议

UNDP 联合国开发计划署

UNIDO 联合国工业发展组织

VAT 增值税

ZDA 赞比亚开发署

ZEMA 赞比亚环境管理署

附录

附录1 赞比亚发展署提供的综合所得税和增值税优惠政策

所得税优惠政策

1. 公司在卢萨卡证券交易所上市的第一年，其农业部门的收入税享受2%的优惠；但是，三分之一以上股权属于赞比亚人的公司在上市的第一年，其农业部门的收入税享受7%的优惠。

2. 在投资后的头两年，用于种植、加工或旅游的工具、机械和设备可以获得50%的折旧补贴。

3. 用于加工、采矿或开宾馆的建筑在第一年享受10%、后面每年享受5%的折旧补贴。

4. 采矿和农业部门所采购的绝大多数固定设备免进口税。

5. 从事种植、化肥生产和非传统产品（除铜和钴之外的所有产品）出口的公司缴纳15%的所得税。

6. 农场用于挖掘树桩、清理土地、防止土壤退化、打井、航空和地理调查、水资源保护等方面的开销享受全额补贴。

7. 种植咖啡、香蕉、柑橘或类似经济作物等所用开销享受10%的发展补贴。

8. 生产改良补贴——用于农场改良的开支在支出当年给予补贴。

9. 在分销公司开展业务的前五年内，农业利润分红免税。

10. 用于工业建筑建造或改善方面开销的10%初始补贴可以从税收中扣除。

11. 企业借外汇用于工商业建筑建设或改善而出现的汇率损失可以通过减免税收来弥补。

12. 组装摩托车、汽车或自行车的公司前五年的红利免税。

13. 结转损失年限：铜矿和钴矿十年、其他矿五年，非矿业类五年，农业和非传统产品出口行业五年。

增值税优惠政策

1. 登记注册的企业在进口符合条件的资本货物时暂缓缴纳增值税（增值税延期）。

2. 应纳税的产品出口时免税。

3. 业务转让后继续经营的暂缓缴纳增值税。

4. 对于申报反向增值税的服务，同等对待其增值税。

5. 用于专业协会如建筑与土木工程承包商协会的资金。

6. 与注册供应商进行交易缴纳进项税时，暂缓缴纳增值税。

7. 对已经开展业务进行增值税登记时，可以要求免除此前三个月的进项税。

8. 免税区的投资人减免增值税。

9. 特定部门增值税的优惠政策如下：

（1）农业：对已经开展业务进行增值税登记时，可以要求免除此前三个月的进项税；免税区的投资人减免增值税。

（2）制造业：通过商业出口项目，从非本地居民业务中购买和出口在赞比亚生产的产品返还增值税；对已经开展的商务进行增值税登记时，可以要求免除此前三个月的进项税；对已经开展的生产活动进行增值税登记时，可以要求免除此前两年的进项税；

（3）矿业：对生产前在勘探上的开销，矿业部门可以要求免除五年的进项税；矿产品出口免税。

（4）旅游业：旅游业一揽子业务免税；其他旅游服务免税，对非本地游客和访客退税；对外国游客临时带入赞比亚的所有商品免进口增值税。

附录 2　据赞比亚发展署收到的排名前 50 名农业投资承诺（1998~2012 年）

年份	公司	投资的具体行业	投资地点	投资者来源国	承诺的雇用人数	承诺的投资额（美元）
2009	乔贝农业有限公司	种植业	卢萨卡	英国	1630	250000000

续表

年份	公司	投资的具体行业	投资地点	投资者来源国	承诺的雇用人数	承诺的投资额（美元）
2012	大康塞恩农业有限公司	种植业	蒙布瓦	英国	92	243434722
2011	赤道农场（赞比亚）有限公司	种植业	缺乏数据	南非	358	164724256
2011	阿曼贸易有限公司	农业相关活动	缺乏数据	马拉维	1992	112000000
2007	ETC 生物能源有限公司	粮食和和生物燃料作物生产	姆蓬圭	印度	0	59648687
2011	内哈赞比亚有限公司	种植业（大米）	缺乏数据	新加坡	78	35000000
2012	黑星农业有限公司	缺乏数据	缺乏数据	南非	100	24000000
1999	扎米塔农场	种植业	卢萨卡	赞比亚	72	20000000
2011	特拉·戈尔德（赞比亚）有限公司	种植业（大米）	缺乏数据	毛里求斯	20	20000000
2011	克朗·米勒斯有限公司	农产品加工	缺乏数据	印度	79	17800000
2005	赞贝齐烟叶有限公司	种植业（烟草）	卢萨卡	英国	233	16109155
2009	多种食用油联合农业加工有限公司	种植业	卢萨卡	尼日利亚	565	15506000
1998	卡隆吉控股公司	缺乏数据	姆皮卡	津巴布韦	1110	15413003
2010	厄斯斯通资源（赞比亚）有限公司	种植业	卢萨卡	印度	1000	15000000
2012	标杆基金有限公司	缺乏数据	缺乏数据	南非	1100	15000000
2012	罗斯·布里德斯赞比亚有限公司	家禽养殖业	缺乏数据	塞舌尔	450	14520000
2003	赞比亚烟叶有限公司	种植业	卢萨卡	津巴布韦	1200	14083500
2006	索莫合资产有限公司	种植业	恩多拉	丹麦	70	14060000
2011	泽塔农场赞比亚有限公司	缺乏数据	缺乏数据	英国	60	13650000
2008	因斯科·戈尔德农业有限公司	家禽养殖业	琼戈韦	英国	178	12579808
2009	哈拉马兹有限公司	园艺业	琼戈韦	英国	170	12500000
2010	巨人物流有限公司	种植业	恩多拉	南非	46	12450000
2012	尤里卡鸡业有限公司	家禽养殖业	缺乏数据	赞比亚	15	12000000

续表

年份	公司	投资的具体行业	投资地点	投资者来源国	承诺的雇用人数	承诺的投资额（美元）
2012	西尔弗兰兹·兰青公司	混合农业	津巴	爱尔兰	62	11914792
2011	姆彭德渔业有限公司	渔业	缺乏数据	赞比亚	37	11572000
1998	弗拉明戈农场有限公司	家禽养殖业	卢安夏	赞比亚	145	11050000
2001	卡姆瓦亚桑卡农场有限公司	花卉种植业	齐邦博	赞比亚	938	10801027
2001	索伊马斯特公司	种植业	卢萨卡	津巴布韦	154	10520165
2011	斯特林农业企业有限公司	农产品加工（制糖）	缺乏数据	毛里求斯	870	10300000
2011	农业科技有限公司	农产品加工业	缺乏数据	中国	104	10001042
2006	D1油料赞比亚有限公司	种植业（生物燃料）	卢萨卡	南非	77	10000000
2008	非洲粮食有限公司	种植业	乔马	赞比亚	0	10000000
2008	普罗格雷斯夫家禽养殖有限公司	家禽养殖业	卢萨卡	南非	64	10000000
2012	西尔弗兰兹公司	混合农业	津巴	爱尔兰	114	9776600
2011	卡里巴·哈韦斯特公司	渔业	缺乏数据	毛里求斯	320	9642000
2006	IACZ农业有限公司	种植业/家禽养殖业	恩多拉	德国	506	9395000
2006	戈尔登·莱有限公司	家禽养殖业	卢安夏	澳大利亚	22	8738371
2012	韦里诺农业产业有限公司	缺乏数据	缺乏数据	英国	45	8000000
2011	约科商品和承包公司	混合农业	缺乏数据	南非	5	7700000
2012	亚列罗有限公司	渔业	希亚丰加	开曼群岛	82	6640000
2009	伦达孜烟草有限公司	种植业（烟草）	隆达济	津巴布韦	2	6506169
2009	CBL农业赞比亚有限公司	种植业（甘蔗）	马扎布卡	南非	缺乏数据	5900000
2010	普罗·阿利亚赞比亚公司	混合农业	卢萨卡	英国	187	5900000

续表

年份	公司	投资的具体行业	投资地点	投资者来源国	承诺的雇用人数	承诺的投资额（美元）
2006	库尔·阿玛茹拉有限公司	缺乏数据	卢萨卡	塞浦路斯	154	5831940
2009	M&Ms 有限公司	种植业	卢安夏	希腊	27	5765301
2011	比利斯农场	缺乏数据	缺乏数据	英属维京群岛	0	5402631
2005	米卡塔农业有限公司	家禽养殖业	恩多拉	爱尔兰	73	5070000
1998	德克卢蒂（非洲）有限公司	种植业	琼戈韦	加拿大	308	5000000
2008	环保生物能源有限公司	生物燃料（种植油料作物）	卢萨卡	英国	254	5000000
2012	萨文达管理服务有限公司	缺乏数据	缺乏数据	赞比亚	248	5000000

印度在赞比亚农业部门的私人投资

——案例研究

〔印度〕 奥博拉吉多·比斯瓦斯

阿贾伊·杜贝 著

马婕 译 *

1 研究介绍

针对目前印度在非洲的活动，印度学者进行了多方面的研究，但大部分在泛非角度上进行，通常关注一些宏大的问题。导致这一情况的原因主要有两个：第一，作为重要的地缘政治学科，非洲研究越来越受到关注；第二，研究某一特定问题或国家的资料极其缺乏，这可能是由于重点研究因资金不足而难以开展。在此情况下，乐施会所提供的，研究印度私人投资者在赞比亚农业部门中作用的机会就显得恰逢其时且意义重大。

印度是非洲日益重要的投资者、贸易伙伴和援助国，基于此，本研究不仅要评估印度在赞比亚不断增多的印迹，还要分析其在赞比亚农业部门直接投资（FDI）的性质和可持续性。自 2000 年以来，印度对非策略发生了重大变化，因此本研究也与印度的宏观非洲政策相关。在增进与非洲关系的过程中，印度并不是只依赖良好的传统声誉，它还将经济理性置于优先考虑的位置。印度政府重新调整的非洲政策就强调了有机可持续的发展模型，这意味着新德里和赞比

---

* 奥博拉吉多·比斯瓦斯：印度孟买大学非洲研究中心教授。相关研究领域包括：印非关系，亚洲和非洲的地区组织以及南部、东南部非洲的其他问题。阿贾伊·杜贝：印度贾瓦哈拉尔尼赫鲁大学非洲研究教授。马婕：北京大学国际关系学院硕士生。

亚首都卢萨卡的关系将包括帮助该国摆脱经济上对采矿业的过度依赖，提升农业等其他部门的经营活动。

然而，这并不意味着忽略了一个事实——在印度的后全球化社会，赞比亚对印度企业家来说具有巨大潜力。重点关注赞比亚农业部门的意义之所以重大，不仅因为它为印度公司提供了尚待开发的投资机会，还因为印度自身的粮食安全问题。印度政府曾公开声明：它确实正在考虑通过私人购买海外农业用地来确保印度的粮食安全。[①]

目前，已有好几个国家通过印度农业部邀请印度人去租地经营农场，例如埃及、埃塞俄比亚、蒙古、塞内加尔、苏丹、特立尼达和多巴哥、突尼斯等，印度农业部已请国内的农业协会和农商组织研究这些提议。印度农业部农业与合作司联合秘书在 2009 年 12 月的一封信中提到，"本部门收到了来自若干国家的很多提议，这为印度公司收购土地办农场以实现其商业目标，为印度农民或其团体利用小块耕地发展农业提供了机会"。这些提议的目的在于提升各国的农业生产，以减少它们对进口粮食的依赖，并将剩余粮食出口到第三世界国家。[②]

在对印度参与赞比亚农业部门的活动进行分析时，本研究涵盖了许多方面。第一，对赞比亚农业部门中的印度投资者及其投资额度进行了确认，列出了赞比亚农业部门中的利益相关者并对其角色进行了说明。第二，对直接投资为小农（尤其是农村妇女）和赞比亚社区生计所带来的影响进行了调查。本文仔细考察了流入赞比亚农业部门的直接投资所带来的各种反响，既包括农业发展和贫困减少等正面影响，也包括强制拆迁等风险，以及因土地和水引发的日益增多的冲突；还对直接投资的其他技术方面，如投资的性质、范围、推动力和形式等进行了评估。第三，对赞比亚和印度各种有助于投资的行政和管理结构进行了分析。

① Dheeraj Tiwari & Rituraj Tiwari, "Food Security: Govt Mulls Private Purchase of Farm Land Abroad," *The Economic Times*, March 5, 2012. http://articles.economictimes.indiatimes.com/2012 – 03 – 05/news/31124242_ 1_ farm – land – foodprocessing – pulses (Accessed on May 1 2013).

② R. Goswami, "African landrush," *InfochangeIndia*, April 5, 2010.

文献回顾是解决这一领域现有知识差距的第一步。本报告分为四部分。第二部分对印非关系和印度直接投资政策进行了综述，前者总结了印非关系由古至今的演变，后者概述了印度实行经济自由化前后的直接投资政策，该综述奠定了本文的基础。第三部分题为"印度在非洲农业部门中的存在"，介绍印度政府的各项举措——如条约和协定、信贷额度等，以及印度的私人投资和直接投资。第四部分"印度与赞比亚的互动"包含两个小节：第一小节对当前关于赞比亚的部分政策、激励措施、法规、税收优惠的文献进行综述，这些政策法规旨在激励印度的私人投资，尤其是对农业部门的投资；第二小节则着重关注了印度在赞比亚的农业投资。

由于印度自身缺乏对该问题的研究，因此综述中所用文献多为来自印度之外的二手资料。还要强调的是，由于解决本文问题的具体资料比较缺乏，因此文献综述中的分析就相对有限。本研究在很大程度上依赖实地调研中收集的一手数据，以便更全面地理解当地的实际情况。

2　总况

2.1　印非关系

印度对非洲的介入可以追溯到该国在 20 世纪 60 年代进行的独立运动的早期甚至更早。如今印度对非洲的介入层次和目的与那时已有很大不同。早期，印度是以第三世界国家中正在出现的、亚非国家团结一致的视角看待非洲国家。通过融资在东非国家修建铁路，印度在非洲基础设施项目中地位显著；此外，印度还在坦桑尼亚和肯尼亚援建小型工业、发展合资纺织企业等。随后几十年里，印度还根据"印度经济技术合作项目"向非洲提供专业技术、医生和奖学金等其他多种形式的援助。

21 世纪开始十多年里，尤其是随着印度崛起为世界经济中的重要成员及其自身对石油等自然资源的需求日益加重，印非合作范围明显扩大。这在印度—非洲论坛峰会中表露无遗：在峰会中，印度为吸引非洲国家，提供了大额贷款、赠款及其他发展援助。在推进与非洲国家关系方面，印度最重要的举措是"聚焦非洲计划"。这是印度工商部 2002 年根据其"进出口政策"（EXIM）提出的一项计划，意在帮助印度公司在非洲经商，其主要目标在于通过识别印非双边贸易投资的潜力领域，提升双方互动。自 2003 年 4 月 1 日生效以来，"聚焦非洲计划"的实施范围已扩大到整个非洲大陆。[①] 通过这个计划，印度政府为众多的贸易促进组织、出口促进委员会、顶尖商会和印度使团提供了资金支持。[②]

印度之所以不断向非洲大陆示好，原因是多方面的。第一，能源安全一直是印度外交政策的重中之重。第二，非洲既是印度商品和服务的重要市场，也是印度经济迅猛发展所需战略性矿产及其他自然资源的重要来源地；[③] 同样，非洲国家也对印度信息技术、农业、卫生及制药业领域中性价比高的中间技术非常感兴趣。第三，随着经济实力的增长，印度决定将军事力量投射到印度洋地区（该地区长期被印度视为自己的势力范围）。鉴于极端组织、犯罪集团（通过在印度洋走私毒品、武器及人口）和海盗的存在，印度已开始大幅扩张它在非洲之角及印度洋地区的军事存在，包括在塞舌尔、马达加斯加和毛里求斯设立侦听站；2009 年底，印度成功邀请马尔代夫加入其南方海军司令部。此外，印度进口的石油中约有 70% 通过印度洋运到国内各港口。[④]

因此，非洲对于印度的优先重点和需要具有至关重要的战略作用，这也确保了印非关系的提升。

2.2 印度海外直接投资政策

海外直接投资是全球化的自然延伸，常始于出口。在这一过程中，各国通过在某些有特定优势的国家扩大海外生产，帮助它们参与全球竞争，努力

---

① Ministry of Commerce Trade and Industry (MCTI), *An Investment Guide to Zambia Opportunities and Conditions 2011*, Government of Zambia, www. mcti. gov. zm (Accessed: 1 July 2013).

② Ministry of Commerce Trade and Industry (MCTI), *An Investment Guide to Zambia Opportunities and Conditions 2011*.

③ Emma Mawdsely and Gerard (eds.), *India in Africa: Changing Geographies of Power*, Pambazuka Press: Nairobi, 2011.

④ Emma Mawdsely and Gerard (eds.), *India in Africa: Changing Geographies of Power*.

进入市场或资源地，逐步降低生产和交易成本。采用这种战略能帮助这些国家赶上竞争对手。[1] 近年来，印度对外的直接投资显著增加。由于全球化是一个双向过程，印度经济与世界其他地区的融合程度不仅反映在更多外国直接投资的流入上，也反映在其更多海外直接投资的流出上。2005 ~ 2007 年，流入印度的直接投资总额为 177.66 亿美元，印度对外直接投资总额为 115.01 亿美元；直接投资流入量增加了 361.9 亿美元，这一趋势在 2011 年继续保持。同样地，2012 年印度外国直接投资流入量达到 255.43 亿美元，对外直接投资为 85.83 亿美元。[2] 国内企业通过进行海外投资，能更好地进入全球网络及市场，并进行技术和技能转移，也能更好地分享研发成果；此外，这也可以作为公司提升品牌形象、有效利用所在国可用原材料的一项战略。对印度来说，海外投资的动机主要是寻求资源、寻求市场，抑或寻求技术。近期，为寻求海外资源，尤其是澳大利亚、印度尼西亚、非洲等地的能源，印度企业海外投资激增。[3]

然而，这并不意味着印度公司的海外投资是 20 世纪 90 年代才出现的新现象。印度公司自 60 年代起就开始在海外投资，但印度的限制性政策使其海外投资局限于发展中国家的少数小型合资企业。印度首个重要的海外投资项目是博拉集团（Birla Group）1959 年在埃塞俄比亚设立的纺织厂。[4] 印度的海外投资主要集中于西非、东非、中东、南亚和东亚，这些地区与印度拥有相同的殖民遗产，保持一定的历史联系。

不同经济体的政策环境的变化，会对一个国家在全球经济中的对外投资

---

① Speech of Harun R Khan, Deputy Governor, Reserve Bank of India at the Bombay Chamber of Commerce & Industry, Mumbai on March 2, 2012.

② UNCTAD, *World Investment Report 2013*, http://unctad. org/sections/dite_ dir/docs/wir2013/wir13_ fs _ in_ en. pdf（Accessed：10 February 2014）.

③ Address by Shri H R Khan, Deputy Governor of the Reserve Bank of India, at the Bombay Chamber of Commerce & Industry, Mumbai, 2 March 2012, http://rbidoc s. rbi. org. in/rdocs/Speeches/PDFs/OV27022012. pdf（Accessed：6 June 2013）.

④ Prema - chandra Athukorala, "Outward Foreign Direct Investment from India," *Asian Development Review*, Vol. 26, No. 2, 2009. Quoted from：Address by Shri H. R. Khan, Deputy Governor of the Reserve Bank of India, at the Bombay Chamber of Commerce & Industry, Mumbai, 2 March 2012, http://rbido- cs. rbi. org. in/rdocs/Speeches/PDFs/OV27022012. pdf（Accessed：6 June 2013）.

模式产生极大影响。尽管如此，出于对资本外流问题的关注，各个国家尤其是新兴和发展中国家都对实行对外投资自由化政策持相对更谨慎的态度。因此，关注印度在这方面的政策演变也是非常重要的。

在印度，企业家认识到在海外创办合资企业及全资子公司是推动全球业务的重要渠道。他们采取的主要方式包括通过合资企业及全资子公司促进对外直接投资，以及通过提供资金支持来推动印度的出口（包括项目的出口）。随着资本流入量的稳步上升（尤其是 2006 ~ 2010 年），外汇储备总体状况的改善使政府能安心逐步放松资本管制，并简化印度对外投资程序。印度对外直接投资政策的演变主要分为三个不同而有所重叠的阶段：[①]

- 第一阶段（1992 ~ 1995 年）：印度经济自由化时期；
- 第二阶段（1995 ~ 2000 年）：创立"快车道"，出台了《外汇管理法》（FEMA）；
- 第三阶段（2000 年至今）：《外汇管理法》下的自由化框架。

印度对外直接投资的形式多为股权投资和贷款。根据联合国贸易和发展会议发布的《2011 年世界投资报告》，印度对外直接投资额名列全球第 21位；根据印度公司的净买入价值，即跨国并购交易总量，2010 年印度仅次于美国、加拿大、日本和中国，排名第五。重要的是，印度国内企业海外投资规模也有所扩大，2010 年印度净购入交易的平均规模已达 1.9 亿美元，仅次于中国的 1.97 亿美元，居第二位。[②]

印度是世界五大新兴经济体之一，其国有企业也日渐向跨国企业发展。近年来，印度国有企业如印度国家电力集团（NTPC）、印度天然气有限公司（GAIL）、印度石油天然气公司（ONGC）和印度国家铝业公司（NALCO）已经进行了大量海外"绿地投资"。[③]

---

① Speech of Harun R. Khan.
② UNCTAD, *World Investment Report 2013*, http：//unctad. org/sections/dite_ dir/docs/wir2013/wirl3_ fs_ in_ en. pdf（Accessed：10 February 2014）.
③ Speech of Harun R. Khan.

虽然海外投资领域的政策变化使印度企业的跨国收购量日益增多，但自 1992 年以来开展的其他结构性改革，如放宽工业管制、放松对外资流入的管制和贸易自由化等，也使印度工业进行了大重组。一项趋势分析显示，自 1999～2000 年度以来，印度对外直接投资总量成倍增长。从 2005～2006 年度到 2009～2010 年度的这一期间，对外投资净流出量急剧上升到 743 亿美元，而 2000～2001 年度到 2004～2005 年度期间这一数额仅为 82 亿美元；尽管印度对外投资在 2009～2010 年度受到一定影响，但在 2010～2011 年度又迅速反弹。

表1　各年度对外直接投资及发放担保金的实际流出量情况

单位：百万美元

年　度	资　产	贷　款	已调用担保	总　计	已发担保
2000～2001	602.12	70.58	4.97	677.67	112.55
2001～2002	878.83	120.82	0.42	1000.07	155.86
2002～2003	1746.28	102.10	0.00	1848.38	139.63
2003～2004	1250.01	316.57	0.00	1566.58	440.53
2004～2005	1481.97	513.19	0.00	1995.16	315.96
2005～2006	6657.82	1195.33	3.34	7856.49	546.78
2006～2007	12062.92	1246.98	0.00	13309.90	2260.96
2007～2008	15431.51	3074.97	0.00	18506.48	6553.47
2008～2009	12477.14	6101.56	0.00	18578.70	3322.45
2009～2010	9392.98	4296.91	24.18	13714.07	7603.04
2010～2011	9234.58	7556.30	52.49	16843.37	27059.02
2011～2012 *	4031.45	4830.01	0.00	8861.46	14993.80
总　计	75247.61	29425.32	85.40	104758.30	63504.05

* 2011 年 4 月至 2012 年 2 月 22 日。

表2　2000～2010 年印度各行业海外投资情况及比例

单位：百万美元

年　度	制造业	金融服务业	非金融服务业	贸　易	其　他	总　计
2000～2001	169 (23.84)	6 (00.85)	470 (66.29)	52 (07.33)	12 (01.69)	709 (100)

年　度	制造业	金融服务业	非金融服务业	贸　易	其　他	总　计
2001～2002	528 (53.82)	4 (00.41)	350 (35.68)	79 (08.05)	20 (02.04)	981 (100)
2002～2003	1271 (70.69)	3 (00.17)	404 (22.47)	82 (04.56)	38 (02.11)	1798 (100)
2003～2004	893 (59.77)	1 (00.07)	456 (30.52)	113 (07.56)	31 (02.07)	1494 (100)
2004～2005	1170 (65.88)	7 (00.39)	304 (17.12)	192 (10.81)	100 (05.63)	1776 (100)
2005～2006	3407 (67.46)	160 (03.17)	895 (17.72)	377 (07.46)	207 (04.10)	5050 (100)
2006～2007	3545 (26.34)	28 (00.21)	7486 (55.62)	1739 (12.92)	656 (04.87)	13459 (100)
2007～2008	6240 (34.84)	26 (00.14)	1635 (09.13)	8993 (50.21)	1010 (05.64)	17910 (100)
2008～2009	6817.0 (42.74)	174.9 (01.97)	1068.0 (06.70)	640.1 (04.01)	7247.8 (45.44)	15947.8 (100)
2009～2010	4443 (43.11)		2895 (28.09)	1174 (11.39)	1794 (17.41)	10306 (100)

资料来源：RBI Annual Reports at www.rbi.org.in/Publications。

近年来，对外直接投资主要是通过融资收购股权或提供贷款的方式进行。尽管发行担保金额一直在增加，但2009～2010年度和2010～2011年度的调用担保金额微乎其微。21世纪头十年，对外直接投资提案的数量在"自动通道"制度下持续上升，体现了印度公司在自由监管制度下拓展海外业务方面日益增长的需求。

2000～2001年度至2009～2010年度，从印度对外直接投资的行业分布看，制造业占了印度对外直接投资的绝大部分（除2000～2001年度和2006～2007年度外），其份额由2000～2001年度的23.84%上升到2009～2010年度的43.11%；非金融服务业的份额在2000～2001年度曾高达66.29%，但在随后几年锐减，不过在2009～2010年度其又回升至28.09%（见表2）。在此期间，金融服务业的份额可以忽略不计。

　　从行业模式看，印度企业逐步扩大海外投资更像是长期战略考量而非对短期利益的追求。例如，维德希有限公司（印度石油天然气公司全资子公司）目前在中东、非洲、独联体国家、远东、拉美地区 14 个国家中的 33 个项目拥有海外资产；印度石油公司（Oil India）在利比亚、加蓬、伊朗、尼日利亚、苏丹等 8 个国家拥有勘探区。同样地，印度煤炭公司也成立了一家子公司——维德希煤炭公司（Coal Videsh）来获取海外煤矿资源，并和其他公司一起成立了一家名为"国际煤炭联合有限公司"的合资企业以在海外获取焦煤和电煤。印度企业在海外采掘业的投资非常重要，因为它支持了国内经济的快速增长、工业化和城市化，并保证印度能在大宗商品价格上涨的背景下长期稳定地获取自然资源。①

　　目前，已有大量研究追踪了全球化世界秩序中印度公司的演变和它们不断扩大的影响力，以及对外直接投资在促进印非关系中的作用。拉克文德·辛格和瓦林德所著的《国家政策影响下印度对外直接投资的新兴模式：宏观视角》一书中提到，已有一些学者注意到印度经济在一个快速全球化的世界中所呈现出的增长活力，并对其进行了评论。事实上，长期以来，印度各界一直通力合作，发展生产要素领域内的战略竞争力，最近已经开始收获竞争力提升带来的回报。随着印度资本尤其是其海外资本的日益强大，它们在全球发起了合作和并购，这种趋势也变得更加明显。本研究包含了对印度经济的这些成就的思考：不仅回顾了有关发展中国家新兴跨国公司的理论及实践，还从发展演变的角度对印度对外直接投资进行了检验；不仅追踪了印度对外直接投资的新模式，还暗示了国家政策在鼓励直接投资流出中的推动作用。②

---

① Lakhwinder Singh and Jain Varinder, "Emerging Pattern of India's Outward Foreign Direct Investment under Influence of State Policy: a Macro – view," MPRA（Munich Personal re – PEC Archive）Paper No. 13439, http：//mpra. ub. uni – muenchen. de/13439/1/MPRA_ paper_ 13439. pdf, 2010（Accessed: 16 July 2013）.

② Lakhwinder Singh and Jain Varinder, "Emerging Pattern of India's Outward Foreign Direct Investment under Influence of State Policy: A Macro – view."

表3　2008～2012年度印度公司各行业海外投资情况

单位：10亿美元

年　度	2008～2009	2009～2010	2010～2011	2011～2012 *	总计
制造业	101.8	53.5	50.4	27.4	233.1
金融保险、房地产及商业服务业	35.5	44.1	65.3	25.3	170.3
批发及零售贸易、餐饮及酒店业	11.7	11.3	18.9	10.0	51.9
农业及相关活动	23.8	9.5	12.1	4.1	49.4
运输、通信及存储服务业	3.1	3.8	8.2	13.4	28.5
建筑业	3.5	3.6	3.8	3.7	14.6
社区、社会及个人服务业	3.9	1.8	7.0	1.8	14.5
电力、天然气及水	1.4	8.4	1.0	0.4	11.9
其他	1.2	1.1	1.8	1.0	5.1
总　计	185.8	137.1	168.4	87.3	578.6

*2011年4月至2012年2月22日。

帕特奈克和巴格维（R. K. Pattanaik & J. Bhargavi）在《对外直接投资：印度的视角》中解释说，印度对外直接投资是经济全球化的主要成果之一，对印度近年来的经济增长和发展做出了巨大贡献。尽管从国际层面来看，发展中国家对外直接投资的巨大流出相对来说还是一个新现象，但印度一些大企业（如塔塔集团和博拉集团）从20世纪60年代早期以来就一直在海外进行投资。然而，印度自1947年独立后就一直实行相对严格的对外投资贸易政策；直到20世纪90年代中期，它才开始大规模进行对外直接投资。即便如此，自90年代初贸易和投资政策逐步自由化以来，印度对外直接投资势头大增；这一势头及对外直接投资的新特点，是印度国家政策变化、企业行为和国际贸易投资发展互动的结果。取消对公司发展的控制措施（如FERA）、废除许可证制度、解除国家对公有及中小私人企业产品市场份额的保护体系、对外国公司实施便利措施、进口关税的大规模削减等，都使得印度的市场竞争越来越激烈。①

---

① R. K. Pattanaik and Bhargavi, "Outward Foreign Direct Investment: An Indian Perspective. Maharashtra Economic Development council," *Monthly Economic Digest*, 2011, pp. 5 - 13.

　　因此，在过去十年里，对外直接投资、公司兼并的质量和数量都有显著提升。根据帕特奈克和巴格维的观点，印度在 2008 年已成为亚洲新兴国家第 7 大、全球第 21 大对外投资国。印度对外直接投资由 1990 年的区区 2 亿美元上升到 2010 年的 790 多亿美元。过去十年来，印度对外直接投资的增长非常惊人（根据联合国贸易和发展会议的对外直接投资数据，增长超过 2000 倍），在 2000 年和 2008 年都仅次于阿联酋和埃及，位列世界第三。[①]

　　印度投资增长在几个行业非常明显：如在 2000～2007 年，石油、天然气和化学产业就贡献了总流出量的近一半。在非洲国家以自然资源为基础的产业中，印度国有石油公司的存在感不断增强，这种趋势正得到越来越多的认可。事实上，另一项研究的作者们也认为，由于丰富的自然资源和良好的发展前景，非洲地区已成为一个竞争日益激烈的经济战场。[②] 佩德森（Jorgrn-Dige Pedersen）的文章《第二波印度海外投资》，通过对比前一波保守得多的海外投资，对近年来印度公司的国际扩张进行了评估；同时，他也对印度政府对外投资政策的演变进行了追踪，认为海外投资增长的重要原因在于：20 世纪 90 年代经济改革后，印度政府逐步放松了对资本外流的限制。印度海外投资的新特征在于，投资分散在多个国家和多个经济部门。另外，最值得注意的是，印度公司目前和欧美公司一样将非洲视为其目标市场，收购当地公司。同时，印度公司继续扩大在其他发展中国家的存在，这也促进了那些国家的经济发展，减少了它们对发达国家的经济依赖。[③]

　　普拉丹（Jaya Prakash Pradhan）在文章《印度跨国公司境外收购的趋势和模式》中写道，印度公司的境外收购也可以看作它们对 20 世纪 90 年代以来全球化竞争的反应。随着贸易、产业、外来投资和技术政策体制的自由化，之前受到保护的印度公司迅速面临全球竞争。印度公司越来越意识到，它们

① B. Chowdhury Mamta, "India's Outward Foreign Direct Investment: Closed Doors to Open Souk," http://mpra. ub. uni - muenchen. de/32828/.
② K. Sauvant and J. Pradhan, *The Rise of Indian Multinationals: Perspectives On Indian Outward Foreign Direct Investment*, New York: Palgrave Macmillan, 2010, p. 18.
③ J. Pedersen, "The Second Wave of Indian Investments Abroad," *Journal of Contemporary Asia*, 38 (4), 2008, pp. 613 - 637.

在过去对国内市场保护制度和进口替代政策的严重依赖，使其目前积累的技术及其他能力明显不足以应对更自由的商业环境所带来的新竞争，这迫使它们迅速提高竞争力并加强在世界市场中的地位。印度公司意识到，与通过在研发、广告等方面的大量投资来提升长期竞争力相比，境外并购的风险和花费相对更小。[1]

拉维和辛格（Ravi Ramamurti & Jitendra V. Singh）主编的《新兴经济体中的新兴跨国公司》一书为理解世界市场的新格局及新竞争结构做出了突出贡献。他们在不同国家所进行的研究显示，新兴经济体中的跨国公司既有很多共同的结构特点，也有特定本土经验的印记。对管理者和企业经营者来说，这本书也为如何塑造新的国际秩序提供了很多宝贵建议。[2]

阿迪苏等人（Kinfu Adisu、Thomas Sharkey & Sam Okoroafo）的文章《对印度对外政策和企业对非战略的分析》中，对印度的对外政策及其企业在非洲的战略进行了调查。除了提及两个地区间的历史联系，他们还提出印度在非洲的海外投资是可持续的。通过运用直接投资和波特竞争优势理论，他们进一步检验了印度在非公司具备的一些优势。塔塔集团、巴蒂集团和信实集团等已广泛运用战略联盟打入市场，快速推动经营活动。[3]

3 印度在非洲农业部门中的存在

3.1 发展合作与农业

已有 40 余年历史的印非农业合作，是支持印非关系发展的重要支柱之一。连续两届印非论坛峰会（2008 年在新德里、2011 年在亚的斯亚贝巴）也使这一合作得到了加强及深化。对印度和非洲领导人来说，印非在农业

---

[1] Jaya Prakash Pradhan, Jaya Prakash (2007), "Trends and Patterns of Overseas Acquisition by Indian Multinational," http：//isidev. nic. in/pdf/WP0710. pdf, accessed on 16th July, 2013.

[2] R. Ramchandani and J. Singh, *Emerging Multi Nationals In Emerging Markets*, Cambridge：Cambridge University, 2010；Lakhwinder Singh and Jain Varinder, "Emerging Pattern of India's Outward Foreign Direct Investment under Influence of State Policy：a Macro – view."

[3] A. Kinfu, T. Sharkey, and S. Okoroafo, "Analyzing Indian Policies and Firm Strategies in Africa," *Journal of Management Research*, 2013. 5 (3), pp. 17 – 27.

领域的互补性很强，合作潜力大，因此农业合作在两届峰会上都被置于优
先地位；同时，印非领导人也都热衷于通过发展非洲农业来保障各自的粮
食安全。①

　　值得关注的是，印度在非洲农业部门合作的目的是提升非洲的长期贸易
及其生产能力；在 2008 年的印非论坛峰会上，印度承诺会确保在这些领域扩
大合作。此外，我们还需注意，过去十多年来印度在非洲农业部门中经济和
技术合作的加强，是在传统援助国加拿大、德国、日本、荷兰、美国等对该
部门的支持下降的背景下进行的。②

　　事实上，在大多数非洲国家，农业支出在政府支出中的比例都大幅下降。
在 2008 年印非论坛峰会通过的《印度—非洲合作框架协议》中，双方一致认
为发展农业是消除贫困、改善民生、保证粮食安全的有效手段，并同意加强
在此领域的合作，以改善非洲的粮食安全，增加其对世界市场的出口。除此
以外，印非还决定将合作扩大到土地开发、水资源管理、农业种植、育种技
术、粮食安全、农产品加工机械、农业病虫害防治、试验示范项目和培训等
方面。③

　　印非农业合作是多层面的。一方面，这是在互惠互利的基础上为促进双
方外交关系、推动"南南合作"所做的努力。印度为非洲提供援助，设立农
业科研机构，并在印度各类农业院校为非洲学生提供奖学金。2008 年首届印
非论坛峰会的成果之一是印度为非洲学者提供了 300 个专项农业奖学金名额
（印度驻埃塞俄比亚大使馆）。④ 作为该项目的一部分，目前有 49 名非洲学生

① Ministry of External Affairs, India - Zambia Relations, Government of India, http：//mea. gov. in/Portal/ForeignRelation/India - Zambia_ Relations. pdf（Accessed：6 July 2013）.
② UK Department for International Development（DFID）, Jamie Morrision, Dirk Bezemer and Catherine Arnold, "Official Development Assistance to Agriculture," November 2004, http：//dfid - agriculture - consultation. nri. org/summaries/wp9. pdf（Accessed：1 May 2013）.
③ African Union, *Africa India Framework for Cooperation*, 2008, http：//summits. au. int/en/sites/default/files/AFRICA - INDIA% 20FRAMEWORK% 20FOR% 20COOPERATION% 20ENGLISH% 20 - % 20FINAL% 20VERSION. doc（Accessed：6 June 2013）.
④ Indian Embassy, Addis Ababa, "Agricultural Scholarships," http：//www. indianembassy. gov. et/? q = agricultural（Accessed：16 August 2013）.

在印度多所农业院校学习。[1]

另一方面，印度和美国在利比里亚、马拉维和肯尼亚开展了农业新合作，以提升粮食安全。为期 3 年的"印美非三方合作伙伴计划"项目，预期将把印度私人和公共部门经过检验的创新成果用于解决目标国家的粮食安全、营养不良及贫困问题。印度已成为一个高效能、低成本的创新中心，以应对气候变化、自然资源减少、耕地质量下降、粮食需求增加等问题带来的挑战。美国国际开发署（USAID）粮食安全办公室主任杜古马（Bahiru Duguma）在美国政府全球饥饿和粮食安全倡议"保障未来粮食供给计划"（Feed the Future）的支持下启动了这一项目。该项目的目的在于提升肯尼亚、利比里亚和马拉维的农业生产力，支持其市场制度。通过斋普尔的乔杜里查兰·辛格全国农业市场营销研究院（NIAM）和海得拉巴的印度农业管理研究院（MANAGE）提供的市场和农业推广管理培训，该计划预期将为这 3 个非洲国家培养 180 名农业专家。项目由 NIAM 和 USAID 领导，其中首个农业培训项目将于 2013 年 1 月在 MANAGE 启动，30 名来自非洲的学员将参加培训（《商业标准报》，2013）。[2] 目前，日本和其他国家也试图在农业部门与印度建立类似的伙伴关系。

印度也承诺提高对非农业部门的授信额度。根据印度进出口银行的报告，截至目前，其批准的最大一笔贷款是旨在促进印度投资的埃塞俄比亚 Tindaho 糖厂项目（6.4 亿美元），这笔贷款不仅是针对 Tindaho 糖厂项目，也是为了复兴 WonjiShoa 和 Fincha 两家糖厂。2006 年，印度进出口银行还为塞内加尔灌溉项目一笔 2700 万美元的授信延长期限，该项目的设备从印度进口。此外，在第二届印非论坛峰会上，曼莫汉·辛格总理宣布将为塞内加尔农业机械化项目的第二阶段拨款 750 亿西非法郎（约 1.6 亿美元）。[3] 根据印度进出

---

[1] Stein Sunstol Eriksen, Aparajita Biswas and Ajay Dubey, "India in Africa: Implications for Norwegian Foreign and Development Policies," NUPI Report 2.

[2] Business Standard, "India and US partner to help improve agriculture in Africa," 30 July 2013.

[3] Second Africa – India Forum Summit 2011, Addis Ababa, *Africa – India Framework for Enhanced Cooperation*, http://indiaafricasummit. nic. in/staticfile/framework – en. pdf; *Plan of Action of The Framework For Cooperation of The India – Africa Forum Summit 2008*, Delhi, India, http://www. indianembassy. gov. et/.../Joint%20Plan%20of%20Action. doc (Accessed: 6 June 2013).

口银行的报告，目前针对外国政府和金融机构的信贷项目共有 140 个，其中近 100 个在非洲，而且绝大多数在农业部门。2013 年，印度进出口银行授信 2.17 亿美元以支持莫桑比克的基础设施项目。①

在 2011 年的第二届印非论坛峰会上，非洲国家和印度重申了加强合作以增加农业产量、在 2015 年前实现饥饿人口减半的"千年发展目标"。峰会上，领导人还着重关注了发展科研的需求：一方面要提高农业生产力，另一方面也要保护土地和环境。其目的在于"确保粮食安全，降低目前上涨的粮价开支，为'非洲农业综合发展计划'（CAADP）的实施提供资金"。②

印非农业合作的主要特点之一，在于印度积极追求能力建设，并分享其自身经验来帮助非洲农业部门发展，其中特别值得关注的是各类农业实践中的研究及知识共享方式。根据一份名为《印度和非洲——发展中的伙伴：能力建设项目和授信》的文件，2011 年印度向赞比亚、埃塞俄比亚和南非等几个非洲国家派遣了来自"印度农业研究理事会"（ICAR）的专家团，其目的在于获取非洲国家如何设法改善其农业实践的第一手资料。③

此外，由国际热带半干旱地区作物研究所（ICRISAT）、国际农业咨询集团（IACG）和印度农业研究理事会（ICAR）共同创立的印非农业合作平台（PIAPA）让各利益相关者能作为合作方参与进来，以提出更好的政策、建立更有效的机构、提升基础设施建设并获得更好的市场准入和更高质量的投入（尤其是为印度和非洲的旱地农民）。

国际热带半干旱地区作物研究所（ICRISAT）还创立了"热带半干旱地区作物研究南南倡议"（IS－SI）来为印非农业部门提供系统有效的合作。通过建立牢固、成功的印非伙伴关系，其作为热带干旱地区繁荣和经济机会驱

---

① African Union, Africa India Framework for Cooperation, http：//summits. au. int/en/sites/default/files/ AFRICA－INDIA% 20FRAMEWORK% 20FOR% 20COOPERATION% 20ENGLISH% 20－% 20FINAL% 20VERSION. doc, 2008 （Accessed：6 June 2013）.

② Second Africa－India Forum Summit 2011, Addis Ababa, *Africa－India Framework for Enhanced Cooperation*.

③ MEA, India & Africa Partners in Development：Capacity Building Programmes & Lines of Credit Mozambique：*Exim Bank of India Opens $ 217 Million Credit Line*, http：//allafrica. com/stories/ 201307090302. html（Accessed：6 June 2013）.

动者的角色得到了进一步加强。① 根据印度农业研究理事会 2011 年 12 月发布的报告，印度农业研究与教育部（DAER）、印度农业研究理事会和埃塞俄比亚农业研究所（EIAR）所长共同签署了一份关于农业研究及教育合作的谅解备忘录，合作的优先领域包括园艺学、作物学、渔业、动物学、农业工程和自然资源管理、农业推广及农业教育等。两国同意通过科学家、学者、技术、文献、信息、种质的交流来扩大合作，并寻求合作开展研究项目；备忘录还就具体合作领域进行了讨论，并形成了两年工作计划草案。②

为进一步开发非洲的人力资源，印度总理提议在农业和农村发展领域设立新的机构。他强调了如下事项的必要性：建立印非纺织业综合集群以支持棉花产业、建立印非食品加工集群来增加附加值、创建区域市场和出口市场、建立印非中期天气预报中心以将卫星技术用于农业和渔业。

来自印度进出口银行和印度工业联盟（CII)③ 的一份名为《关键主张和文件》的文件，指出了会议讨论过程中特别关注的五大关键领域为：双边贸易的扩大、印度在非投资、能力建设、粮食安全和能源安全。文件声明，两地代表对加大农业及农产品加工合作的需要进行了探讨，这将对印非粮食安全形势产生重大影响。尽管非洲农业的增长很大程度上依赖是否有充足的技术投入，但其生产总值仍有望在 2030 年达到 1 万亿美元的规模。④ 代表们还就非洲如何学习印度的绿色革命、白色革命⑤和农业加工业的扩张进行了讨论。非洲农业部门的拖拉机化被认为是一个重要的领域：尽管北非和南非部

---

① African Union, Africa India Framework for Cooperation, 2008, http：//summits. au. int/en/sites/default/files/AFRICA – INDIA% 20FRAMEWORK% 20FOR% 20COOPERATION% 20ENGLISH% 20 – % 20FINAL% 20VERSION. doc（Accessed：6 June 2013）.

② ICAR, ICAR signed Mou with the Ethiopian Institute for Agricultural Research, http：//www. icar. org. in/node/4151（Accessed：6 June 2013）.

③ CII – EXIM Bank Conclave on India – Africa, 2013. 9 th CII – EXIM Bank Conclave on India – Africa Project Partnership（online）, http：//www. ciiafricaconclave. com/images/Report% 20% 20 – % 209th% 20CII – EXIM% 20Bank% 20IndiaAfrica% 20Conclave% 202013. pdf（Accessed：16 July 2013）.

④ CII – EXIM Bank Conclave on India – Africa, 2013. 9 th CII – EXIM Bank Conclave on India – Africa Project Partnership（online）, http：//www. ciiafricaconclave. com/images/Report% 20% 20 – % 209th% 20CII – EXIM% 20Bank% 20India – Africa% 20Conclave% 202013. pdf（Accessed：16 July 2013）.

⑤ "白色革命"，指印度的农民提高牛奶产量的举措。——译者注

分地区越来越多地将拖拉机用于农业，但非洲大部分地区的农民仍依赖手工农具。

专家建议印度公司可以通过以下方式帮助非洲农业部门发展：农业机械化、农产品加工及仓储、农业部门人力资源的培训和开发投资、创造就业机会、"绿地投资"、开发本土供应商、对邻国的农业出口、建立非洲农业产业园、发展园艺花卉业及订单农业等。[①]

3.2 印度对非农业投资

过去几年中外国投资者对非洲适宜耕地的需求迅猛增加。尽管他们对农业和土地的投资并不是新现象，但他们将种植的大部分粮食供应国内市场，作为本国粮食安全战略的一部分，这种行为在各个国际论坛中引发争论。世界银行的一份报告指出，外国对非洲农业的投资主要在撒哈拉以南地区；2002~2009年，仅苏丹、埃塞俄比亚、加纳、尼日利亚和莫桑比克就占据了全球土地投资项目的23%。[②]

根据联合国粮农组织的统计，近年来对非农业投资的主要形式是长期租赁土地（最高达99年）。土地投资的规模很大：许多投资土地面积超过1万公顷，有些甚至超过50万公顷。由于不同的文化、政治、商业联系，以及对投资基金的地理限制，不同双边投资流动的特定模式也随之出现。例如，海湾国家更偏好投资苏丹及其他伊斯兰会议组织（OIC）的非洲成员国；而亚洲国家则倾向于投资赞比亚、安哥拉和莫桑比克。然而，这些模式的分界正变得日渐模糊。[③]

近期一份土地交易数据库的报告指出，自2000年以来，约5%的非洲农

---

① CII – EXIM Bank Conclave on India – Africa, 2013. 9 th CII – EXIM Bank Conclave on India – Africa Project Partnership（online），http：//www. ciiafricaconclave. com/images/Report% 20% 20 – % 209th% 20CII – EXIM% 20Bank% 20India – Africa% 20Conclave% 202013. pdf（Accessed：16 July 2013）.

② World Bank，"Rising Global Interest in Farmland"，The World Bank，Washington D. C.，2010.

③ Gerlach Christin and Liu Pascal，*Resource Seeking Foreign Direct Investment In African Agriculture：A Review of Country Case Studies*，FAO Commodity And Trade Policy Research Working Paper，No. 31，http：// www. fao. org/fileadmin/templates/est/ PUBLICATIONS/Comm_ Working Papers/_ EST – WP31. Pdf （Accessed：6 June 2013）.

地已被投资者购买或租赁。研究者估计，2000～2010年，购买或租赁的土地超过2亿公顷，大概相当于8个英国的面积。新的国际土地交易数据库也显示出一股购买非洲土地的热潮①。

令人不安的是，目前尚未有关于这些投资规模、性质和影响的具体数据。已有的直接投资数据缺乏足够的细节，而且对了解当地农业投资数量及投资形式来说，也过于笼统。因此近期的投资究竟是一种全新的发展，还是现有趋势的延伸，还难有定论。②

联合国粮农组织一项名为"寻求非洲农业资源的直接投资"的研究，对8个选定非洲国家——乌干达、马里、马达加斯加、苏丹、摩洛哥、加纳、塞内加尔和埃及——的案例研究的主要结论进行了综述。由于直接投资对各国及一国之内不同地区造成的影响差异很大（取决于很多因素，包括投资合同内容、实行的商业模式、所在国当地的体制等），因此研究展现的也是一幅喜忧参半的画面。东道国可以预期的主要好处是经济利益，如创造就业、提升生产力、改善小农融资及进入市场的渠道、技术转让和生产标准的执行。但一些研究发现直接投资并未产生这些预期效益，有两项研究甚至认为投资项目使当地农民失去了创收的机会。研究还发现，针对土地征收、土地登记、土地使用和小农权益的法律框架及法律程序大多不清晰、不透明。未经相关研究及公众咨询以确保实现投资项目的社会、环境和经济可行性，就贸然出让土地，也被视为可能对当地社区造成不利影响的重要问题。为了使风险最小化、国际投资的积极影响最大化，政府需要确认现有政策、规章制度是否完善，前期研究及咨询是否已覆盖所有利益相关方。③

---

① The Guardian, Claire Provost, "New International Land Deals Database Reveals Rush to Buy Up Africa," 2012, http：//www. theguardian. com/global – development/2012/apr/27/internationalland – deals – database – africa? guni = Article：in%20 body%20link（Accessed：10 February 2014）.

② Gerlach Christin and Liu Pascal, Resource Seeking Foreign Direct Investment In African Agriculture：A Review of Country Case Studies.

③ Gerlach Christin and Liu Pascal, "Resource – Seeking Foreign Direct Investment In African Agriculture：A Review of Country Case Studies," Fao Commodity And Trade Policy Research Working Paper, No. 31, http：//www. fao. org/fileadmin/templates/est/PUBLICATIONS/Comm _ Working _ Papers/EST – WP31. pdf（Accessed：6 June 2013）.

印度公司在非洲、南美和东南亚租赁或购买的土地中，相当大一部分用来种植粮食、豆类和食用油作物。近期印度海外农地投资回升的一个主要潜在原因是对其粮食安全的关注。印度自身的粮食生产增长的速度赶不上人口日益增长的速度。食用油的进口是印度第二大外汇消耗去向，仅次于原油。豆类（扁豆）的形势更为严峻，因为它是印度人食物中蛋白质的主要来源。

情况如此危急，以至于印度总理专门组建了三个委员会来为控制通货膨胀和促进农业生产提供建议，委员会由位高权重的各邦首席部长和中央内阁部长组成。农业生产工作组由哈里亚纳邦首席部长胡达先生（BS Hooda）主持，成员包含西孟加拉邦、旁遮普邦和比哈尔邦三个邦的首席部长。该委员会建议，印度应像其他很多"在海外购买土地种植农作物以满足国内消费需求"的国家一样，鼓励印度公司在海外购买土地来进行豆类和食用油作物的生产。"我们应该认真考虑这些选择"，委员会建议说，"在 15 ~ 20 年每年至少生产 200 万吨豆类和 500 万吨食用油"①。

印度政府采取了多种方式来促进印度公司海外粮食生产的外包进程。政府带领很多由农民组成的贸易代表团前往各个国家和地区，并在主要的地区贸易和商业峰会上为促进印度海外农业投资者的进入提供帮助。政府为众多不同的方案提供支持以促进印度农业公司在非洲和其他地区的海外投资，包括对传统新绿地直接投资的全面支持，并购、购买现有公司，公私合作模式（PPPs），出口到印度的农产品的特定关税减免政策，协商地区双边贸易投资协定（BITs）和避免双重征税协定（DTAs）。

印度政府在经济上促进该进程的另一主要方式是通过印度进出口银行为各发展中国家政府、银行、金融机构及区域金融机构提供优惠信贷。这类信贷一般用于国家发展项目，如果这些项目与农业发展相关，印度海外投资者就有望以直接投资的形式赢得优惠信贷和项目合同。

印度进出口银行还直接向印度公司提供软贷款和信贷，尽管对公众来说很难获得有关特定公司此类活动的详细信息。例如，印度为赞比亚发展项目

---

① Biraj Patnaik, "The New Shifting Agriculture: Shopping for Fields Overseas," *Indian Times*, 9 July 2010.

授信 7500 万美元，拨款 500 万美元用于健康、教育和社会等行业的项目；印度进出口银行与赞比亚财政和国家计划部签署了一份贷款协议，把给赞比亚 5000 万美元的授信投放至伊泰济泰济（Itezhi‐Tezhi）水电项目，而印度塔塔集团和赞比亚国家电力公司均为该项目的合资方。[1]

此外，塔塔集团在乌干达成功租赁了一块土地进行农业试点项目，斋浦里亚（Jaipurias of RJ Corp）公司获得了 50 英亩示范奶牛场的租约。印度主要建筑公司孟买工程和建筑公司（Shapoorji Pallonji & Co）在埃塞俄比亚获得了 5 万公顷土地的租约，在未来可能会发展农业项目。不仅仅是大型印度公司，印度中小企业也在考虑进入非洲商业农业领域，这些公司涉及的行业从香料、茶到化工原料制品，范围极广。

由于得到了全面支持，通过合同进入非洲的印度公司基本上都获得了收益，但其对非洲农民利益保障或环境保护的回报很少。事实上，在地下水利用和环境污染，有关劳工权益、劳工工资和工作环境、技术转让、本土商品服务购买等公司责任方面，印度公司几乎都没有限制。[2]

表 4　印度公司的非洲农地投资示例

序号	公司名	国　家	详细信息
1	卡鲁图里农产品公司（Karuturi Ago Products Plc）	埃塞俄比亚	购买了甘贝拉州 Jikao 和 Itang 地区的 10 万公顷土地，用于棕榈树、谷类和豆类种植，并可能在一定条件下获得另外 20 万公顷土地。卡鲁图里农产品公司（Karuturi Ago Products）是卡鲁图里全球有限公司（Karuturi Global Ltd）的一家子公司。
2	鲁齐豆业公司（Ruchi Soya）	埃塞俄比亚	获得甘贝拉州和本尚古勒‐古马兹州 152649 公顷土地 25 年的租约，用于大豆种植和处理。
3	韦丹塔收获公司（Verdanta Harvests Plc）	埃塞俄比亚	获得甘贝拉州 5000 公顷土地 50 年的租约，用于茶叶和香料种植。

---

[1]　High Commission of India, Lusaka, India‐Zambia Bilateral Relations, http：//www. hcizambia. com/india‐zambia% 20bilateral% 20relations. htm（Accessed：6 July 2013）.

[2]　R. Rowden, *India's Role in the New Global Farmland Grab*（report）, New Delhi：Grainand Economics Research Foundation, 2011.

续表

序号	公司名	国 家	详细信息
4	查达农业公司（Chadha Agro Plc）	埃塞俄比亚	获得奥罗米亚州 Guji 区最多 10 万公顷的土地，用于糖业发展项目。
5	瓦伦国际（Varun International）	马达加斯加	子公司 Varun Agriculture Sarl 租赁或购买了 232000 公顷土地，用于水稻、玉米和豆类种植。
6	乌塔姆糖业技术公司（Uttam Sucrotech）	埃塞俄比亚	赢得一份价值 1 亿美元的合同，用于 Wonji - Shoa 糖厂的扩大。
7	麦克劳德拉塞尔印度公司（McLeod Russel India）	乌干达	购买了价值 2500 万美元的茶园，包括乌干达 Rwenzori Tea Investments 公司。麦克劳德拉塞尔印度公司为 BM Khaitan 集团所有。
8	阿迪史瓦棉花工业公司（ACIL Cotton Industries）	巴西、刚果、埃塞俄比亚	计划投资近 1500 万美元在巴西、刚果和埃塞俄比亚租赁土地，以开展豆类和咖啡的订单农业。
9	阿达尼集团（Adani Group）	非洲、巴西、阿根廷、印度尼西亚、马来西亚	计划（自 2010 年 10 月起）建立农场，用于食用油作物和豆类种植。
10	萨纳提农业企业公司（Sannati Agro Farm Enterprise Pvt. Ltd）	埃塞俄比亚	获得甘贝拉州 Dimi 区 1 万公顷土地 25 年的租约，用于水稻、豆类和谷物种植。
11	杰西瑞茶叶工业公司（Jay Shree Tea & Industries）	卢旺达、乌干达	获得卢旺达的 2 个茶园和乌干达的 1 个茶园。该公司由比克 - 贝拉（BK Birla）集团控制。
12	阿迪史瓦棉花工业公司（ACIL Cotton Industries）	巴西、刚果、埃塞俄比亚	于 2011 年 1 月宣布其计划投资近 1500 万美元，在巴西、刚果和埃塞俄比亚开展如豆类、咖啡等作物的订单农业。
13	BHO 生物制品公司（BHO Bio Products Plc）	埃塞俄比亚	获得 27 万公顷土地，用于谷物、豆类和食用油作物的种植。
14	印度国营五矿贸易公司（MMTC Ltd）	肯尼亚、坦桑尼亚	计划（自 2010 年 10 月起）种植豆类。

资料来源：Rowden, R. Grain and Economics Research Foundation。

印度对此类投资的观点

研究团队联系了一些印度公司的负责人，了解他们在这个问题上的参与情况和看法，包括印度工业联盟（CII）的穆蕾（Indrayani Mulay）女士和印度工商联合会（FICCI）的苏打卡兰（Shiela Sudhakaran）女士。穆蕾女士提供了 2013 年 3 月 17～19 日在新德里召开的"印度与非洲项目合作伙伴论坛"中有关第九届印度工业联盟——进出口银行召开的会议详情，为如何看待印非经济关系提供了一个不同的视角。印度和各非洲国家——尤其是赞比亚、布隆迪和喀麦隆的多名高官参与了论坛活动，其中有几次会议专门讨论农业部门。穆蕾女士提到，通过大大小小的会议，该组织为实现各代表和投资者在同一张桌子上讨论提供了平台；在会议上，印度工业联盟扮演了调停者的角色，并强调了机遇的重要性。

苏打卡兰女士强调，赞比亚拥有稳定的政治环境和新兴的经济环境，这对印度投资者来说具有巨大潜力。她进一步指出，印度工商联合会一直与孔科拉铜矿的主要印度投资者——韦丹塔集团（Vedanta）的能源审计团队保持密切联系。工商联合会致力于推动印度对非农业领域的投资。为此，印度工商联合会在 2016 年 2 月举办了印度—非洲农业商务论坛，包含赞比亚在内的多个非洲国家参与了论坛活动。

除了上述两位女士，本团队还联系了"印度社会行动论坛"（INSAF）的威尔弗雷德（Wilfred）先生、非政府组织卡尔帕日什（Kalpavriksh）的主任科思瑞（Ashish Kothari）先生和印度和平组织的乔杜里（AnilChowdhary）先生，他们均为笔者提供了有关争夺非洲土地的信息。科思瑞先生写过一些有关非洲土地争夺问题的报告，但由于其大部分工作在埃塞俄比亚开展，因此没能提供与赞比亚特别相关的信息。乔杜里先生提供了有关非洲土地争夺问题的各类报告和研究发现。团队还联系了印度非政府组织"矿山、矿产和人民"（MM&P）的斯瑞德哈尔（R. Sreedhar）先生，他是一位反对韦丹塔集团的合法请愿者。他告诉笔者，投资者都寻求与可为其带来激励措施的当地官员和部落领袖建立联系，而不是寻求与当地居民达成共识。他认为，投资者寻求的是像埃塞俄比亚和莫桑比克这样的"软柿子"。他进一步指出，在赋权的名义下有可能发生"资源诅咒"，并预计未来情况会很糟糕：公司为了提升自身投资和利益，不断破坏自然环境。

　　研究团队还与印度粮食和农业卓越中心（Food and Agriculture Centre of Excellence）的冈古丽（Kavery Ganguly）女士、阿维聂姆（Avignam）集团的普尔加尔（Abhilash Puljal）先生和进出口银行的苏布拉马尼亚姆（Sriram Subramaniam）先生举行了会谈。普尔加尔先生谈了中国因素。比起中国和西方投资者，埃塞俄比亚等非洲国家更青睐印度投资者，原因在于：印度公司能与当地人共事，并主张能力建设；而中国公司则引入中国员工，事实上它们还运来囚犯从事劳动密集型工作。他认为，某种类型的土地争夺问题肯定是存在的，但媒体展现的画面过于极端，一定程度上偏离了真实情况。

4　印度与赞比亚的互动

4.1　赞比亚的农业政策

　　农业在赞比亚经济中发挥着巨大作用，有可能成为其发展和减贫的主要动力。赞比亚农业的主要特点是二元结构：集中在铁路线附近的少数大型商业农场，与分散于各地的小农及小型商业农场并存。后者往往面临严重困境，难以进入资金技术等生产投入市场和加工销售等终端销售市场。据估计，约40%的农户仅从事维生农业。由于政府倾向于城市并一味强调种植玉米以实现粮食自给自足，农业部门长期被忽视；在农村地区尤其是偏远农村地区，基础设施、技术推广服务和农业科技的研发依然很落后。①

　　自20世纪90年代早期起，赞比亚农业政策经历了巨大变化，由强大的政府干预转向自由经济体系，目的在于支持私营部门加入农业生产的各个领域，如要素供给、加工、销售及技术推广服务等。作为政府退出的一部分，农林渔业部通过创立农业信托基金，大胆与私营企业建立公私合作伙伴关系，

---

① Federico Bonaglia, "Zambia: Sustaining Agricultural Diversification," OECD Business for Development, http://g-fras.org/en/world-wide-extension-study/africa/eastern-africa/zambia.html#references (Accessed: September 2013).

授权这些企业在商业经营的基础上管理公共资产，提供研究、咨询和培训服务等。① 然而，由赞比亚政府和援助者共同设计，以促进农业向市场经济过渡的 1996～2001 年农业投资计划，却并未带来预期效果。连续干旱加上变幻莫测的商业环境的不利影响，减少了私营部门进入并填补政府干预退出所留下空间的动力。②

赞比亚新的 2004～2015 年国家农业政策（NAP）提出了农业部门的总体构想和政策框架，并将私营部门视为关键角色，期待它们提供更多的服务。农业与合作部（MACO）预计将专注于其核心职能（政策制定、法律法规执行），同时也会发展与该领域其他利益方的关系以确保技术推广、农业研究和监督评估。它鼓励援助者在农业政策、计划执行中提供金融、技术和其他支持，为利益方提供能力建设。农业与合作部利用从国家到基层的工作人员来执行推广计划。③ 在国家层面，根据印度外交部（MEA）2011 年发表的报告④，赞比亚公共推广部门共有普通职员 742 人，高级管理人员 308 人。在高级管理人员中，7 人拥有博士学位，31 人达到理学硕士水平，女性占 13%。整个推广部门有 64 名专门技术专家、323 名基层技术推广人员和 26 名信息通信技术人员。报告指出，公共部门没有雇用在职培训人员。

赞比亚政府通过多种渠道对外展现可行的投资机会。赞比亚商业贸易和工业部部长办公室及赞比亚发展署（ZDA）、赞比亚国际贸易投资中心等组织发布了各类报告和研究，强调了赞比亚巨大的投资潜力。联合国在 2011 年发布了一项名为"赞比亚投资指南——机遇和条件"的综合性研究，全面提供

---

① Federico Bonaglia, "Zambia: Sustaining Agricultural Diversification," OECD Business for Development, http://g - fras. org/en/world - wide - extension - study/africa/eastern - africa/zambia. html # references (Accessed: September 2013).

② Katharina Felgenhauer, "A Brief History of Public Extension Policies, Resources and Advisory Activities in Zambia," http://www. worldwide - extension. org/africa/zambia/s - zambia/, 2007 (Accessed: August 2013).

③ Federico Bonaglia, "Zambia: Sustaining Agricultural Diversification".

④ Ministry of External Affairs, *India & Africa Partners in Development: Capacity Building Programmes & Lines of Credit Mozambique: Exim Bank of India Opens $ 217 Million Credit Line*, http://allafrica. com/ stories/201307090302. html (Accessed: 6 June 2013).

了各种情况的有关信息,列出建议投资赞比亚的四大理由:友好的投资环境、开放的市场、丰富的资源和大量的机会。关于赞比亚该如何努力创造和分配财富、发展经济、创造就业和提高人民生活水平,有很多争论,但其中有一条共同主线即对外国投资关键作用的认同。随着印度与非洲大部分地区联系的加强,赞比亚各官方机构也为其提供了现有数据和信息,以帮助潜在的投资者。[①]

一份由"非洲发展新伙伴计划"(NEPAD)和经合组织(OECD)共同发布、名为《非洲加快改革:基础设施和农业投资动员——赞比亚投资政策框架要点》的综合性报告,涵盖了与赞比亚相关的各种话题。报告讨论了赞比亚经济由国家主导型向私营部门驱动型过渡过程中政府实施的各项改革,意在改变之前由国家主导的经济体系,推动由私营部门驱动的市场经济。赞比亚颁布了多项法律,成立了众多法定机构来实施这些改革,这些机构包括赞比亚投资中心(ZIC)、赞比亚出口委员会(EBZ)、赞比亚私有化委员会(ZPA)、赞比亚出口加工区管理局(ZEPZA)和小企业发展局,每一个都肩负着促进该国贸易投资的特定任务。此外,报告还详述了保护投资者的各项协议,推动投资的各项战略,保障企业治理框架基础,以促进总体经济表现和市场透明有效的各项步骤等。[②]

史蒂芬(Steven Haggblade)为"粮食安全研究项目"赞比亚部分准备的一份名为《回到农业投资》的报告中,一开始就强调了农业投资在确保赞比亚经济快速发展及减少贫困方面的重要性。关于自"非洲发展新伙伴计划"实施以来的各项政策措施及结构性缺陷如何阻碍了赞比亚的发展,他给出了详尽的解释。例如,在资金分配上,赞比亚经常将大部分可支配的农业预算用于补贴私人农业投入(主要是化肥),但在农村基础设施和技术发展上的投

---

① UNCTAD, "An Investment Guide to Zambia—Opportunities and Conditions," United Nations, New York and Geneva (Accessed: 23 April 2013), http://unctad.org/en/Docs/diaepcb201008_en.pdf, 2011 (Accessed: 8 July 2013).

② Organisation for Economic Co-operation and Development (OECD), "Zambia's Policy Framework for Investment – OECD," http://www.oecd.org/daf/inv/investmentfordevelopment/47662751.pdf (Accessed: 1 July 2013).

入要少得多。①

非政府组织奥克兰研究所（Oakland Institute）等机构为我们提供了有关非洲投资交易各方面的深入分析。在关于赞比亚的报告中，它着重关注了目前研究中不足的方面，如缺乏对各方争夺土地的本质和对赞比亚社会造成的经济、社会、环境影响的研究。②

相应地，德国全球和区域问题研究所（GIGA）发表了诺尔特（Kerstin-Nolte）一篇名为《不良土地管理下的大规模农业投资：赞比亚案例中的参与者和制度》的工作报告，其中有不少有趣的见解。报告对赞比亚土地管理系统及其演变、对投资者获取土地的必经流程和确定流程的负责方进行了细致观察，强调在土地获取流程中，正式规则的执行较为宽松。该研究还对包括投资者、地方当局、中央政府在内的所有利益相关方进行了影响力分析，认为当地土地使用者扮演的角色越来越微不足道。报告还强调，这些交易的土地有很大的发展机遇，仅将其归类为富有的"强大投资者"所进行的"土地掠夺"未免太简单化了。③ 穆仁佳（Fison Mujenja）和沃娜妮（Charlott Wonani）在论文《农业投资的长期后果：赞比亚的教训》中，对赞比亚的两个农业投资项目进行了讨论：卡利亚小业主公司（Kaleya Smallholders Company Ltd，KASCOL）和姆庞伟发展有限公司（Mpongwe Development Company Ltd，MDC）及其继任者ETC生物能源公司和赞比亚牛肉公司（Zambeef）投资的能源项目。这两个项目源自20世纪70年代及80年代早期赞比亚政府和英联邦发展公司（Commonwealth Development Corporation，CDC）成立

① Steven Joe Haggblade, "Returns to Investment in Agriculture," *Food Security Collaborative Policy Briefs 2013*, http：//econpapers. repec. org/paper/agsmidcpb/54625. htm（Accessed：8 July 2013）.

② The Oakland Institute, *Understanding Land Investment Deals in Africa：Country Report - Zambia*, 2013, http：//www. oaklandinstitute. org/sites/oaklandinstitute. org/files/OI_ country _ report _ zambia. pdf（Accessed：8 July 2013）.

③ German Institute of Global and Area Studies（GIGA）, *Large - Scale Agricultural Investments under Poor Land Governance Systems：Actors and Institutions in the Case of Zambia*, GIGA Research Programme：Socio - Economic Challenges in the Context of Globalisation, Working paper 2013, No. 221（report）, Germany：GIGA. http：//www. giga - hamburg. de/dl/download. php? d =/content/publikationen/pdf/wp221 _ knolte. pdf（Accessed：8 July 2013）.

的合资公司，最近已被私有化。英联邦发展公司的参与反映了这两个项目最开始的发展方向。鉴于两个项目实施的重要背景和重要时段，对它们的案例研究可以为最佳农业投资实践及其长期发展结果提供一些有价值的见解，这些见解也可以为当今世界有关农业投资的争论做些贡献。[①]

在农业部门，赞比亚政府提供的常规税收优惠和补贴政策如下（赞比亚发展署，2011）:[②]

- 农业和非传统产品出口所得税为15%；
- 全额补贴农场平整土地、清理杂草、防止水土流失、打井、蓄水、大气或地质勘探所带来的开销；
- 对于种植咖啡、香蕉、柑橘或类似作物的企业，给予资本性支出10%的发展津贴；
- 农业改良补贴——当年全额补贴用于农业改良的资本性支出；
- 公司农业经营前5年的红利免税；
- 亏损弥补期为5年。

除此之外，《赞比亚发展署法》还为在下列与农业相关的优先行业投资50万美元以上的投资者提供了额外的激励政策。这些行业包括：花卉业、园艺业、食品、普通饮料和酒精饮料的生产行业、棉花、棉纱和布料等纺织品的生产和加工行业、农业加工业、牛皮、半硝革、皮革产品、服装等皮革产品的生产和加工业。额外激励政策如下：

- 首次盈利后5年内免征利润所得税；
- 第6~8年，只对50%的利润征税；第9年和第10年，只对75%的利润征税；

---

① Fison Mujenja, Charlot Wonani, *Long - term Outcomes of Agricultural Investments: Lessons from Zambia*, International Institute for Environment and Development, 2012, http://pubs.iied.org/pdfs/12571IIED.pdf（Accessed: 6 July 2013）.

② Zambia Development Agency, *Zambia Agriculture Sector Profile*, 2011, http://www.zda.org.zm/sites/default/files/Sector% 20Profile% 20 - % 20Agriculture.pdf（Accessed: 1 May 2013）.

- 分红自首次申报起 5 年内免税；
- 用于改善或升级基础设施的资本性支出可 100% 申请改进补贴；
- 机器设备 5 年内免征进口关税。

4.2 印度在赞比亚的农业投资

赞比亚的农业部门有着巨大的潜力。赞比亚拥有 6000 万公顷肥沃的可耕地（但仅开垦了 15%），充足的地表和地下水，以及适宜于耕种小麦、大豆、咖啡、棉花、烟草、糖、辣椒等多种作物的气候条件。同时，赞比亚政府也通过各种方式推动这一部门的发展，如将铁路和公路网附近的大片土地分配给潜在投资者，并加强这些区域的电气化建设。此外，政府还鼓励本地开展农产品加工（包括小麦、大豆、棉花、烟草、香料、糖和蔬菜）以实现增值，并向商业农民和小农提供特殊的激励政策。在森林资源方面，赞比亚拥有大量的松树和桉树储备林，但有过度砍伐的危险。在渔业方面，每年的商业化生产约为 7 万吨；政府和私营部门都参与其中，共同致力于实现渔业可持续生产计划。[①]

对印度政府来说，赞比亚也是其“聚焦非洲”计划中最重要的国家之一，而推动制定各种新政策的主要平台之一就是印度—非洲论坛峰会，详细列出各种贸易刺激政策的报告很容易找到。例如，印度—非洲论坛峰会将对非信用额度从 21.5 亿美元提高到 54 亿美元（到 2012 年），资金将通过印度进出口银行进行支付。其他措施还包括：覆盖印度 85% 税目的出口产品享受免关税待遇；对非洲 33 个最不发达国家，另有 9% 税目下的产品可享受优惠关税待遇；赞比亚工商贸易部部长还在 2010 年 5 月与印度签订了使用《印度免关税优惠方案》（DETP）的意向书，随着这一意向书的签订和相关文件的完成，赞比亚将有 94% 的产品可出口到印度市场。此外，印度还提议在赞比亚设立 3 个机构——人居环境中心、企业家发展学院和生

---

① Government of India, *Focus Africa*, *Investment oppertunties*: *Zambia*, http://focusafrica.gov.in/Investment_ Opportunities_ in_ Zambia. html（Accessed: 1 May 2013）.

物质气化炉系统群。①

　　印赞两国还保持着高级别的政治、商业互访交流，并通过这些会面不断推出鼓励投资的新招商政策。例如，2007 年 8 月 17 日，印度和赞比亚成功完成了对双方签订的避免双重征税协定所进行的审查。此外，2010 年 7 月 29 日至 8 月 5 日，一个以赞比亚财政和国家规划部副部长菲力（David Phiri）和工商贸易部副部长普玛（Lwipa Puma）为首的赞比亚代表团访问了印度德里和孟买，其目的在于通过公私合作模式（PPP）吸引更多印度投资；大约有 30 家印度公司利用公私合作模式对赞比亚进行了各类证券投资组合。

　　赞比亚工商贸易部部长穆塔提（Felix Mutati）称，赞比亚在过去 3 年从印度投资中获益已超过 30 亿美元。如世界最大食糖生产企业之一、印度的瑞纳卡（Shree Renuka）公司将为赞比亚南部省份的一个"交钥匙"项目投资约 2000 亿美元，② 建立甘蔗种植园和糖厂，以缓解该省长期以来的食糖短缺问题；该公司向马扎布卡区区委会承诺它将在农村地区创造 6000 个新岗位，并建立一家糖厂，在制糖的同时还利用甘蔗残渣来生产乙醇及发电。

4.3　赞比亚实地考察

　　在实地调研过程中，笔者与多家在赞比亚投资的公司进行了交流。丹马公司（Danma）是一家园艺企业，2011 年 1 月开始营业，其老板之前从事建筑业；该公司有 25 英亩土地（其中包括 4 个温室、包装和冷藏场所），种植西红柿、辣椒、草莓、卷心菜、胡萝卜、花椰菜和西兰花，其中主要盈利作物为红黄灯笼椒和草莓，种子从韩国和南非进口。公司至今还未进行过社会或环境影响评估，也没有投资过重大基础设施。在供应链方面，4 个温室和灌溉设施从南非进口，椰纤土从印度和斯里兰卡进口，紫甘蓝种子来自以色列，西红柿种子来自南非，草莓苗来自当地供应商（使用加州大学授权的专利）；咨询服务则来自一名以色列农学家。公司的产品目前主要供应当地市场，特

---

① High Commission of India, Lusaka, *India – Zambia Bilateral Relations*, http：//www. hcizambia. com/in-dia – zambia%20bilateral%20relations. htm（Accessed：6 July 2013）.

② 英文如此。查找资料显示，应该是 2 亿美元，赞比亚 2012 年 GDP 仅 206 亿美元。——译者注

别是 Shoprite、Spar 和 Pick and Pay 三大连锁超市；二级产品则主要销往索韦托。公司还计划增加产量，将产品以更高价格出口到安哥拉。在劳动力方面，公司一共雇用了 80 名员工，70% 为女性；这些员工中，1/4 为永久雇员，每天工资为 16 克瓦查外加一顿饭（每月总计约 400 克瓦查）。公司的员工也是赞比亚全国农民联盟的成员。

调研团队接触的第二家公司是印度出口贸易集团（ETG）。在过去 40 年中，该公司在埃塞俄比亚、肯尼亚、坦桑尼亚、乌干达、马拉维、莫桑比克和赞比亚都进行过农业研究。ETG 公司成立于 1967 年，1986 年被现在的董事收购，在非洲拥有并管理着一条垂直完整的农业供应链，业务包含采购、加工、仓储、分销和销售。该公司在全球 45 个国家拥有分部，集团总部位于达累斯萨拉姆，财务总部设在毛里求斯，共有雇员 6500 人，其中赞比亚有 73 人；此外，公司业务还涉及农产品加工、清洗和包装业务等中下游产业。目前，该公司在非洲和亚洲运营着 26 家这样的工厂，负责将玉米、大米、腰果、小麦、干豆、大豆、芝麻、咖啡和化肥转化为地区和国际销售网络中的畅销产品。

ETG 公司年产量超过 2500 万吨，主营农业贸易，进口化肥并促进农作物多样化；关注农产品的采购和运输、农资供应及最佳农业实践支持。

2002 年，集团大幅增加农产品加工方面的投资。目前，ETG 公司已在赞比亚、马拉维、坦桑尼亚、乌干达、埃塞俄比亚、印度和莫桑比克拥有 21 个加工中心，这些农产品加工工厂不仅帮助当地社区创造了新岗位，还帮助所在国赚取外汇收入。

ETG 公司也采用订单农业：从小农手中采购玉米，存储在仓库中，然后出口到南非和马拉维；同时以固定、享受补贴的价格向小农提供种子和肥料。目前，公司拥有一处约 12000 公顷的甘蔗种植园（其中只有 4000 公顷宜耕），但仅种植了 100 公顷；它还力图尽快建立一家糖厂，以加工小农生产的甘蔗。

调研团队访谈的第三家公司是马德生公司（Motherson）。这原本是一家水泥制造公司，之后尝试转向小麦和玉米生产，并在 2015 年涉足农业部门。根据一份 99 年的长期租约，该公司拥有 234 公顷土地的使用权，用来生产玉米和大豆。公司所有者计划从印度引入机器，并从泰国和印度进口种子。为了方便获得土地，传统土地必须转化为私人可以租用的国有法定土地。该公司所租的 234 公顷土地在租约上的租金为 500 美元/公顷，但他们不得不和地方首领及酋长谈判，实际租金约为 600 美元/公顷。公司并不清楚赞比亚发展署在谈判中的角色，还指出由于赞比亚是一个内陆国，设备在这里也往往更贵。

调研团队接触的另一家公司是新加坡的奥兰国际公司（Olam），它自称是全球领先的农产品与食品配料连锁供应商。奥兰在全球大多数主要农产品生产国都有直接采购或加工业务，为全球 13600 名顾客提供服务。根据公司网站显示，奥兰的员工数达 23000 名，经营范围包括可可、咖啡、腰果、芝麻、大米、棉花和木材制品等。

奥兰最早是由在尼日利亚的印度人创办的，但它目前已是一家总部设于新加坡的跨国公司，在全球 66 个国家都有业务（其中有 24 个非洲国家），年营业额达 55 亿美元。奥兰赞比亚分公司一共有员工 1200 名，其中 200 人是长期工。公司内部联系紧密，包括在坦桑尼亚的一家腰果加工厂。由于赞比亚缺乏维权方面的地方法规，公司已在当地进行了环境和社会影响评估，并遵守国际金融中心（IFC）的相关规定。在企业社会责任方面，公司已进行的活动包括"社区许可证"、替代就业机会等，及与非政府组织合作致力于教育和卫生方面的提升。

表5　赞比亚农业部门利益相关方

在赞比亚的印度公司	政府、公共研究及教育机构	农民组织
尼哈（Neha）国际股份有限公司	农业研究与发展（ASTI）	赞比亚出口种植者协会（ZEGA）
赞比亚斯特林农业股份有限公司（SAEL）——印度SP集团子公司	赞比亚发展署（ZDA）	赞比亚全国农民联盟（ZNFU）
	赞比亚农产品交易所（ZAMACE）	赞比亚有机产品协会（OPPAZ）
	赞比亚农业与合作社部（MACD）	赞比亚粮食交易协会（GTAZ）
韦丹塔（Vedanta）资源公司	赞比亚土地协会	赞比亚轧棉协会（ZCGA）
	赞比亚农业研究所（ZARI）	赞比亚种子交易协会（ZSTA）

在赞比亚的印度公司	政府、公共研究及教育机构	农民组织
摩汉（Mohan）出口公司	国家科学工业研究所（NISIR）	农业保护单位（CFU）
	国家农业信息服务部（NAIS）	农业组织支持计划（FOSUP）
	赞比亚大学农学院，农业经济与拓展系	全国农民和小农协会
		大规模商业农场代表组织

5 印度团队研究成果概述

5.1 研究方法

为达到研究目的，本研究团队首先阐述了"印度公司"的定义：为印度人或是赞比亚印度移民组织（Indian Diaspora in Zambia）的成员所有及管理的公司。这些公司的总部大多设在印度之外，业务遍及含印度在内的世界各地区：如丹马（Danma）公司就从 2011 年 1 月开始在卢萨卡运营；同样，ETG 公司总部设于达累斯萨拉姆，财务总部则在毛里求斯。

为了批判性地评价这些公司更广范围内的影响，本研究决定不使用印度企业事务部 2011 年颁布的国家自愿准则（NVG）中的标准。首先，因为这些规则是根据印度的生产经营环境制定的，这些标准明显是根据印度的背景环境设计的，与有关印度征地、劳工、最低工资、环境等方面的强制性法律相关联；但将同样的准则延伸至公司在印度海外的活动是不合适的，因为在这些地方，此类法律可能不同、较弱甚至完全缺失。此外，这些准则的框架主要由印度公司与其他利益相关者磋商（未必达成一致）后制定，并由印度政府公告。在执行方面，即使是在印度，这些原则也是在"应用否则解释"（apply or explain）的原则上才要求执行的；可以想见，在海外对这些规则的遵守就更弱了。因此，要理解私营部门农业投资的影响，就要采取另一种研究方法：按照赞比亚土地局等机构颁布和监督实施的当地法律法规和地方管理条例，对其进行调查和评估。

表6　受访公司信息

公司名	丹马公司（Danma）	印度出口贸易集团（ETG）	马德生公司（Motherson）	奥兰国际公司（Olam）
背景信息	公司自 2011 年 1 月开始运营； 早期涉及建筑业，有 25 公顷土地； 2011 年 9 月完成首笔交易/出产； 4 个温室设施、土地、包装和冷藏。 园艺：番茄、辣椒、草莓、卷心菜、胡萝卜、花椰菜、西兰花； 盈利作物：红黄灯笼椒、草莓； 计划尽快进行农产品加工（番茄酱、沙拉包）； 种子进口于韩国和南非； 以 8000 美元/英亩的价格购买了 25 英亩土地； 下属租赁土地或公地：租约剩余 76 年（原为赞比亚本地农民所有，不知具体是何人）	集团东非总部位于达累斯萨拉姆，财务总部位于毛里求斯。在 45 个国家（含 30 个非洲国家）设有分公司。共有 6500 名雇员，其中赞比亚 73 人。ETG 增加了当地就业，并通过投资中下游农产品加工、清洗包装业务给当地经济创造了更多价值。目前，ETG 在亚非拥有 26 个这样的工厂，将玉米、水稻、腰果、坚果、小麦、豆类、芝麻、种子、咖啡和化肥转化为适销商品在地区和全球销售，年产超过 2500 万吨；农业贸易，进口化肥；促进作物多样化，在 12000 公顷土地上，种植了甘蔗和木豆。未与赞比亚开发署签订协定。积极跟进各类企业社会责任活动	始于水泥制造业，2015 年开始涉足农业，期望生产小麦和玉米； 拥有 234 公顷土地的 99 年租约； 目前生产玉米和黄豆； 公司计划引进印度机器。种子从泰国和印度进口	跨国公司，总部设于新加坡，但管理部门和新闻处在印度； 由在尼日利亚的印度人创立； 在 66 国（含 24 个非洲国家）设有分部； 拥有 1200 名员工（其中 200 名是长期工）； 供应链管理和合同农业模式，是 SHA 农民和原材料消费者（雀巢、卡夫、玛氏）的中间人； 目前营业额达 55 亿美元（66 国，其中 26 个位于非洲），有很强的前向连锁支持，在坦桑尼亚有一个腰果加工厂； 农业加工的产品：棉花和腰果； 在赞比亚本地投入生产玉米、小麦、糖和棉花； 为 SHA 农民提供培训及最佳实践知识； 在卡萨马附近拥有 2000 公顷的咖啡园、棕地，但缺乏基础设施； 进行了环境和社会影响评估，遵循国际金融中心（IFC）要求； 企业社会责任活动：获得"社区许可证"，通过与禾众基金会（Solidaridad）等 NGO 的合作提供交替就业机会、教育和医疗卫生服务

公司名	丹马公司（Danma）	印度出口贸易集团（ETG）	马德生公司（Motherson）	奥兰国际公司（Olam）
供应链	4个温室及灌溉设备自韩国进口；椰纤土从印度和斯里兰卡进口；紫甘蓝种子来自以色列，番茄种子来自南非；草莓幼株来自当地供应商（签协议，供应商与加利福尼亚大学也有协议）；咨询服务来自一位以色列农学家；产品供应当地市场，主要是 Shoprite、Spar 和 Pick and Pay；二级产品供应索韦托市场；未来计划：增加产量，并（以更高价格）向安哥拉出口	拥有并管理在非洲次大陆的大多数垂直农业一体化供应链，业务范围包括采购、加工、仓储、分销和推销		将小农包含于供应链中，以增加其收入、传授农业和商业技能，并通过改善当地基础设施、提供针对食品安全及水紧张等问题的解决方案来发展更繁荣的社区；与大规模农户合作，将可持续农业实践嵌入其中，尤其是水、碳和能源领域，目标在于增产（在不增加化肥和水使用量的前提下）以实现农地利用最大化；使用标记滴灌设施以提升水资源利用率，保证每一滴水能产出更多作物
劳工	雇员 80 人，其中 70% 是女性，25% 是长期工；员工是赞比亚国家农民联合会成员；工人工资为 16 克瓦查/天加一顿饭（每月总计约 400 克瓦查）	有 120 个赞比亚工人，其中 80 个为长期工；零工工资为 30 克瓦查/天		

续表

公司名	丹马公司（Danma）	印度出口贸易集团（ETG）	马德生公司（Motherson）	奥兰国际公司（Olam）
生产模型	农产品交易：玉米、糖、大豆和花生； 合同农业：（最多10000公顷，无规定）存储小农生产的玉米，然后出口到南非和马拉维； 按固定的补贴率向SHA农民提供种子和肥料； 计划近期设立一个糖厂以进行农产品加工； 拥有一个占地约12000公顷（其中4000公顷可耕）的糖料种植园，但仅种植了100公顷； 赞比亚开发署在促进投资方面的作用有限； 未来计划通过作物多样化来减少化肥使用（与本地NGO合作），并增加木豆产量； 通过4个关键步骤确保未来可持续增长：为现有小农提供更大市场、新产品、新地区，通过纵向联合实现增值	专业在于农产品加工和包装，也推广作物多样化、进口化肥。在当地购买种子并进行生产，但产品用于国际消费，因此出口占很大一部分； 公司也雇用小农	逐步停止生产，234公顷土地中仅用40公顷（可耕）； 预期额：2500美元/单位产量玉米； 计划从印度进口设备，从泰国和印度进口种子； 计划在40公顷耕地上投资4万美元，并期待在4个月内获得2.5倍收益（玉米）； 玉米供应给当地连锁店	全球大米贸易的领导者之一。涉及从起源到分销的整个价值链。有一些创新想法，如其尼日利亚分公司最近就采用了一种由洛克菲勒基金会支持的生产模式（这一模式计划自2018年，每年提供1.6万吨大米）

公司名	丹马公司（Danma）	印度出口贸易集团（ETG）	马德生公司（Motherson）	奥兰国际公司（Olam）
征地			传统土地必须转化为私有的国有土地（Mumbwa）；以 500 美元/公顷的价格租赁了 234 公顷土地；但必须和酋长谈判，实际支付约为 600 美元/公顷；赞比亚开发署在谈判中的角色不清；对受影响者的补偿：承诺提供电力、建学校、提前完成计划；由于赞比亚是内陆国家，设备相对更贵	

5.2 赞比亚发展署（ZDA）

赞比亚发展署 2006 年由议会通过立法成立，2007 年 1 月正式开始运作，它由过去 5 个法定机构合并而成，即赞比亚投资中心（ZIC）、赞比亚私有化委员会（ZPA）、赞比亚出口委员会（EBZ）、小企业发展局（SEDB）和赞比亚出口加工区管理局（ZEPZA）。合并之前，这五大机构一直独立运作，它们通过高效协调、由私营部门带动的经济发展战略，促进贸易和投资，推动经济增长和发展。它们的使命是对投资设施进行事前和事后监管，招募投资者，对他们进行培训，并为他们提供跟踪服务。它们在使经济资源多元化方面十分活跃，致力于发展包括铜矿开发在内的多个领域，也热衷于发展公私合营模式（PPPs）。

《赞比亚发展署法》赋予了发展署在多个关键领域的权力，包括发展贸易、促进投资、企业重组、绿地项目发展、小企业发展、贸易及产业基金管理和技能培训发展推动等。发展署理事会的成员包括公私部门和民间团体，均由工商部部长任命，且署长和副署长均来自私营部门，因此它也算是一个半自治机构。发展署的总部设在卢萨卡，并在奇帕塔、基特韦、卡萨马、利文斯敦、曼萨、索卢韦齐和芒古设有地区办事处。

发展署的主要职能如下。

● 通过高效协调、由私营部门带动的经济发展战略，负责促进贸易和投资、推动经济增长和发展。

● 通过推动高技能的创新、生产性投资和贸易增长，努力使赞比亚经济具有国际竞争力。

● 主要通过提高效率、增加投资、提高商业竞争力、加强出口等方式，进一步推动经济发展；简化经营许可证等各项手续的办理流程，降低企业过高的经营成本。

● 通过促进资金流入、资本形成和增加就业机会来建立和完善赞比亚作为投资者的形象；通过一系列激励措施推动国内经济的长期可持续发展，以促进中小企业成长。

● 对所有投资者提供一站式服务，证明赞比亚欢迎一切投资者来从事经营活动。

在研究团队与各公司管理者的交流中，后者指出赞比亚发展署帮助了不少投资者，促进了投资；它还协助办理工作许可证。发展署的一项功能是把传统法管辖之下的土地转化为国家成文法管理，在区一级有两个委员会负责对土地进行随机调查。根据赞比亚发展署一名官员所说，酋长最多只能提供250公顷土地，剩下的则要看国家批准。同时，赞比亚发展署鼓励发展包括种植、加工和销售的综合农业。发展署还在全国所有10个省引进了农业片区项目，并加强基础设施建设以推动其发展。

5.3 赞比亚土地协会

赞比亚土地协会由7个非政府组织（NGO）组成，它们致力于推动制定公正合理的土地政策法规，并确保充分考虑到赞比亚穷人的利益。这些非政府组织在各区都有分支机构。土地协会成立于1997年，主要是为了应对政府的土地法规：非政府组织希望能保护传统土地，不希望跨国公司在此投资——尽管习惯法规定个人无权买卖土地，但他们发现一些酋长还是在向私营企业出售土地。

根据习惯法，在传统土地上生活的当地人相信他们拥有对土地的权利。但习惯法体系往往是非正式的，因此，政府想方设法整顿传统土地的转让，并将它纳入国家的控制之下。土地协会则试图通过游说、倡议、研究和社区参与等方式，使他们对土地的使用权、所有权和控制权更有保障。根据土地协会的网站，其总体目标包括：为实现包容性的政策、法规和行政制度进行游说和倡议；研究与土地相关的问题；加强在土地权利、性别等方面的意识；通过与一系列相关组织的交流与合作，实现土地问题方面的经验共享。

5.4 赞比亚实地调研中的观察和发现

- 在赞比亚农业部门中，印度投资所占份额很小；且主要是个人投资，没有印度政府支持。
- 必须区分印度人的投资和在赞比亚的印度移民的投资。
- 印度农场的主要竞争对手是南非和津巴布韦农民。
- 由于农产品市场价格的波动和缺乏与农业下游产业之间的联系，印度农民遭受了一定损失。
- 赞比亚仅6%的土地为国有土地，剩下的均为传统土地。赞比亚政府希望重新制定土地政策以促进传统土地权利的私有化。1995年，赞比亚政府颁布了一部支持投资的法律以吸引外国投资，因而随着外国投资的不断增加，大片传统土地被转为私人所有。
- 投资者可以通过有效期不超过14年的临时租用证书来获取土地。根据

1971 年的《土地测量法》，在提交合法的边界测量 6 年后，投资者可以申请毫无争议的 99 年产权证书。

• 尽管《土地法》承认传统地区土地的现有权利，但它也允许外国投资者将传统地区土地转化为租赁占有的土地，并最后获取产权证书。

• 要获得土地，投资者可以通过与村落酋长磋商后直接获得大酋长的同意，或者让由土地部与发展署人员组成的工作小组代表与对方协商土地转让。如果对方同意转让土地，酋长就会发出批准函。随后，投资者必须在村落酋长的陪同下，根据示意图划分地块边界。批准函和示意图都要提交区议会，然后由它向土地专员发推荐信，最后由土地专员推荐或直接提交总统批准。

• 近年来，政府在"私营部门发展改革计划"下采取了许多举措以鼓励外国投资者，这些措施包括：设立由发展署和土地部人员组成的土地工作小组；支持农业片区项目发展。

• 迄今为止，还没有发生过因土地重新分配或拆迁引发的民众抗议。

6　在德里的访谈

作为研究的一部分，研究团队还在德里采访了一些政府官员、私营机构和非政府组织。本部分主要阐述与他们交流后的看法。受访者就印度在非洲和赞比亚的投资提出了深刻见解，尽管印度工业联盟（CII）和印度工商联合会（FICCI）对印度政府在非活动相对乐观，也采取了一些促进措施，但非政府组织的看法恰恰相反。此外，尽管团队多次尝试联系印度对外事务部官员，但最后还是不得而终；赞比亚驻孟买领事馆和驻德里大使馆也同样未接受采访；在驻孟买领事馆，我们也未找到与本主题相关的文件资料。

6.1　推动印非经济合作

印度工业联盟（CII）副总干事穆蕾（Indrayani Mulay）女士认为，印度工业联盟为印非合作提供了平台，是最重要的组织之一。她详细介绍了 2013 年 3 月 17 ~ 19 日在新德里举行的第 9 届工业联盟—进出口银行印非项目伙伴关系会议，此会议展现了印非经济关系的新维度，其中有关农业的会议成果如下。

- 由莎尔玛（Naresh Kumar Sharma）先生（塔塔工程有限公司市场传播部主管）和史达仁（Amit Sridharan）先生（塔塔化工 Pulses 总经理及业务主管）主导的"建立基础设施和农业项目合作伙伴关系"会议召开。
- 由基洛斯卡（Sanjay Kirloskar）先生（基洛斯卡兄弟有限公司董事长兼总经理）主持、以"实现非洲粮食自给自足——合作的机会"为主题的全体大会召开，会议关注了印非普遍关心的粮食安全问题。
- 就推动印度对非农业投资所需的各步骤进行了讨论。
- 提出以下问题：印度农业技术是否能将非洲发展成全球的粮袋子？印度和非洲国家该如何加强农业研发合作？
- 召开了关于赞比亚的分会，着力关注如何加强印赞双边贸易和投资。
- 包括赞比亚副总统斯科特在内的赞比亚多名部门官员参与了此次会议。
- 斯科特副总统在演讲中提到非洲经济体应注意学习印度工业成长的经验，他鼓励印度企业来非洲尤其是赞比亚投资，因为这里可以带来最高回报。
- 在该会议的第三天，举办了"发展流动性、电力和农业技术繁荣中的伙伴关系"分会。
- 在会议最后，总价值 640 亿美元的 475 个项目被提交讨论，而 2015 年的第 8 届会议仅提出了 300 亿美元的项目，因此本届会议宣告成功。

由于参会代表在会后没有向印度工业联盟确认伙伴关系的进展，因此印度工业联盟未能提供有关会议后续活动的具体数据。穆蕾女士进一步表示，印度对非洲国家尤其是农业部门的援助并未得到正确引导。若考虑长期商业机会，那么在投资之外，印度也应该对当地人尤其是农村妇女赋权并进行培训，因为这将作为一个社会要素以提升印度品牌形象。她还谈到了印度工业联盟的"非洲使命"计划：为了扩大印度尤其是印度东部地区的影响、促进定期对话交流、加深相互理解并建立战略合作伙伴关系，2013 年 6 月 22 日至 7 月 2 日，前印度工业联盟东部地区主席查克拉沃提（Sandipan Chakravortty）

先生率领一个 14 人的代表团对赞比亚、南非和肯尼亚三国进行了商务访问，其重点在于加深非洲国家与印度之间的联系；访问期间，代表团和当地行业领袖、商会成员、政府官员及外交官进行了交流，以加强双边商贸关系，并为印度企业寻找投资机会。

访问的最后，代表团团长查克拉沃提先生与卢萨卡工商业商会（LCCI）主席罗西（Rossi）先生签订了一份备忘录：印度工业联盟和卢萨卡工商业商会承诺将共同发展双边贸易、促进投资，而作为承诺的一部分，它们会在商业机会的推广和发展方面互帮互助——在所有经济、商业、工业、农业事务方面交换信息，并促进投资。印度工业联盟—粮农卓越中心（Food and Agriculture Centre of Excellence，CII – FACE）的冈古丽（Kaveri Ganguly）女士表示，与美国国际开发署（USAID）这样的技术合作伙伴一起，他们在利用技术创新来提升生产力、减少农业环境影响的同时，还努力加强能力建设。冈古丽女士简要介绍了当前在肯尼亚、马拉维和利比里亚农业部门，与塔塔汽车公司合作、致力于能力建设措施的一个风险项目，但表示协会未来也会发展在赞比亚、肯尼亚和埃塞俄比亚的项目。

6.2　粮食安全之外的事项

2013 年 2 月 6 日，印度社会行动论坛（INSAF）、卡尔帕日什（Kalpavriksh）、印度和平组织（PEACE）、奥克兰研究所等非政府组织召集印度和埃塞俄比亚抵制圈地社会活动家，在新德里的印度国际中心召开了一整天的公民社会峰会。上述机构表示，该会议开创性地为埃塞俄比亚小农、土地维权人士及其印度同伴之间的对话提供了一个机会，为直接受土地掠夺影响的人提供了空间来分享其经历、苦难及制定针对机构、企业等土地掠夺者的战略。

乔杜里（Chowdhary）先生透露，印度和平组织正致力于圈地事务，而此次会议的目的就在于为受影响国家提供一个发表意见的平台。他还指出，驱动印度海外农业投资的各种因素，既包括印度粮食安全问题，又包含了越来越严重的水资源短缺问题和谋利动机。

6.3 印度对赞比亚农业的投资

粮食安全并非印度外包粮食生产的唯一动因，非洲农业的低成本、赞比亚等发展中国家的招商引资政策也是吸引印度企业投资的重要因素。赞比亚之所以关注农业，是因为这是其减少对单一商品（铜）的依赖以实现经济多样化的重要方式，其他所述原因还包括改善粮食安全（国家及家庭水平）、提升出口收入、继续进行世界银行结构调整计划所要求的改革。

通过低税收等众多激励措施，赞比亚创造了一个极具吸引力的投资环境。不完善的土地市场下较低的土地成本（尤其是直接来源于酋长的土地）、丰富的土地及水资源（用水无限制）、良好的耕作条件、南部非洲市场的中央位置、稳定的政治环境也是赞比亚吸引投资者的重要原因。

赞比亚为农业部门的投资提供了众多激励措施，列举如下。

● 首次实现盈利后5年内免征利润所得税；第6~8年，只对50%的利润征税；第9年和第10年，只对75%的利润征税。

● 红利自首次申报起5年内免税。

● 机器设备免征进口关税。

● 对进口的某些农资，包括有机、无机化肥及农药等减免关税。

●其他税收激励措施，包括：对农业机械耗损每年补贴50%；对用于农业改进的资本性支出，前5年每年补贴20%；直到投产的第二年，对用于种植咖啡、茶、香蕉、柑橘或类似作物的资本性支出每年补贴10%；全额补贴农场平整土地、清理杂草、防止水土流失、打井、蓄水、大气或地质勘探所带来的开销。

● 用于农业的机器设备，可在前2年享受每年50%的折旧补贴。

● 用于农场改进的资本性支出，可在前5年享受每年20%的补贴。

● 直到投产的第一年，用于种植咖啡、茶、香蕉、柑橘或类似作物的资本性支出可享受每年10%的发展津贴。

而且根据《赞比亚发展署法》，这还仅仅是投资激励措施的一小部分。

乔杜里先生提到，根据他所在非政府组织已进行的工作，印度政府也通过支持各类行动促进印度农业企业在非洲的投资，支持范围包括：传统新绿地直接投资、企业并购、收购现有公司、降低农产品进口关税、公私合作、避免双重征税协议、为在海外获得特许经营合同的印度公司提供信贷等。

征用土地带来的冲击则主要由当地人承受。不同来源的报告都显示，当地人的不满主要有：不人道行为及低工资、高度机械化作业引起的就业不足、化学污染引起的环境恶化、不良生产活动对水土的负面影响等。

6.4　双边交往的背面

斯瑞达（R. Sreedhar）先生表示，企业寻找的目标是那些政府组织相对软弱无力的非洲国家。2007 年，韦丹塔集团以 4830 万美元的价格买下了赞比亚孔科拉（Konkola）铜矿，首付 2530 万美元，并签订合同规定每年支付 500 万美元；2008 年，公司盈利达 2.08 亿美元。但过去的这几年里，印度公司对赞比亚采矿业的投资却并不十分热心，因为印度自身的采矿业也处于一个糟糕的阶段。他总结道："由于印度具备组织发展和技能发展的潜力，也就具备在全球进行管理的能力，因此它不应通过企业部门过于冒进。"

普尔加尔（Puljal）先生指出，非洲国家缺乏土地投资的原因在于土地可以租赁之前未进行过测绘，且小规模征地往往比大规模的更为成功；他甚至点了一些公司的名，这些公司获得 10 万公顷土地，却无法充分利用土地潜力，在所在国也成为一场闹剧。此外，圈地使得公司在原始资本和技术投入后，把后续资金用于购买更多的土地，而不是用于项目发展，这在一定程度上也是社会产生悲观氛围的原因之一。

普尔加尔先生相信，赞比亚当前政策中有些缺陷急需处理，建议政府在土地投资中更多支持中小企业。他还指出，赞比亚以前的班达政府比较亲中，因此中国对赞比亚土地和农业的投资都非常大；但当前政府对所有投资者都较为开放，尤其是对印度投资者，这在近期举办的印度工业联盟—进出口银行会议中表现得非常明显。

6.5 印度——关键伙伴

印度在非洲持有 450 万公顷土地，在农地征用方面扮演着非常重要的角色。尽管印度在赞比亚的投资还处于初期阶段，但赞比亚政府提供的众多激励措施应该会激起更多投资者的兴趣。此外，与在埃塞俄比亚和马达加斯加的投资（在这两个国家，外国投资者的大规模征地导致了不少当地人流离失所）相比，印度在赞比亚的投资似乎争议较小。赞比亚拥有大片可供出售的农业用地，因此外国投资者获得土地的机会非常大。此外，通过低税收等众多激励措施，赞比亚政府创造了一个极具吸引力的投资环境，其国家农业政策也促进了农业部门直接投资的增加；因此，外国公司的投资额也非常大。就印度来说，类似印度工业联盟（CII）和印度工商联合会（FICCI）组织和"聚焦非洲"等政府计划，都增进了印度工商业对赞比亚的兴趣。赞比亚相对他国更为稳定的政治经济环境，也是其产业发展的重要推动力。

在赞比亚的印度农业公司处于不同的发展阶段。冠军食品（Champions Food）等一些公司的功能还不完善，丹马等公司则刚开始在赞比亚开展业务。本研究提供了一个初步的概念框架，有助于更好地理解印度对赞比亚农业投资的特点和形态；但仍有必要对这些投资所带来的经济社会影响做进一步详细分析和评估。实地考察期间收集的实例证据显示：到目前为止，赞比亚土地征用导致当地人流离失所的负面影响还比较有限。但是，系统性证据的缺失使我们难以评估这些投资对减少农村贫困、提升小农生活的影响。此外，由于赞比亚法律中缺乏明确的征地拆迁安置政策，而在印度也没有规范印度公司海外活动的约束机制，未来发生"圈地"的风险仍较高。虽然目前看来圈地还不是一个迫切的威胁，但若继续保持当前的投资趋势，印度公司继续不承担它们的社会、经济和环保责任，将来它就很可能成为一个迫切的威胁。

附录

附录 1　已有研究及其方法

联系及会面的数据和细节（农场参访等）；联系人及联系信息（email、电话等）如下。

公司	活动及反应	联系人姓名及职位	联系信息
丹马有限公司 （Danma Corporation Limited）	2013 年 9 月 16 日/正式会面/农场参访	Dhruv Singh/总经理	+260 973 310 738 Dhruv. danmacorp@ gmail. com
奥兰国际有限公司 （Olam International Limited）	2013 年 9 月 19 日/正式会面/办公室参访	Varun Mahajan/地区主管	+260 974 770631 varun. mahajan@ olamnet. com
奥斯特罗控股有限公司 （Astro Holdings Ltd）	2013 年 9 月 17 日/正式会面/办公室参访	SM Arora/执行董事	+260 211 229939 arora@ astroholdings. co. zm
ETG	2013 年 9 月 17 日/正式会面/办公室参访	Mahesh Patel	
赞比亚印度商会 Indian Business Council of Zambia	2013 年 9 月 17 日/正式会面/办公室参访	Teza Sikasula/行政经理 Binod P. Menon/执行秘书	+260 977 781168 ibczsecretariat@ gmail. com
印度高级专员署 Indian High Commission	2013 年 9 月 18 日/正式会面/办公室参访	Mr. J. S. Variaah　/高级专员	info. lusaka@ mea. gov. in
马德生有限公司 （Motherson Enterprises Limited）	2013 年 9 月 16 日/正式会面/办公室参访	Gunasingh Prabahar/总经理	+260 0967 204173 mothersonenterprises@ yahoo. com
赞比亚开发署（ZDA）	2013 年 9 月 19 日/正式会面/办公室参访	Moses K. Mwanakatwe/业务拓展经理	+260 9778 77683 mmwanakatwe@ zda. org. zm

续表

公　司	活动及反应	联系人姓名及职位	联系信息
赞比亚土地协会 （ZLA）	2013年9月18日/ 正式会面/办公室 参访	Henry Machina/执行董事 Dimuna Phiri /研究员	+ 260 977 240823 henrymachina@ gmail. com
赞比亚大学	2013年9月17日/ 正式会面/办公室 参访	Kamini Krishna J. B. Phiri	Kaminik04@ yahoo. com + 260 977 804459 Jube56@ yahoo. com

附录2　受访者列表

A. 公司

Danma Corporation Limited

ETG Trading Company Limited

Motherson Enterprises Limited

Olam International Limited

Astro Holdings（Ex – director of Tata Zambia）

B. 政府/公共部门

赞比亚开发署

赞比亚印度商会

印度高级专员署

赞比亚大学

印度工业联盟（CII）

印度工商联合会（FICCI）

印度社会行动论坛（INSAF）

印度和平组织（PEACE）

卡尔帕日什（Kalpavriksh）

赞比亚大使馆

印度国家基金会（NFI）

外交部

矿、矿产和人民

粮农卓越中心（Food and Agriculture Centre of Excellence）

Avignam 集团

印度进出口银行

C. 公民社会组织

赞比亚土地协会

D. 公司选择的标准

来自于印度（Indian origin）

涉足赞比亚农业部类（Involvement in agriculture sector in Zambia）

以专利公司形式注册（Registered in the Patents and Companies）

注册代理（Registration Agency）

对于访问给予良好且快速的回复（Good and quick response to enquiry）

E. 一些公司被省略，因为：没有回复电话或邮件，或未在印度注册

F. 在赞比亚，研究队伍联系了如下公司及组织

1. 公司

Danma Corporation Limited

ETG Trading Company Limited

Motherson Enterprises Limited

Olam International Limited

2. 政府/公共部门

赞比亚开发署

赞比亚印度商会

印度高级专员署

赞比亚大学

3. 公民社会组织

赞比亚土地协会

4. 信息收集来源

赞比亚专利和公司注册局（PACRA）

赞比亚印度商会（IBCZ）

网络搜索

大学、学术机构等其他来源

5. 未能联系到的公司及组织

Export Trading Group

S. P. Group

Continental Ginery

Savanna Streams

Crown Millers Ltd

Zambian National Farmers Union

Satkar Limited

Earthstone Limited

Induszam Limited

Champions Limited

附录 3　在德里联系的专家列表

机构/公司	回应	联系人姓名/职位	联系信息
印度工业联盟（CII）	积极	Ms. Indrayani Mulay 国际部副总干事	地址：The Mantosh Sondhi Centre, 23 Institutional Area, Lodi Road, NewDelhi－110003 电话：91 11 24629994－7 Extn 368 /24653092（D） 传真：91 11 24601298 手机：91 9810750611 Email：indrayani. mulay@ cii. in 网址：www. cii. in
印度工商联合会（FICCI）	积极	Ms. Shiela Sudhakaran 非洲处助理秘书长	地址：FICCI, Federation House, Tansen Marg, New Delhi－110001 电话：＋91 11 23738760－70 Ext. ：380, 23322564（D） 传真：＋91 11 23765316（D）, 23320714 Email：shiela. jbc@ ficci. com

续表

机构/公司	回　应	联系人姓名/职位	联系信息
印度社会行动论坛（INSAF）	积极	Mr. Wilfred	地址：A 124/6 Katwaria Sarai，New Delhi 110016 电话：+91 11 26517814 传真：+91 11 26517814 Email：insafdelhi@ gmail. com
印度和平组织（PEACE）	积极	Mr. Anil Chowdhary	地址：F - 93，Katwaria Sarai New Delhi 110016 手机：9811119347 Email：anilpeace@ gmail. com
卡尔帕日什（Kalpavriksh）	积极	Mr. Ashish Kothari	地址：Flat no 5，2nd Floor，Shri Dutta Krupa，908，Deccan Gymkhana，Pune 411004，Maharashtra，India 电话：+91 - 20 - 25670979，25675450 传真：+91 - 20 - 25654239 Email：kalpavriksh. info@ gmail. com kalpavriksh. delhi@ gmail. com chikikothari@ gmail. com
赞比亚驻印度大使馆	未回应		地址：Zambian High Commission in New Delhi，IndiaD/54，Vasant Vihar New Delhi India 电话： （ +91）11 - 2615 0271 （ +91）11 - 26150270 Email：zambiand@ sify. com
印度国家基金会（NFI）	没有与研究相关的所需信息	Mr. Amitabh Behar 执行董事	Email：amitabh. behar@ gmail. com
印度外交部	跟进中	Mr. Alok Ranjan Jha 东南非处副处长	地址：Ministry of External Affairs Room 67 - C，South Block New Delhi - 110 011 电话：011 - 23010364 Email：dsesa@ mea. gov. in
矿、矿产和人民	积极	Mr. R. Sreedhar	

机构/公司	回　应	联系人姓名/职位	联系信息
粮农卓越中心（Food and Agriculture Centre of Excellence）	积极	Ms. Kavery Ganguly	地址：India Habitat Centre, Core 4A, 4th Floor, Lodi Road, New Delhi－110003 电话：2468 2230－35 传真：24682226 Email：face@ face－cii. in/info@ face－cii. in Website：www. face－cii. in By mail：kavery. ganguly@ cii. in
Avignam 集团	积极	Mr. Abhilash Puljal 总经理	地址：First Floor, 8 School Lane, Bengali Market, New Delhi－110001, India 电话：+91 8800969966 传真：+91 9873109966 手机：+91 9871133726 Email：abhilash. puljal@ avignam. com 网站：www. avignam. com twitter：@ avignamgroup facebook：www. facebook. com/avignamgroup
印度进出口银行		Mr. Sriram Subramaniam	电话：91－11－23326375 Email：eximndro@ eximbankindia. in 传真：91－11－23322758

附录4　未联系到的机构

大使馆：研究团队通过邮件联系了东南非处副处长 Alok Ranjan Jha 先生，他建议联系处长 Mahaveer Singhvi 先生和负责赞比亚的 Srikant Chaterjee 先生。团队联系了这两个人，但由于其日程安排原因未能成功约定时间。

进出口银行：通过邮件联系了相关人员，但未收到回复。

Report One

Agricultural Foreign Direct Investment in Zambia: Opportunities and Challenges for Poverty Reduction and Development*

An Overview of Trends and Policies

Jessica M. Chu **

Executive Summary

There is a renewed interest in foreign investments in agriculture in sub – Saharan Africa. The call for greater investment in agriculture can be a direct route to improve the lives of the rural poor; however, if such investments are not properly conducted, they can also serve to further impoverish rural communities by excluding them from natural resources.

This report serves to investigate how such trends are manifested in Zambia. In recent years, Zambia has experienced a large amount of economic growth, largely due to foreign investment and benefitting from current high copper prices. However,

---

*   This report was commissioned by Oxfam and written by Jessica M. Chu. The views expressed in the report are those of the author and do not necessarily represent the views of Oxfam.

**   The author would like to thank her fellow researchers and colleagues from Oxfam for undertaking investor case studies. In particular, the author would like to thank Professor Liu Haifang and Wan Ru (University of Peking), and Professors Aparajita Biswas (University of Mumbai) and Ajay Dubey (Jawaharlal Nehru University) for their help and insights into China – Africa and India – Africa relations, as well as colleagues from Oxfam (Mthandazo Ndlovu, Supriya Roychoudhury, Kevin May and Robert Nash). There are also many interviewees who took the time to answer the questions from the research team, including the questionnaire respondents and the representatives from the Zambia Development Agency – many thanks to all those who took part in the research. The author thanks all those from various Oxfam organisations who provided critical and constructive reviews of the drafts of the report, and to Oxfam for their support of this study.

such investment has not resulted in a corresponding level of poverty reduction. Therefore, this report serves to provide an overview of the trends and policies in foreign direct investment (FDI) in agriculture in Zambia, as the first step to understanding the potential relationship between FDI in agriculture and poverty reduction. As agricultural investment trends continue to rise, there is a need for a close examination of what they entail and how they proceed.

This report uses extensive literature review, key stakeholder interviews, and descriptive analysis of a dataset of pledged agricultural investments from the Zambia Development Agency (ZDA). Although the dataset can be considered incomplete and inconclusive in many respects, it remains the most comprehensive source of information about agricultural investment trends. There are notable limitations to this dataset, which can also be used to identify recommendations to ZDA.

While the agricultural sector is playing an increasing influence in the overall economic growth strategy for the Zambian government, there is a disconnect between agricultural growth policies and rural poverty reduction strategies. Policies to improve agricultural productivity have focused on the intensification of agricultural production, while other research suggests that smallholder farmers, despite the perception of an abundance of land, face land access constraints that limit their growth. However, while the linkages between agricultural livelihoods and rural poverty are clear, there has not yet been an emphasis to link the commercialisation of agriculture in rural areas to poverty reduction.

ZDA is the main body responsible for attracting investments, both foreign and domestic, in all sectors. With regards to agriculture, it facilitates applications for licenses and permits, as well as the acquisition of land. It is also the main body that can monitor investment patterns, through the recording of investment pledges. Although investment policy has been successful thus far in *attracting* investment to Zambia, there are still several shortcomings in Zambia's investment policies. In particular, these surround the regulatory mechanisms that help ensure that Zambia is able to adapt to changing needs. These include better monitoring mechanisms and data gathering, and better institutional operation and consultative mechanisms to provide feedback and facilitate changes.

The analysis of ZDA's investment pledges reveals that agricultural investments are indeed on the rise, with total values pledged increasing in recent years. It also presents a number of extremely large investments in recent years. Despite ZDA investments into prioritizing high value agricultural products, a large number of agricultural investments pledges have been in the crop farming sector. However, the dataset was not able to offer any insight into the ways in which agricultural investments contributed to growth in the processing and manufacturing sector. Lastly, ZDA was not able to offer information about how much land has been transferred via agricultural investments, although a preliminary list was compiled.

The use of ZDA data has allowed for a more comprehensive national understanding of agricultural investments in Zambia. Data from ZDA shows interest in investments of both large – scale and of the SME level, and investments from traditional investors such as the UK, Zimbabwe, and South Africa, who continue to dominate agricultural investments, but as well from a number of new actors including emerging economies (such as China and India), and investments following complex financial chains, facilitated through known financial conduit nations. However, there are also limitations to the data in that there is little data on the rate of realisation of investments, and it is expected that SME level investments are underreported. However, regardless of the origin of agricultural investments, all investments are subject to the same constraints and policy regulations in Zambia.

This report has also identified the policy gaps related to the facilitation of agricultural investment. Transparency of information remains a key area of concern. This applies to both the willingness of government agencies and companies to participate in research, but importantly, it also applies to the availability of information. Even with cooperation, it was often found that data important to the monitoring and evaluation of investment, such as rates of realisation of investments from pledges, was not available. EIAs remain the most important public source of information about investments, but many are not publically available, despite being public documents. The capacity of both ZDA and ZEMA must be strengthened in order to effectively monitor incoming agricultural investments, both with regards to data collection, as well as creating regulatory mechanisms with which to assess investments and their impacts. These mechanisms should look to new international guidelines, such as the Voluntary Guidelines, as models.

With regards to identifying the impacts of agricultural investments thus far, a few early conclusions can be made. While ZDA has attempted to create land banks and farm blocks for the attraction of agricultural investment, it appears that investors favour the acquisition of existing statutory land from willing sellers. Zambian land laws provide more security to statutory land, and there is a colonially – produced, agriculturally – rich supply of commercial farmland. While the acquisition of statutory land may limit displacements thus far, there must also be equal attention to how agricultural land investments further encourage the conversion of land from customary to statutory land. If the demand for agricultural land continues, there are very few mechanisms that will ensure the security of customary land tenure of the smallholder farmers.

The key area of employment and labour, as well as agricultural markets and food security, have been identified as areas in which investments are able to contribute both positive and negatively. However, there is no one mechanism in which agricultural investments will follow in order to determine impact; much of this depends on the agricultural model of the investment. Thus far, a large number of investment pledges that have proceeded through ZDA appear to favour large-scale commercial and plantation models, with low employment provision and little integration into local communities. Despite policy intentions, there has been little ability for ZDA to thus far, influence the use of pro-poor agricultural models of investments.

Agricultural investment policy needs to be reconsidered in order to effectively promote agricultural models that can incorporate smallholder farmers and rural communities into their value chains. While it is likely too early to be able to quantitatively assess such changes, stubborn rural poverty and the desire (and often desperation) for wage income facilitate cheap labour for agricultural investment in more rural areas.

The expansion of secondary sectors such as processing and manufacturing should also be encouraged in rural areas, and not just limited to cities. Lastly, there needs to be a greater understanding of the accessibility of such agricultural employment, for local residents, and for women. Agricultural investments must also provide skills and technology transfers, either through worker programmes or through the opening of markets for affordable technology. While low productivity and diversification remain barriers for food security, there is also a need to understand the impacts of agricultural investments to the household smallholder farmer level. This includes understanding the changes to the choice of crop, domestic consumption, local food prices, and household income and spending.

This report hopes to begin the process of understanding how FDI in agriculture can serve to impact, positively and negatively, Zambia's poorest and most vulnerable. While Zambia still contains land that has not been fully utilized for agriculture, there continues to be the need to understand how and why smallholder farmers face land access restrictions, while encouraging better utilization of land that has already been designated for agricultural purposes.

For foreign agricultural investments to contribute to poverty reduction for smallholder farmers, there must be an understanding of:

— *Does the investment exacerbate land tenure pressures?*

— *Does the investment provide sustainable and meaningful employment for local communities?*

— *Does the investment contribute to upstream and downstream development along the agri-*

cultural value chain?

But in order for these elements to hold, the government of Zambia must take measures to improve the monitoring and regulation of agricultural investments.

1) Introduction

There has been increased attention to the rise of foreign investment in agriculture and the acquisition of land in sub-Saharan Africa. Much of this attention has focused on the potential negative impacts of such agricultural investments to host countries. Often called 'land grabs', these investments are thought to allow foreign companies and governments to profit, at the expense of the rural poor. However, there is also an increasing recognition of the complexity and diversity within this trend of agricultural investment, prompting the question: can foreign direct investment (FDI) in agriculture contribute much needed capital and growth to developing economies, as well as to poverty reduction?

In order to begin understanding this question, there first must be a exploration of what FDI in agriculture entails. This report asks this question for the case study of Zambia. Zambia is situated within the 'Guinea Savannah' zone in Sub-Saharan Africa and has been increasingly attracting the attention of investors from all over the world for its high 'yield gap', [1] perceived availability of land, stable government, and a supportive policy climate for investment. Indeed, there appears to be a 'rush' of interest in foreign investment in Zambia agriculture. To understand the repercussions of agricultural FDI in Zambia, this report seeks to investigate the question of *who* is taking part in foreign investment in agriculture, and what are the processes that guide agricultural investment. The fine line between the contribution of agricultural investments to both economic growth and poverty reduction is often

---

[1] "Yield gap can be defined as the gap between potential and realised agricultural yields," See Deininger and Byerlee (2011).

borne by governance processes and regulatory mechanisms. Therefore, the potential for agricultural investment to contribute to both growth and poverty reduction comes down to Zambia's capacity to cope with increased interest in its agricultural sector and land.

There are two important trends that underlie the motivations for this research. First, although agriculture forms a smaller contribution to Zambia's overall GDP and FDI inflows, particularly in relation to mining, it is playing an increasingly larger role. Secondly, there appears to be a trend that, while traditional investors such as the United Kingdom (UK) and South Africa continue to play large roles in agricultural investment, there is a growing role played by emerging economies India and China, suggesting that there are new actors playing an additional role in agricultural development in Zambia that warrants further exploration.

Table 1   Ranking of the top 10 nations in pledged agricultural investment by value (1998 – 2012)

Nationality	Number of pledged investments	Total value of pledged investments (USD)	Average value of pledged investment (USD)
British	64	596249513	9316399
South African	50	273639189	5472784
Malawian	2	113319000	56659500
Indian	21	112061375	5336256
Zambian	32	107188553	3349643
Zimbabwean	70	99445907	1420656
Mauritian	5	43427000	8685400
Singaporean	1	35000000	35000000
Chinese	34	33301378	979452
Ireland	3	26761392	8920464

Source: ZDA (2013).

Other investigations into the rise of agricultural investments in Zambia have either approached the topic via case studies of specific investments,① or through the examination of the general processes related to investment.② While these questions are also discussed in this report, this report instead focuses on an examination of these processes from the perspective of both the functions of agricultural investment policy and the efficacy of these policies, by looking more closely at investor trends revealed through data made available from Zambia's main investment facilitator, the Zambia Development Agency (ZDA). Although this approach has limitations (which will be discussed in the methodology section) it is hoped that this analysis contributes to the wider literature on foreign investments in agriculture in Zambia by providing a means to understand trends in investor interest and behaviour. Furthermore, an assessment of the data provided by ZDA also provides a means of evaluating ZDA's processes and policies.

It is hoped that the information in this report will contribute to a better engagement with policy advocacy on agricultural investment trends. The findings of this report can help civil society better engagement with the Zambian government's promotion of agricultural investment, and thus begin to find ways to understand the impacts of agricultural investments and assess if agricultural investments can contribute to poverty reduction.

2) Methodology

A. The Data

This report employs extensive literature review and key stakeholder interviews, while the bulk of the discussion relies on descriptive analysis of a dataset of pledged agricultural investors provided by ZDA. For the purposes of this report, agricultural

---

① Such as: Action Aid (2013); FAO (2013a); Mujenja and Wonani (2013).
② Such as: FAO (2013b); German et al. (2013); Nolte (2014).

investments are defined as instances of FDI[①] in the primary agricultural sector. However, this report relies mostly on the designation of 'investor' as employed by ZDA. As the main vehicle for investment facilitation (both foreign and domestic), ZDA offer investment licenses, which provide access to a set of investment incentives (further discussed in Section 4). ZDA maintains a database of investment licensees, categorized by sector, which provides the basis for the list of pledged investors employed by this report. Thus, within this report, the pledged investments listed under ZDA's database under the primary agriculture sector, are considered agricultural investors.

Comprehensive literature reviews were conducted on not only on secondary sources about FDI in Zambia, but also on policy documents in Zambia pertaining to investment. These were complemented by key informant interviews. [②] Fieldwork and interviews for the report were conducted in July 2012, July 2013, and September 2013. Semi-structured interviews were conducted with a number of key stakeholders, which included representatives from ZDA and Zambia Environmental Management Agency (ZEMA), as well as from a range of civil society organizations and non-governmental organizations, and academic experts. Interviews were held in informants' offices and each lasted approximately one hour in length. Semi-structured interviews covered information on understandings of the extent of foreign investment in agriculture, in particular, information on key investors, as well as concerns and information on impacts arising from such investments. It was noted that very little ground-level research has been conducted on the impacts of FDI in agriculture, both by government bodies and by other civil society organizations.

---

① A useful definition of FDI can be found at UNIDO, which understands FDI to be 'investment that reflects the objective of a resident entity in one economy obtaining a lasting interest in an enterprise resident in another economy', or more specifically, when the foreign investor owns equity capital stake of at least 10% of ordinary shares, or the equivalent (2008: 3).

② See References for the complete list of informants and documents analysed.

Access to FDI and investor data remains the largest limitation to this study. While Zambia is reported to be one of 14 countries in which national inventories of land investments are available, previous research in this field has noted that the data available is of questionable reliability. [1] As accessing much of the data on FDI is challenging and at times unreliable, this report therefore mostly provides descriptive statistics deriving from the data to suggest trends, which was corroborated with the information derived from the literature and interviews.

Another noted limitation to this report is the changing research environment in Zambia. There was a noticeable change over time in the limitation of government agencies to engage and share information with researchers. This has two sources: the first stems from efforts among government bodies to more properly direct and control information that is provided from various employees. This is part of an effort to ensure that information is obtained and channeled through authorized bodies, thus reducing the risk of unprofessionalism and corruption. However, the corollary effect has been that the ability to conduct research is severely hampered by bureaucratic mechanisms, primarily in delays experienced while waiting for authorizations. However, overall, government bodies appeared to be willing participants in facilitating research, in particular, ZDA.

The dataset used for the analysis of agricultural FDI is based on the data made available by the Research Unit of ZDA. The data provided by ZDA reports the levels of pledged investments in the agricultural sector for investment licenses granted by ZDA. The ZDA data contains information about the registered company name (or name of the individual, if not through a company), the year in which the investment pledge was made, the reported nationality of the investor, and the size of pledged investment (expressed in American dollars). The status of the companies (such as private or public) was not available, nor was information on other regis-

---

[1] See Deininger and Byerlee (2011).

tered or affiliated companies. ① However, when possible, information on companies
was checked against data made available by the Patents and Company Registration A-
gency (PACRA) and the ZEMA, and verified with public information made available by the companies.

This research focuses on a fifteen-year time frame of 1998 – 2012. This time frame
was selected based on the desire to focus on recent changes in agricultural investment. Importantly, the time frame encompasses the years of 2006 – 2008, which
saw significant global events such as crises in food prices, global finance, and fuel
prices, and the restructuring of Zambia's investment policy through the consolidation
of ZDA in 2006. ②

Other data employed in this report was gathered from the public data made available by United Nations agencies [namely the Food and Agriculture Organization
(FAO) and the United Nations Conference on Trade and Development
(UNCTAD)]. An effort was made to ensure consistency in data used, although
with regards to data on foreign direct investment, this was difficult. Inconsistencies in
data point to a larger issue of data availability and transparency, which is a noted issue
in the topic of FDI, and is beyond the scope of this report to discuss.

B. Limitations

Several limitations of this report have already been noted, which includes data a-
vailable on FDI. The use of the ZDA data is meant to help bridge the gaps in understanding agricultural FDI, but this in itself holds another set of limitations, which is
discussed in this section. While data on agricultural investment pledges is made available to the public upon request, there appears to be inconsistencies in data keeping by

---

① Although details of the investments such as the farm size and the status of the company were not available
from the ZDA data set, occasionally this data can be derived from the PACRA, using the name registered at
ZDA.

② The repercussions of this to FDI levels will be explained in later sections.

ZDA and infrequent updating and correcting. The data gathered by ZDA derives from self-reporting questionnaires from the investors themselves, but thus far ZDA's ability to monitor and evaluate the reliability of self-reported answers is limited. Thus, errors are common within the data, which may derive from incorrect or calculated changes to reported data by companies.

In addition, the percentage of investors that operate through ZDA is not available, nor is the rate of realization of pledged investment projects known. ZDA believes that through its incentives programme, a large number of investors *do* proceed through ZDA, even if they do not necessarily follow up with the ZDA after receiving their investment license. Thus, figures provided by ZDA should be taken as an indicator of trends, rather than a precise quantification.

Table 2　FDI inflow versus total value of pledged investments in agriculture (1998 – 2012)

Year	FDI inflows (USD)	ZDA reported pledged investments, total value (USD)
1998	238000000	(not known)
1999	86000000	(not known)
2000	121700000	82095718
2001	145300000	115108990
2002	298400000	82935945
2003	347000000	119797798
2004	364000000	124994483
2005	356900000	252645995
2006	615800000	737512040
2007	1323900000	1986144108
2008	938600000	10883998005
2009	694800000	2010202370
2010	1729300000	4809365296
2011	1108000000	5464446729
2012	1066000000	6287305537

Source: ZDA (2013); UNCTAD Stats (2013)

A brief comparison of the FDI inflows and the data reported by ZDA suggests that for most years, ZDA's reported pledged investments does vary with reported FDI figures, ranging from forming a proportion of FDI (in particular, from 2000 – 05), to out-valuing FDI inflows in recent years. This discrepancy has a number of factors, including difficulty in maintaining data records, but also the changes in the latter years points to greater numbers of speculative investments that may be unrealized, or a lag between pledged investments and FDI reporting. However, importantly, they both demonstrate similar trends upwards, with a marked change around 2006 – 07.

The data from ZDA also provides a simplification to much of the details on aspects such as investor origin and investment sector and subsector; investors that derive their origin from a number of countries, or indeed are transnational, are not accurately reflected in the data, nor are companies that have invested in a number of sectors (such as those other than agriculture such as mining, transportation, construction) or in a variety of subsectors (such as crop farming, mixed farming, horticulture, floriculture, livestock, or primary production versus secondary processing or value-addition).

Although the flaws in ZDA data have been recognised,[1] there is also an acknowledgement for improvement needed in the mechanisms for data collection within ZDA. ZDA has recently restructured its Research Unit to provide greater capacity to record information and data that follows the investment pledge. This is part of an effort to create better 'aftercare' of investors and to promote a longer-term engagement with individual investors to move past investment attraction to investment sustainability. As part of this, ZDA have begun gathering more systematic and comprehensive information on the status and progress of each investment pledge; it is anticipated that such information in the future will contribute more greatly to understanding the outcomes of FDI, in particular, in a sector such as agriculture, which en-

---

[1] See CUTS International (2003).

compasses longer time frames for outcomes and successes. ①

3) Zambia's Development and Agricultural Context

A. Zambia and Development

In order to contextualise the importance of understanding the nature of foreign investment in agriculture to Zambia's economic growth and poverty reduction strategies, this section seeks to provide some details about Zambia's current development trajectories, as well as the relevance of the agriculture sector. Zambia is a rapidly changing country. Recent years have seen great changes in Zambia's economic landscape, symbolized by Zambia's recent graduation into the lower-middle income country (LMIC) group. These changes are the result of Zambia's recent economic growth, which can be seen in the rise of GDP as well as sustained economic growth rates. These rates of growth continued even through 2007 – 2008, which saw the decline of growth in Western countries, which undoubtedly had impacts on FDI inflows to Zambia. These changes ensured that Zambia has met its macroeconomic goals set forth in the first year of its Sixth National Development Plan (SNDP) (2011 – 15).

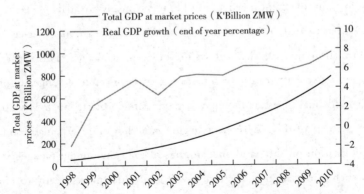

Figure 1   Total GDP and real GDP growth in Zambia (1998 – 2012)

Source: CSO (2013).

---

① Interview, ZDA representative (2013).

However, despite macroeconomic success, the equivalent improvements have not been seen for social indicators. The 2011 SNDP Annual Progress Report outlines either backwards progress or stagnation in the government's efforts to improve the criminal justice system, reduce numbers of persons infected with HIV/AIDs, lower gender – based violence, address deforestation or environmental degradation, and in efforts to raise the issue of disability and accessibility. ① Zambia's slow progress on social indicators is corroborated by the United Nations Development Programme's (UNDP's) Human Development Index (HDI) rankings. Zambia was ranked 163 out of 187 on the HDI, placing it in the low human development category. While Zambia has seen gradual gains since 1980 (increasing an average of 11 percent, or 0.3 percent annually), it still remains behind several of its neighbours and continental economic counterparts. ②

Table 3   Zambia's trends in human development indicators (1980 – 2012)

	Life expectancy at birth	Expected years of schooling	Mean years of schooling	GNI per capita (2005 PPP $)	HDI value
1980	52	7.7	3.3	1, 424	0.405
1985	51.2	7.7	4	1, 185	0.405
1990	47.5	7.9	4.7	1, 135	0.398
1995	43.5	7.9	6.1	959	0.385
2000	42	7.9	5.9	981	0.376
2005	44.4	7.9	6.4	1, 060	0.399
2010	48.5	8.5	6.7	1, 234	0.438
2011	49	7.9	6.5	1, 307	0.43
2012	49.4	8.5	6.7	1, 358	0.448

Source: UNDP (2013a).

Zambia has made slow gains towards several Millennium Development Goals (MDGs). In particular, Zambia has made progress in MDG 2 (Achieve Universal

①   GRZ (2012).
②   UNDP (2013a).

Primary Education), MDG 3 (Promote Gender Equality), and MDG 6 (Combat HIV and AIDS, Malaria and other Diseases), while maintaining good status for MDG 8 (Develop a Global Partnership for Development). However, progress in the remainder has been lacking, despite strong economic growth. Zambia has made little progress in areas such as halving the proportion of people living in extreme poverty and addressing growing inequality, as measured by the GINI coefficient. [1]

B. Profile of Agriculture in Zambia

Despite strong economic growth, these slow gains in several measurements of development indicate that growth has not resulted in improvements to the lives of a large number of Zambia's poorest communities. [2] This indicates that despite economic success, there must be a greater investigation into the areas of growth and how to translate such growth to the wider Zambian population.

One way to address this is to focus on the agricultural sector in Zambia. Despite playing a relatively small role in the Zambian economy, agriculture remains one of the greatest concerns for both the majority of the Zambian population, as well as for the Zambian government. Agriculture provides employment for the majority of the Zambian population, employing approximately 66.7 percent of the population in 2010. While the percentage of the overall population employed in agriculture has decreased since 2006 (71 percent in 2006), the *number* of households engaged in agriculture has still increased from 1551952 in 2006 to 1631000 in 2009, stressing that agriculture *continues* to be an important source of employment.

Furthermore, agriculture provides employment for the majority of those living in rural areas. This has tremendous poverty reduction implications, as the majority of those living below the poverty line (60.5 percent of the Zambian population), live in rural areas. In

---

[1] In 2010, the last date for which it was calculated, Zambia's GINI coefficient was calculated at 0.65; the target for 2015 is 0.34, which it is unlike to reach (UNDP, 2013c).

[2] Resnick and Thurlow (2014).

2010, the rural poverty rate was 77.9, compared to 27.5 percent in urban areas. [1]

Thus, agriculture remains the most important sector for poverty reduction and rural development in Zambia. This is not only because of the high proportion of rural livelihoods that are derived from agriculture, but also due the close linkages between agricultural livelihoods and other key rural development indicators such as food security. Agriculture also remains politically important, as it constitutes a large voter base, and economically important as a means to diversify the economy away from the mining sector. This section details current Zambian agricultural policy directions, and then provides a brief breakdown of some key trends and issues in the Zambian agricultural sector.

Historically, the agricultural sector has long been seen as complementary to the mining sector. Originally envisioned to support growing urban centres and mining labour, this supported the growth of a dual-purpose agricultural economy, with a concentrated commercialised farming sector in addition to the widespread rural smallholder economy. Although successive plans since Independence have prioritised the growth of agriculture as a diversification from the mining sector, in practice, little attention had been placed on agricultural policy. [2] The collapse of the copper prices and much of the mining economy in the mid-1970s, alongside the implementation of Structural Adjustment Policies (SAPs) in the 1980s and 1990s, prompted a wave of liberalisation policies, which were particularly targeted towards maize production.

The history of agricultural policy in Zambia was thus limitedly successful in creating broad based growth and poverty reduction. Agricultural contributions to GDP were led by high-value crops, primarily concentrated in large-scale commercial farms. Although agricultural production declined in the wake of SAPs and agricultural liberalisation, there has been a slow recovery of the agriculture sector in the 2000s. Presently, agriculture is once again seen as a means for economic diversification and poverty reduction.

---

[1] GRZ (2010).

[2] Wood (1990).

Zambia's current agricultural policy is guided by the National Agricultural Policy (NAP) (2004 – 15). The aim of the NAP is to 'promote development of an efficient, competitive, and sustainable agricultural sector, which assures food security and increased income', emphasizing increased production, sector liberalisation, commercialisation, the promotion of public and private sector partnerships, and the provision of effective services. [1] Once again the NAP aims to promote both large-scale, export – led commercial agriculture and measures to promote smallholder growth. These policies are closely echoed by other guiding policy principles such as the national Vision 2030 plan (2006) and the current national development plan, the SNDP (2011 – 15).

The goal of Vision 2030 for the agricultural sector is to achieve 'an efficient, competitive, sustainable and export-led agriculture sector that assures food security and increased income by 2030'. Vision 2030 identifies three categories of farmers who will contribute to these goals: the 'peasant farmer', [2] the commercially oriented 'peasant farmer' [3] and the large commercial farmer. The report envisions that increasing agricultural productivity, particularly amongst smallholder farmers, can significantly contribute greater agricultural development; targets such as increasing irrigated land, agricultural machinery, livestock, and fish populations appear to target the category of smallholder farmer. Although the gender categories are not taken into account with regards to references to smallholder farmers, Vision 2030 acknowledges that women face greater disadvantages when it comes to accessing land under both customary and statutory systems. [4]

---

[1] GRZ MACO (2004).

[2] While Vision 2030 report refers to 'peasant farmers', most often, the smallest category of farmers is called 'smallholder farmers', which is the term that will be used within the report. Typically, the definition of a 'smallholder farmer' is one that holds less than 20ha of land, while the GRZ further refers to smallholder farmers as those that hold less than 5ha (Sitko and Jayne, 2012).

[3] Also referred to as the 'emergent farmer', who typically cultivates between 5 – 20ha of land, and contains a number of other traits, including business skills, access to capital, and innovation and dynamism (Sitko and Jayne, 2012).

[4] GRZ (2006: 23).

Both Vision 2030 and Zambia's National Agricultural Investment Plan (NAIP; 2014 – 18) set forth the road map to help achieve the goals of the Comprehensive Africa Agriculture Development Programme (CAADP), launched by the African U-nion and the New Partnership for Africa's Development in 2003. As a signatory to CAADP, Zambia seeks to achieve 6 percent annual growth in the agricultural sector, through the allocation of at least 10 percent of the national budget to agriculture. [1]

Throughout the GRZ's recent articulated agricultural policy documents (such as NAP, Vision 2030, and NAIP), there is a clear emphasis towards a vision of not only increased agricultural production, but also the development of an export – ori-ented, value-added agricultural sector, meant to also reduce the dependence on the volatility of food prices and copper prices as the mainstay for economic growth. All of these are in the name of aggressively diversifying the economy away from a de-pendence on the mining sector. However, while the linkages between agricultural livelihoods and rural poverty are clear, there has not yet been an emphasis to link the commercialisation of agriculture in rural areas to poverty reduction.

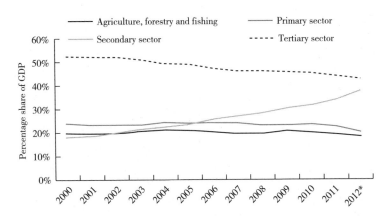

Figure 2　Percentage share of GDP by economic sector, and agriculture (2000 – 12)
* represents estimate.

Source: CSO (2013).

---

[1]　NAIP (2013).

Agriculture has steadily contributed approximately 20 percent to the Zambian GDP over the past 12 years. When examined under a longer-term context, agriculture has been the fastest growing sector from 1965 – 2001, at an average annual growth rate of 3.1 percent, with the majority of the growth after the post-market reform period starting in 1992.[①] Figure 2 demonstrates the percentage share of GDP of different sectors. The primary sector includes mining and quarrying, as well as agriculture, forestry and fishing, with the latter forming the greatest proportion of the primary sector GDP contribution. This was estimated to have a slight decrease from 2011 at 18.4 percent. However, the sector with the largest growth in GDP is the secondary sector.

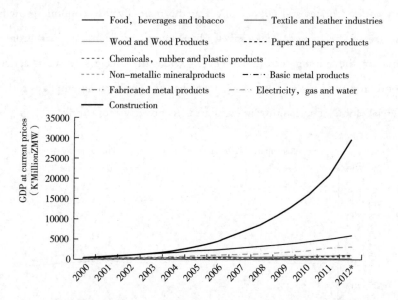

Figure 3: Secondary sector GDP contributions (2000 – 12)

* represents estimate.

Source: CSO (2013).

Within the secondary sector, construction remains the largest growth sector, but it is important to note that the food, beverages and tobacco sector follows, with

---

① GRZ (2006).

notable growth over recent years (see Figure 3). Figure 4 demonstrates that within
the components of the primary agriculture sector, while growth rates in agriculture
and forestry are normally high, they have both seen a slight decline in recent years
while fishing shows a slight resurgence; it is also important to note that growth rates
have been inconsistent over recent years pointing to some volatility.

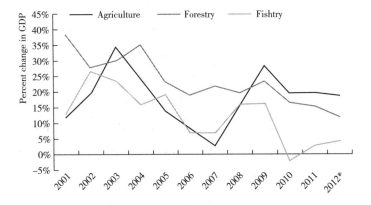

**Figure 4: Agricultural sector growth rates as percentage
change at current prices (2001 – 12)**

Source: CSO (2013).

The inconsistencies in agricultural growth rates in recent years may speak to the
reasons why agricultural growth rates have not necessarily translated into a marked reduction of poverty amongst smallholder farmers. NAIP identifies productivity and
low diversification as two of the greatest challenges to Zambian agriculture, particularly at the smallholder level. The dominance of hybrid seed maize is well known; in
2010, 82 percent of all smallholder farmers reported growing maize.[1] This is the
consequence of cultural demand (with maize as the staple crop) and historical and
current government economic incentives for both inputs and output markets. In addition to maize, other notable smallholder crops are cassava, groundnuts, and sweet

---

[1]   NAIP (2013).

potatoes. Cotton and tobacco remain important cash crops for export for smallholder farmers.

An additional factor is often singled out as a restraint to smallholder productivity: restricted land size. The Central Statistics Office (CSO) estimates that 72.7 percent of small-scale farmers cultivate less than 2ha of land. [1] The restriction of land cultivated is often thought to be the consequence of access to labour and capital, rather than availability of land. However, there is increasing evidence that this is due to land constraints through land access, rather than land availability. [2] Small-scale farmers in customary land areas have trouble accessing additional land near their villages, while farmer surveys reveal that farmers believe that there is no additional unallocated land available in their communities. Importantly, there is additional research that has demonstrated that increasing the land cultivated for this smallest sector of small-scale farmers helps provide the most dramatic increases in agricultural sales, with an increase of 1ha improving smallholder agricultural sales by 319 – 788 percent for the bottom two quartiles of smallholder farmers. [3]

There continues to be a disconnect between agricultural growth policies and rural poverty reduction strategies. Policies to improve agricultural productivity have focused on the intensification of agricultural production, while other research suggests that smallholder farmers, despite the perception of an abundance of land, face land access constraints that limit their growth. Despite the targeting of smallholder farmers in CAADP strategies, modelling of CAADP scenarios demonstrate that much of the public investment in agriculture is still favoured towards large-scale commercial producers. [4] The emphasis on export-led crops, rather than broad-based agricultural growth through the appropriate targeting of smallholder crops, will result in the limit-

---

① NAIP (2013).
② Sitko and Jayne (2012).
③ Hichaambwa and Jayne (2012).
④ Thurlow et al (2008).

ed success of Zambia's agricultural growth plans.

The question remains how foreign investments in agriculture in Zambia can translate into benefits for the smallholder farmers and the rural poor, who already face a
number of large barriers in benefitting from Zambia's recent economic growth.
However a number of promising spaces for cooperation remain, in that Zambia has a
growing manufacturing sector, particularly in food and beverage processing areas,
which has the possibility of contributing to growth without adding to further land
constraints.

4) Zambia's Investment Environment

A. Recent Investment Trends in Zambia

Much of Zambia's recent economic growth is owed to strong levels of FDI;[1]
therefore, in understanding trends in agricultural investment, it is important to understand the wider trends in investment in Zambia and the roles played by investment
policy in Zambia's wider economic strategy. It is believed that FDI can provide linkages and connections to the global market, act as capital for other forms of investment
and growth, in addition to acting as a source of skills, technology and know –
how.[2] This section provides a brief background on recent investment trends, and
some factors in the determination of investment, such as trade, aid, and Zambia's investment framework.

Beginning with the privatization programme in 1992 and the liberalisation of trade
regimes in the early 1990s, Zambia has been attracting increasing levels of foreign investment inflows. A comparison of FDI inflows during 1980 – 2010 in several developing countries shows that the Zambian economy continues to depend much more
heavily on FDI inflows, than other countries such as Uganda, Ghana, Mali, Tanza-

---

① NEPAD OECD (2011).
② FAO (2013).

nia and Senegal. Much of this is due to the historical and continued dominance of the copper mining industry in Zambia.

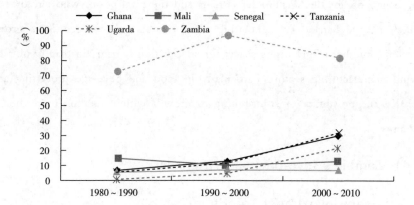

Figure 5: Comparative contribution of FDI stocks to GDP in select African economies
Source: Adapted from FAO (2013).

ZDA outline a number of attractive facets of the Zambian political system for investors (such as stability, investor-friendly environment), but also emphasize the abundant natural resources of Zambia, which continues to bring in investment. Table 4 (below) demonstrates that within FDI flows, mining and quarrying continue to dominate, with strong performances in the manufacturing sector. Agriculture ranks in the middle of the sectors, forming only 1.8 percent of the total FDI inflows for the year 2010.

Table 4   FDI inflows in Zambia by sector (2007 – 2010)

Sector	2007	2008	2009	2010
Agriculture	$ 3800000	$ 2700000	$ – 14100000	$ 45600000
Mining and quarrying	$ 671600000	$ 554360000	$ 367000000	$ 1652600000
Manufacturing	$ 108700000	$ 77100000. 00	$ 285000000	$ 423700000
Construction	$ 9200000	$ 6530000	$ 44200000	$ 17400000
Wholesale and retail	$ 80400000	$ 57030000	$ 65000000	$ – 2200000
Tourism	$ 12700000	$ 9010000	$ 40900000	$ 4300000

续表

Sector	2007	2008	2009	2010
Transport and communication	$ 67800000	$ 48090000	$ − 10700000	$ 204300000
Financial institutions	$ 111500000	$ 79080000	$ − 83500000	$ − 11200000
Real estate	$ 2900000	$ 2060000	$ − 400000	$ − 4500000
Other	$ 255300000	$ 103060000	$ 600000	$ 166400000
TOTAL	$ 1323900000	$ 939020000	$ 694000000	$ 2496400000

Source: ZDA (2013).

Zambia continues to put in place a number of different policies to encourage the continued growth of FDI trends. These include not only the harmonisation of investment regulations, but also in trade regulations and reform of the private sector.

B. Trade and Aid

Trade and aid both also play important roles in the Zambian economy. Export − led trade has helped investment promotion in Zambia by demonstrating Zambia's importance in growing markets; this is particularly relevant with regards to agricultural investments. Previous agricultural export markets focused on high-value products, such as horticulture and floriculture; however, the market remains small. As a country with no natural ports, the Zambian government has started to promote Zambia as 'land-linked', in order to emphasize the potential of Zambia as an export hub to neighbouring growing markets, as opposed to overseas exports.

Trade agreements form another integral part of Zambia's ability to attract foreign investors, as well as ability to ensure economic growth resulting from such investment flows. As a landlocked country, Zambia relies on trade with its neighbours for key markets. Neighbours such as the Democratic Republic of Congo (DRC) and Zimbabwe remain two key trading partners, alongside South Africa; internationally, it relies on the European Union and Switzerland as export markets. Zambia is part of both the Southern African Development Community (SADC)[1] and the Common Market for Eastern and Southern Africa (COMESA),[2] and the efforts to establish the tripartite free trade area between SADC, COMESA, and the East Africa Community.[3] In addition, Zambia is part of the African Growth and Opportunity Act (AGOA) with the USA, which permits duty free entry into the USA for certain goods; thus far, AGOA permits the transit of textiles and apparel goods, cut flowers, horticulture, and automotive and steel.[4]

Zambia's main export products are intermediate goods, such as copper cathodes and refined copper (accounting for a total of 86.3 percent of Zambia's total export value), while consumer goods, capital goods, and raw materials made up the remaining 13.6 percent.[5] The Zambian government is currently undergoing efforts to diversify their export portfolio, not only away from mining, but towards mining by-products as well.[6] As of 2013, Asia was ranked as the largest market for Zambia's total exports in terms of value, at 30.2 percent. This is primarily accounted for by trade with China (at 78.4 percent of trade with Asia), but notably includes the United Arab Emirates (16 percent), Singapore (3.3 percent), Japan (1.2 percent), and India (0.5 percent). The SADC region ranks second, holding 23.8 percent of Zambia's export shares by value, dominated by the DRC (43.7 percent of the SADC region's exports), followed by South Africa (34.6 percent). With regards to imports, Zambia's SADC and COMESA neighbours play a particularly important role as sources of machinery and construction materials, as well as mineral

---

[1] SADC Countries: Angola, Botswana, Democratic Republic of Congo, Lesotho, Madagascar, Malawi, Mauritius, Mozambique, Namibia, South Africa, Swaziland, Tanzania, Zambia and Zimbabwe.

[2] COMESA Countries: Burundi, Comoros, Democratic Republic of Congo, Djibouti, Egypt, Eritrea, Ethiopia, Kenya, Libya, Madagascar, Malawi, Mauritius, Rwanda, Seychelles, Somalia, Swaziland, Uganda, Zambia and Zimbabwe.

[3] OECD (2012).

[4] ZDA (2013).

[5] CSO (2013).

[6] OECD (2012).

products. South Africa was Zambia's main source of imports at 31. 2 percent, while China and India collectively accounted for 11. 5 percent at fourth and fifth respectively. [1]

It is clear that Zambia is increasingly seeing itself as a regional exporter, particularly in light of its efforts to diversify trade away from copper exports, towards other non-traditional exports, which include agricultural products, and its efforts to continue the harmonisation of trade policy and the improvement of border posts at Chirundu (to Zimbabwe), Katima Mulilo (to Namibia), Kazungula (to Botswana), Nakonde (to Tanzania), and Kasumbelesa (to DRC).

With regards to aid, in recent years, Zambia has experienced a decrease in overseas development assistance (ODA), particularly from members of the OECD's Development Assistance Committee (DAC). Zambia saw ODA decrease by almost half, from 2000 ($ 1. 5 billion USD) to 2010 (to $ 852 million). [2] In addition, Zambia saw much its foreign debt forgiven by the IMF and World Bank, under the Heavily Indebted Poor Country initiative and the Multilateral Debt Relief Initiative. [3] Donors argued that Zambia's diversification of its development finance sources and its new LMIC status has provided confidence for the reduction of dependence on ODA. As ODA levels decrease, FDI inflows will form a greater percentage of Zambia's GDP than ODA. These factors will likely contribute to favourable Zambian policy conditions to continue attracting greater amounts of FDI, as an alternate source of income to ODA.

Within development assistance volumes, there has been a global rise in non-traditional development assistance (NTDA), which is defined as 'cross-border sources of finance that are provided to developing countries for a public or philanthropic purpose, and which have an element of concessionality, but are not traditional bilat-

---

[1] CSO (2013).

[2] Prizzon (2013).

[3] Prizzon (2013); OECD (2012).

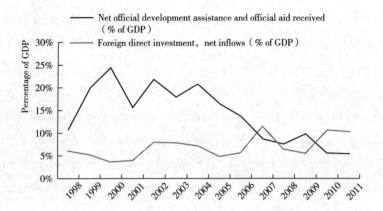

Figure 6: ODA versus FDI as percentages of Zambia's GDP (1998 – 2011)
Source: World Bank Stats (2013).

eral or multilateral ODA. '[1] These derive from a number of different sources, including philanthropic organizations such as the Gates Foundation and the Clinton Initiative, but also non-DAC countries, such as the BRICS countries. NTDA still only
forms a small percentage of the world's ODA, and is dominated by global health
funds; however, China has become the largest non-DAC donor, and as NTDA
continues to rise, so will China's contribution. [2]

　There is a global shift away from aid that is prompting a greater policy movement
towards the attraction of, and emphasis on, increasing FDI inflows. This holds true
for emerging economies, such as the BRICS nations, but also for rising LMICs such
as Zambia. This also provides a space in which BRICS nations can play a greater role
in the economies of developing countries through the provision of NTDA. While
this may contribute to home country investors seeing Zambia as part of a more viable
and stable investment strategy, it also increases Zambia's dependence on such sources
of revenue. This puts even greater impetus that Zambian investment policy be shaped
in such a way that ensures that FDI inflows translate into shared benefits throughout

---

① Prizzon (2013).

② Prizzon (2013).

the Zambian economy, and that investments do not take precedent over the livelihoods of the Zambian people.

C. Investment Policy and the Role of the Zambia Development Agency

In recent years, Zambia has considered itself a success in attracting foreign investment. It has risen in rankings such as the World Bank's 'Doing Business' index, on
which it currently ranks 83rd in the world (7th in sub-Saharan Africa). [1] Such indices
are meant to assess Zambia's ability to attract investment, by ranking the difficulty for
investors to start businesses, get credit, acquire permits, and the ease of paying taxes.
Therefore, while indices such as the 'Doing Business' index rank Zambia highly in
comparison to a number of its sub-Saharan African neighbours, a more useful analysis
is to ask *how* does Zambia's investment policies affect its ability to attract agricultural
investment, and *what kind* of agricultural investments does it attract.

Zambia's investment aims are articulated in national planning policies such as the
SNDP and Vision 2030. These national planning policies seek to re-orient the Zambian economy towards a diversified (and sustainable) economic base. [2] The goals of
the SNDP and Vision 2030 are mandated through the Zambia Development Act of
2006. The Zambia Development Act sets forth not only the creation and powers of
ZDA, but also defines the investment incentives that guide the operations of
ZDA. ZDA remains the most important body in attracting foreign investment, and
increasingly, in the maintenance and aftercare of foreign investment and investors.
ZDA is a semi-autonomous body, formed in 2006 from the amalgamation of several
bodies, namely the Zambia Privatization Agency, the Zambia Investment Centre,
Export Board of Zambia, Zambia Export Processing Zones Authority, and the Small

---

[1]   World Bank (2013).

[2]   GRZ (2006).

Enterprises Development Board. ZDA's main function is to 'further economic development through promotion of investments and exports in Zambia', primarily through investment facilitation, market development, business development, and support services for small and medium enterprises. [①] In addition to working with investors and promoting business, it has the mandate of collecting data. In conjunction with the Bank of Zambia and the CSO, it is the main source of data on foreign investment and other similar economic indicators.

While not all foreign investments in Zambia are obligated to proceed through ZDA, for investors, the motivations to invest through ZDA take the form of the tax incentives, which are following the application and successful granting of investment licences. ZDA offers a series of general incentives (see Appendix 1), in addition to special incentives offered to a number of categories of investors. Primarily, these take the form of income tax incentives, which are meant to promote investments in certain, incentivized sectors, while value added tax (VAT) incentives are meant to facilitate the development of the agriculture, mining, manufacturing and tourism sectors.

Currently, the priority sectors set forth by the Zambian government for agriculture include:

— *Primary*: *floriculture* (*fresh and dried flowers*); *horticulture* (*fresh and dried vegetables*); *tea and tea products, coffee and coffee products, cotton and cotton yarn.*

— *Secondary*: *processed foods* (*wheat flour and other processed foods*); *production of leather goods, fabric and garments, wood and wood products, palm oil and their derivatives, pulp, paper and paper board, textile and textile products.* [②]

These incentives are meant to favour high value products, as well as to encourage additional development in the manufacturing and processing sectors.

---

① ZDA (2012b).
② The most recent edition as of the date of writing is February 2013 edition.

ZDA provides additional incentives to investors according to categories defined by how much an investor pledges to invest. For instance, investments of $ 10 million USD and above qualify for additional negotiation with the GRZ for additional incentives. Investments of above $ 500000 USD in priority sectors and in a Multi Facility Economic Zones (MFEZ) are entitled to the following incentives:

a. Zero percent tax rate on dividends for 5 years from the first year of declaration of dividends

b. Zero percent tax on profits for 5 years from the first year profits are made. For year 6 – 8 only 50 percent of profits are taxable and years 9 and 10 only 75 percent of profits are taxable

c. Zero percent import duty rate on raw materials, capital goods, machinery including trucks and specialized motor vehicles for five years

d. Deferment of VAT on machinery and equipment including trucks and specialized motor vehicles.

In general, investments must be over $ 500000 USD and in priority sectors in order to qualify for the general incentives (outlined in Appendix 1), although investments by 'Micro and Small Enterprises' are sometimes eligible for tax exemptions.

A number of lingering questions remain, which are beyond the scope of the current report, with regards to Zambia's taxation system. Tax policy, with regards to foreign investment, has been a controversial discussion, particularly with regards to mining investments, but increasingly with agricultural investments. [1] The OECD and other organisations have noted Zambia's continual struggle and efforts to harmonise and stabilise taxation policies, as well as to strengthen the administration of tax collection. [2] With regards to the relationship to foreign investment, some remaining questions for further exploration are:

---

[1]   See: Action Aid (2013).

[2]   OECD (2012); NEPAD OECD (2011).

1) Does the Zambian government have the capacity to enforce the taxation rules as set forth by ZDA? Is compliance high? Are there ways for foreign investors to skirt these?

2) What kind of losses in taxation revenue results from such incentives? With the incentives, is the amount of revenue from taxation enough for poor rural communities to see the benefit?

In addition to providing incentives, ZDA plays a role in providing services to facilitate investments. These include the acquisition of land, obtaining infrastructure for water, electricity, transportation and communication, the acquisition of licenses for particular sectors, and the acquisition of self-employment permits and employment permits for expatriates. It offers a number of guarantees, such as: free repatriation of profits and dividends, guarantee against compulsory acquisition by the government, and protection against non – commercial risks, as signatories of World Bank's Multi-Lateral Investment Guarantee Agency and Africa Trade Insurance Agency.

ZDA has created a 'land bank' in an effort to mediate the acquisition of customary land. [1] Through the Land Bank Development Officer, ZDA has taken the role of negotiating with chiefs for parcels of customary land for the purposes of attracting investment. This is meant to control the acquisition of land to investors and to ensure that allocated land is used for its designated purposes, but also to help 'fast-track' the land allocation applications. However, this puts the power of allocation in the hands of the government, who under the Lands Acquisition Act (1975), have the power to compulsorily acquire land, particularly rural land. The land bank programme includes the farm block programme (see Table 5), the MFEZ programme, but also the creation of agricultural 'clusters'. This is a new project started by ZDA in 2012 for the promotion of primary agriculture alongside the development of manufacturing

---

① AfDB (2011); Oakland Institute (2011).

and processing sectors. [1] This builds on the pre-existing programmes that sought to promote cotton (primarily in Eastern Province) and as well, biofuels.

Table 5　ZDA's farm block programme

Name of farm block	Location	Prospective size
Nansanga	Serenje, Central Province	155000ha
Kalumwange	Kaoma, Western Province	100000ha
Luena	Kawambwa, Luapula Province	100000ha
Manshya	Mpika, Muchinga Province	147000ha
Luma/Mikelenge	Solwezi, Northwestern Province	100000ha
Musakashi (SADA)	Mufulira, Copperbelt Province	100000ha
Muku	Kafue, Lusaka Province	100000ha
Simango	Livingstone, Southern Province	100000ha
Mwase – Phangwe	Lundazi, Eastern Province	100000ha

Source: NEPAD OECD, 2011

While Zambia's steady ability to continue attracting FDI in various sectors perhaps speaks to the successes of ZDA thus far, there is little research that has looked at whether the majority of investors operate through ZDA, and the types of investors that prefer to operate via ZDA (for instance: domestic versus international firms, size of firms, etc.), and lastly, which incentives provide the most compelling reasons for investment. Do such incentives result in long-term, sustainable business and employment creation? These questions are explored in the following sections

5) Overview of Agricultural Investments in Zambia

A. Overview of Agricultural Investment Pledges (1998 – 2012)

Mining continues to dominate FDI inflows into Zambia (see Table 6, below),

---

[1]　Interview, ZDA Representative (2013).

despite the impetus to use agricultural investment to contribute to economic diversification and poverty reduction. However, shifts in the global aid framework are beginning to favour a strategy of FDI, for both home country investors, and for framing investment attraction policies in host countries, such as Zambia.

Therefore, this section provides an overview analysis of agricultural investments in Zambia through the lens of agricultural investment pledges declared by ZDA. This will provide greater insight into the ways and processes in which Zambia facilitates agricultural investments, including the benefits and shortfalls of the ways in which Zambian investment policy is currently functioning to bring investment into the agricultural sector.

In order to evaluate Zambian investment policy, it is useful to then turn to an overview analysis of the kinds of agricultural investments being made. This can then begin the discussion of disaggregating agricultural investments by home nations, and thus understanding the specific role played by new investor nations.

This section more closely examines the trends deduced from the dataset of agricultural investment pledges made to ZDA from 1998 – 2012. Although, as discussed earlier in the report, these figures do not correspond to figures of *realized* agricultural investment, they provide the most comprehensive dataset on agricultural investments and thus are useful indicators of wider trends of and characteristics of agricultural investment.

Table 6 Total pledged investments by sector for the past 5 years (2008 – 12)

Sector	Total value of pledged investments
Mining	$ 13824878263
Manufacturing	$ 5417330197
Energy	$ 3314843645
Real Estate	$ 2466840101
Tourism	$ 1491984249
Agriculture	$ 1139480207

续表

Sector	Total value of pledged investments
Service	$ 584158168
Construction	$ 269976744
Education	$ 242278633
ICT	$ 197562050
Transport	$ 189899326
Finance *	$ 180183954
Health	$ 135902400

Source: ZDA (2013). ①

Although agricultural investment enjoys a number of policy preferences and has garnered international attention, it continues to play a comparatively small role in terms of sectors with pledged investments, with mining playing the largest role, followed by manufacturing, energy, real estate, and tourism.

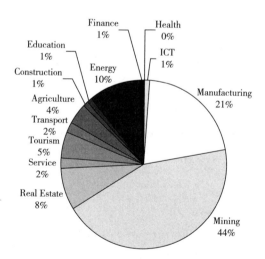

Figure 7   Percentage of total investment pledges by sector (1998 – 2012)
Source: ZDA (2013).

---

①   Figures for the finance sector were incomplete. Data were not available for the years 2008 and 2010 and were not included in this sum.

Table 6 and Figure 7 both reinforce the dominance of the mining sector in both FDI inflows as well as pledged investments, with the manufacturing industry following in second. However, Figure 8 shows the percentage changes in pledged investments, between 2008 – 12.

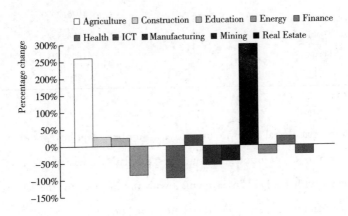

Figure 8   Percentage changes in pledged investments by sector（2008 – 12）

Source: ZDA（2013）. [1]

Clear growth is seen in the agricultural sector and the real estate sector, with small amounts of growth in construction, tourism, education, and ICT. While negative changes are present, this speaks more to the volatility and speculative behaviour in pledged investments rather than necessarily of negative growth.

Although in total figures, agricultural investments appear to play a lesser role in FDI inflows into Zambia, it is clear that agricultural investments are playing an increasingly role, and that indeed there has been a rise of interest from abroad into Zambian agriculture. Figure 9 shows the rise of pledged investments in agriculture in 2009; although there was a dip for 2010, the levels rose once again for 2011 and were sustained for 2012. This is consistent with the literature on agricultural investments that speculates a rise following the 2007 – 08 global food price crisis, which

---

[1]   Real estate figures reach 945 percent.

saw peaks of world food prices in key staple crops. While it may be too early to dis-
cern the mechanisms of the translation of such world food prices to investment patterns, the results of the pledged investments are also slightly skewed by several key
large investments.

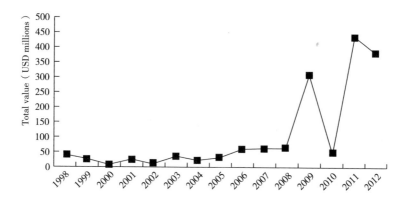

Figure 9   Total value of pledged agricultural investments (1998 – 2012)
Source: ZDA (2013).

There is an important trend towards investment in primary agriculture, as opposed to investment in upstream sectors (such as agro – processing, beverages, and
other similar sectors). The next section delves into a breakdown of what these recent
investments in agriculture have been.

B. Characteristics of Agricultural Investments in Zambia

The ZDA data on agricultural investment pledges can be further broken down
by the top investing countries and the top investments. Table 1 in the Introduction of this report provided a list of the top 10 investing countries over the period
1998 – 2012 and Appendix 2 provides a list of the top 50 investments from 1998 –
2012. Table 7 (below) reiterates similar trends in recent years of the top investing
countries, as broken down by total investment size and average size of investment,
remain.

Table 7   Top 20 agricultural investment pledging nations（2008 – 12）

Rank	Country	By total amount	Country	By average investment size
1	British	$ 596249513	Malawian	$ 56659500
2	South African	$ 273639189	Singaporean	$ 35000000
3	Malawian	$ 113319000	Seychelles	$ 14520000
4	Indian	$ 112061375	German	$ 9395000
5	Zambian	$ 107188553	British	$ 9316399
6	Zimbabwean	$ 99445900	Ireland	$ 8920464
7	Mauritian	$ 43427000	Mauritian	$ 8685400
8	Singaporean	$ 35000000	Nigerian	$ 7878000
9	Chinese	$ 33301378	Cayman Islands	$ 6640000
10	Ireland	$ 26761392	South African	$ 5472784
11	Danish	$ 18014920	Indian	$ 5336256
12	Nigerian	$ 15756000	Danish	$ 4503730
13	Seychelles	$ 14520000	Cypriot	$ 3895970
14	Australian	$ 14172371	Zambian	$ 3349642
15	Greek	$ 11760301	Canadian	$ 3000000
16	German	$ 9395000	Australian	$ 2362062
17	Cypriot	$ 7791940	Greek	$ 1960050
18	Cayman Islands	$ 6640000	Zimbabwean	$ 1420656
19	American	$ 6548390	American	$ 1091398
20	Canadian	$ 6000000	Chinese	$ 979452

Source: ZDA (2013).

While historical investors in Zambia (such as the UK, Zimbabwe, South Africa, and domestic investments) still dominate the list of top total investors by total amount, the list now include a number of newer investors, notably India and China, as well as a number of large singular investments that derive from known financial conduits, such as Mauritius, Singapore, Ireland, Seychelles, and the Cayman Islands. An analysis of 'average investment size' also indicates that the total size of investments pledges from such financial conduits is notably larger than the average size of investments from new emergent market investors, such as China and India.

However, it is important to note here that the categorization of investments by investor country is complicated by the presence of such financial conduit countries, where in reality the money and investment interests may be derived from other sources. ZDA characterize 'investor home country' through shareholder lists provided by investors, thereby making it difficult to categorize the home country of the investment. Lastly, many investments also have multiple investor home countries, which again complicates the question of investment origin.

The cumulative value of the investments from the top 50 companies is $ 1341248169 USD, which forms approximately 85 percent of the total pledges for 1998 – 2012 (out of a total of 344 recorded pledges); however, the top 50 investors only account for 39 percent of employment pledges. Within the top 50 investing companies, 68 percent (34 companies) made their investments in 2008 or after, while a smaller portion (32 percent, or 16 companies) investing prior to 2008. This suggests that indeed, there is a growing difference in size of agricultural investments being made, with a number of large investments dominating the figures, and also coming in recent years, following 2008. The top 5 investments alone, all dating from 2007 – 12, contribute to 64 percent of the total amount pledged by the top 50.

Looking more closely at the top 50 investors (Appendix 2), although data is not available for the subsectors of investments for all years, within the top 50 pledges, the majority of the investment pledges lay in the crop farming subsector, while other investment pledges lay in the subsectors of mixed farming, poultry and livestock, and agro-processing while horticulture/floriculture, and fish farming play a smaller role. ZDA does not further disaggregate the types of crops within crop farming, but there is a small, but visible presence in crops such as sugar, tobacco, and rice, in addition to conventional crops such as maize, wheat, and soya. Notably, there was a role played by biofuels investments, although it is generally considered that the wave of interests in biofuels in Zambia has largely subsided. [1]

There is also a strong role to be played by the agro-processing sector that appears to be underreported by the dataset. ZDA keeps separate lists of investments listed under the agricultural sector and the manufacturing sector; the categorization of an investment under one list or another is unclear, particularly when an investment may be made which includes both sectors. Thus, although a preliminary scan was conducted on the list provided by ZDA on the manufacturing sector, this analysis remains focused on the primary agricultural sector, and it is surmised that this remains a limitation of this analysis.

Table 8   Summary of known land acquisitions

Name of company	Size and designation of land acquisition	Location	Sources
Chobe Agrivision Company Ltd	4155ha (Statutory)	Mkushi, Central Province	Chobe Agrivision (2011a), (2011b), (2012).
Amatheon Agri Zambia Ltd	14237ha (Statutory)	Mumbwa, Central Province	Amatheon Agri (2012), (2013).
ETC Bioenergy Ltd * since acquired by Zambeef	46876ha (Statutory)	Mpongwe, Copperbelt Province	Mujenja and Wonani (2012).
Somawhe Estates Ltd * since acquired by Chobe Agrivision	12822ha (Statutory)	Mpongwe, Copperbelt Province	Chobe Agrivision (2012).
Silverlands Ranching	19090ha (Statutory)	Zimba, Southern Province	http://www.miga.org/projects/index.cfm? pid=1248
African Crops Ltd	25000ha (Statutory)	Choma and KalZmo, Southern Province	http://www.africancropszambia.com
CBL Agric Zambia Ltd	438ha (Statutory)	Mazabuka, Southern Province	Interview with farm manager (2013).

[1] Locke and Henley (2013).

续表

Name of company	Size and designation of land acquisition	Location	Sources
Pro Alia Zambia	2325ha (Statutory)	Kazungula, Southern Province	http://www. emvest. com/ Emvest_ Livingstone. html

Source: compiled by the author.

Importantly, the dataset does not include information about land acquired (by size), although some datasets include the location listed by investor. However, the dataset does include figures on pledged employment production. These are self – reported by the investors, with no evidence of reliability or enforceability, at the time that the investment pledge is made, and remains one of the important areas in which ZDA has identified that requires follow – up in their monitoring of investment progress and realization. There does not appear to be any correlation in the size of investment, the type of investment (as revealed by sub – sector) and the number of jobs pledged, which seems to indicate that the figures are fairly arbitrary.

C. Mapping New and Old Agricultural Investors

Many reviews of foreign investments in Africa have provided macro – level analysis of FDI trends,[1] with a growing focus on the rising FDI levels from emerging investors, such as China and India. [2] These reviews have focused on questions of trade, government cooperation, and aid, and examine a variety of economic sectors. However, there has also been a growing focus in the literature that specifically addresses foreign investment in agriculture in Africa. [3] These reports rely on examina-

---

[1] See: Bhinda et al. (1999); UNIDO (2008); McKinsey (2010).

[2] See: O' Neill (2001); OECD (2006); Cheru and Obi (2010); Mawdsley and McCann (2011); Hofman and Ho (2012); Carmody (2013).

[3] See: World Bank (2007), (2009); OECD (2010); Deininger and Byerlee (2011); Oakland Institute (2011); FAO (2013b).

tions at a micro-scale, looking case-by-case at selected investments in various countries, and then comparatively across countries. Sources include anecdotes and media sources focusing on specific investment cases. Lastly, there has been growing attention specifically to the question of outward agricultural investments by China (and increasingly India) , but provide a different approach to the literature that has examined agricultural investments more widely. Such works have, as with the literature on BRICS in general, put more explicit emphasis on the spaces for government-level cooperation, and have not examined private investors as such. ①

As previously indicated in the Introduction, there is a growing role played new investor nations in FDI into developing countries around the world, and particularly throughout sub-Saharan Africa. ② For instance, with regards to the BRICS nations, there are significant roles played by India, China, and South Africa; Russia has only two recorded investments (in the same property) , while Brazil has none. ③

Box 1   Russian investments in Zambia

Russia has just one investment registered in agriculture in Zambia. Although registered as two separate investments (Zambika and Ambika) , they are believed to be investments in the same farm. Located in Mkushi district, the Ambika investment comes from Mr. Mikail Orlov, a Russian businessman responsible for setting up Black Earth Farming and its spinoff, Ambika Agro. ④ Black Earth Farming held up to 815450 acres of land in Russia, before Orlov quit in 2008 and began a new project in Zambia

① See: Yan and Sautman (2009); Brautigam and Tang (2009); Brautigam and Zhang (2013); Li et al (2012); Cheru and Modi (2013).

② Mlachila and Takebe (2011).

③ This is according to investments up until 2012. The Russian investment is discussed in Box 1, while a discussion of the role of Brazilian interests in Zambia is discussed in Box 2.

④ http: //ambika – agro. com/index. html.

for the production of wheat and livestock. ①

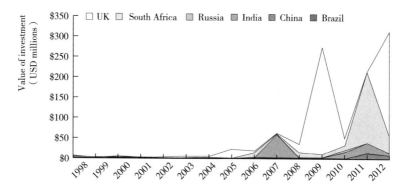

**Figure 10   Value of pledged agricultural investments by the
UK and BRICS nations (1998 – 2012)**

Source: ZDA (2013).

The UK and South Africa rank at the top of the number of investments pledges
contributed to Zambia (see Table 1). ② In addition, the UK forms slightly greater
than one third of the agricultural investment pledge value with 38 percent, while the
BRICS combined form 26 percent, and the remaining countries contributing 36 percent (see Figure 11 below). Interestingly, each country has seen corresponding
spikes in investments in 2007, and then again in 2011, as demonstrated in Figure
10. While the UK has always played a role in investing in Zambian agriculture
through colonial ties and ODA, another set of emerging interests may coincide with
the UK's growing role as a financial conduit. The role of the UK as a financial conduit, alongside a number of other investments from other known hubs of financial
transaction (such as the Seychelles, Mauritius, etc.), perhaps confirms that the
UK's domination is both attributable to historical ties, as well as the growing role of
private equity in agricultural investments in Zambia. To a certain extent, this same

---

① RBTH (2013).

② These two countries are only exceeded by Zimbabwe.

trend can be seen coming from South Africa as well. ①

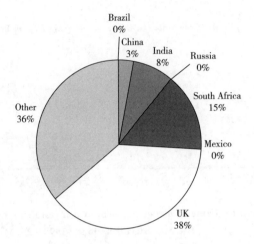

**Figure 11　Total pledged agricultural investments by value by BRICS,
the UK and other countries (1998 – 2012)**

Source: ZDA (2013).

Box 2　Biofuels and BRICS

Although it does not emerge in from the dataset of agricultural investment pledges, one field in which BRICS countries have demonstrated a large amount of interest has been investments in biofuels related projects. In addition to having invested heavily in the mining and mining equipment sectors, China has pledged investments in biofuels, while Brazil having taken part in a Memorandum of Understanding for capacity building and experience sharing in the biofuels sector. ②

China's largest recorded pledged investment under the manufacturing sector involves a company called Kaidi Biomass, a partnership between Wuhan's Sunshine Kaidi Energy Group and Zambia's Biomass Development PLC, for $450 million USD

---

① Bhinda et al. (1999).

② Lusaka Times (2010).

in 2010. The company pledged investment to develop a joint production and processing of a variety of feedstocks including jatropha; they initially proposed the acquisition
of 2 million ha, but were instead offered approximately 78, 000ha in Nakonde and Iso-
ka districts. ① However, the investor has since pulled out,② citing difficulty with the
speed of progress of government approvals, particularly with regards to the land allocation.

Although Brazil thus far has had no official investments in the agricultural sector,
their interest in the energy sector is growing. Brazil's largest investments thus far have
been in the mining sector (Vale). Brazil have a notable expertise in biofuels feedstocks such as sugar cane and soya; with the failure of jatropha projects to take off in
Zambia,③ Brazil is well poised to contribute expertise, technology, and equipment to
help Zambia produce biofuels with feedstocks that are much more proven in Zambian
agriculture.

However, there is a distinction that can be seen between investment pledge
trends from India and China, versus the UK and South Africa. Referring back to Table 1, both China and India contributed a significant number of investment pledges.

Table 9   Ranking of Top 10 pledged agricultural investments by nationality
and total value of pledged investments (1998 – 2012), ordered by
number of pledged investments

Nationality	Number of Pledged Investments	Total Value of Pledged Investments (USD)	Average Value of Pledged Investment (USD)
Zimbabwean	70	$ 99445907	$ 1420656
British	64	$ 596249513	$ 9316399
South African	50	$ 273639189	$ 5472784
Chinese	34	$ 33301378	$ 979452
Zambian	32	$ 107188553	$ 3349642

① The Post (2012).

② Times of Zambia (2013).

③ Locke and Henley (2013).

Nationality	Number of Pledged Investments	Total Value of Pledged Investments (USD)	Average Value of Pledged Investment (USD)
Indian	21	$ 112061375	$ 5336256
Mauritian	5	$ 43427000	$ 8685400
Ireland	3	$ 26761392	$ 8920464
Malawian	2	$ 113319000	$ 56659500
Singaporean	1	$ 35000000	$ 35000000

Source: ZDA (2013).

It can also be seen from this table that the average size (by value) of the Chinese investment pledges is significantly less than those of the Indian and South African, and then the British. Interestingly, the Indian and South African average investment pledge size are quite close, suggesting perhaps that there is an element of similarity in the types of investments made, which could derive from similarly-sized agribusiness expansion. This emphasizes the potentially important role played by small and medium enterprises (SMEs) with regards to Chinese investments, also reinforcing the idea of the importance of taking into account the potential differences in modes of operation[1] of agricultural investments from each investing nation.

This next section provides a brief discussion of some policy push factors for agricultural investment abroad by India, China, South Africa and the UK, as a sample of investing countries. Investor country home policies certainly do have an impact in encouraging the outward movement of individual investors; however, these are not specific to Zambia, per se. Instead, the Chinese and Indian governments employ specific discourses to encourage outward investment abroad more generally, while South African and British investments are facilitated through liberal business environ-

---

[1] Modes of operation refer to the different agricultural models that could be employed in agricultural investments. Different models include plantation, contract, and commercial farming (Smalley, 2013).

ments, in conjunction with historical linkages with commercial farming communities in Zambia.

India

Since 2000, the Government of India (GOI) has changed its approach to Africa, from one of historical goodwill, to that of furthering economic relations. The GOI has attempted to reorient its Africa policy from dependence on the extractive industries sector, towards one of sustainable and organic development, which lends itself to engagement in agriculture. Indian entrepreneurs have found a home for investments in Zambian agriculture, not only because of the relatively underdeveloped market, but also because of the rhetoric of food security concerns within India itself. The GOI has stated that it has considered the purchase of private farmland overseas in order to ensure food security domestically.

The GOI has classified Zambia as one of the important countries in their 'Focus Africa' programme and actively publicises its India – Zambia relations to encourage the outward movement of Indian entrepreneurs. Agreements exist at various levels between the two, including an array of trade agreements, collaborations and cooperation with India's Confederation of Indian Industry and Memorandum of Understandings between agricultural research centres in Zambia and India. A number of high level political and business delegations have been exchanged across both countries. One example of such political relations is the India Africa Forum Summit, which helps facilitate credit lines from India to Africa. At the forefront of India's strategic engagement in Africa, and Zambia, is an awareness of energy security. Second is the growing role that Africa plays as a market for Indian goods and services, as well as a source of natural resources for India's manufacturing sector. In exchange, India has provided cost effective and intermediary technology, particularly in the fields of information technology, agriculture, health, and the pharmaceutical industry.

Despite historical ties and growing and stable trade relations in Zambia, attention has been growing to India's international role in acquiring large amounts of land in other parts of sub-Saharan Africa, most notably in areas of East Africa, and in particular, Ethiopia. ① However, it would be incorrect to categorize this as the acquisition of land by 'India', but rather, by private entrepreneurs, who are expanding towards sub-Saharan Africa in a number of sectors including agriculture. Despite great interest in the topic, there remain few empirical studies on Indian involvement in agriculture in Zambia.

China

The literature on China's relationship with Africa, and in particular, Zambia, is becoming a more established topic of study. Zambia remains one of the key destinations for Chinese FDI in sub-Saharan Africa, not only for agriculture, but also for a number of other sectors such as mining, construction, telecommunications, and manufacturing. The growing Chinese role in the Zambian economy is noticeable in Zambia's urban centres, where the numbers of Chinese population are growing. As of November 2013, China was ranked the second major destination for Zambia's exports (at 23. 7 percent), primarily in Copper blister and other metal ore, but also in tobacco as the fourth major imports from Zambia. ②

While it has been assumed that China's strategy in agricultural investments has been to secure agricultural land for food security (whether through direct imports or through an overall increase in production levels), a number of studies have shown that China's engagement in African agriculture has instead followed a number of historical stages. ③ A first wave of involvement in African agriculture can be characterized as 'agro-socialist', characterized by a number of forms of cooperation through

---

① See: Rahmato (2013) and Rowden (2013), both in Cheru and Modi, eds (2013).

② CSO (2013).

③ See for instance, Brautigam and Tang (2009); Sautman and Yan (2010), and Smaller, Qiu and Liu (2012). Other notable discussions on Chinese investments in Zambia include German et. al. (2011), while other wider assessments of Chinese agriculture in sub-Saharan Africa include Sun (2011), Brautigam (2012), Hofman and Ho (2012), and Brautigam and Zhang (2013).

aid in relatively small agricultural demonstration projects. Since the 1990s, Chinese agricultural investments have been described as 'agro-capitalist', which continued in the legacy of agricultural cooperation projects, but had a greater emphasis on profit making in order to ensure the projects were economically self-sufficient. A new form of 'agro-imperialist' Chinese engagement in African agriculture remains a unseen, as thus far the majority of Chinese investments are thought to be characterized by either state-run agricultural cooperation projects (such as the China – Zambia Friendship farm, and the Johnken[①] Estates and Johnken Friendship farm),[②] or a new wave of individual, private entrepreneurs that have been encouraged as part of China's 'Going Global' strategy, which has been supported by the Forum on China – Africa Cooperation (FOCAC), and financing from key banking Chinese banking institutions such as the China Development Bank and the China Export Import Bank.

South Africa

Zambia features among the top countries conducting trade with South Africa. A number of trade agreements and bilateral cooperation exist between the two countries, which have a long relationship. South African companies have had a particular role in the retail, mining, security, and agricultural sectors, with a particular emphasis on agro – processing as an emerging area. The Department of Trade and Industry in South Africa is responsible for trade relationships, with the development of the Export Marketing and Investment Assistance scheme, developed to help build export markets for South African products and services, while promoting new FDI into South Africa.

Until 1990, South Africa – Zambia relations were shaped by Zambia's support for anti-apartheid movements within South Africa; it was one of the leaders of the frontline states against South Africa and had even provided safe haven for members of the

---

① Also referred to as 'Zhongken' in the literature [see for instance, Sautman and Yan (2009); Brautigam and Tang (2009) and Brautigam (2012)].

② As described in Sautman and Yan (2009) and Brautigam (2012).

Africa National Congress, which had its headquarters in Lusaka in the 1980s. With the dismantling of apartheid in the early 1990s, the two countries re – established diplomatic ties, followed by a number of high – level visits, which normalized trade relations. By this point, Zambia had already been South Africa's second largest African trading partner. South Africa continues to be a main source of machinery and mechanical goods for Zambia. In November 2013, South Africa was ranked the fourth major export destination for Zambian products (primarily mining), and second to China amongst the BRICS nations. [1]

Drivers for South African investments in Zambia include a taxation and income repatriation policy that is flexible for investors, low political risk and a less politicized labour regime, as well as environment factors such as fertile soils and untapped water sources. The move by South African interests into other areas of sub-Saharan Africa, notably Southern Africa, is characterized by migration of individual Afrikaner farmers, as well as the expansion of South African agribusinesses. Individual commercial farmers began exiting agriculture in South Africa in the 1990s, following a series of domestic changes that included the introduction agricultural deregulation, the sharp price increase in farming inputs such as diesel and electricity, and policy changes such as the introduction of basic labour rights for farm workers, the extension of tenure rights to farm workers, and historical land claims to large areas of farmland. [2] Transformation and land reform continue to be a concern in South Africa. The result saw movements of South African farmers, and notably their farming expertise, to areas such as Zambia. Although the wave of migration was not necessarily sustained, this provided precedent for the outward-looking orientation of organizations such as one of the South African farmers' union, AgriSA. Importantly, in Zambia, the political climate was welcoming to such farming expertise. [3] In addition to farmers, South Af-

---

[1] CSO (2013).

[2] Hall (2012).

[3] Hall (2012).

rican agribusiness, such as sugar giant Illovo, have set up notable operations in Zambia, with some controversy. ① Less researched, but notably visible, has been the entry of a number of South African agribusinesses that supply farming inputs and supplies in order to diversify exposure and seek more returns, which have been supported by changes to South African investment laws.

United Kingdom

The UK does not necessarily hold a particular strategy of engagement for Zambia, although the UK's historical linkages with its former colony are evident. Much of the historical commercial farmland areas had been established under the colonial government for the specific use of British settlers. Thus, alongside South Africans, the British have had the longest and most established involvement in Zambian commercial agriculture. There has been little attention to the specific role of British companies in acquiring agricultural land in Africa, ② despite these historical linkages.

Disaggregating British investors is not always easy, as many long – time residents of Zambia with British heritage still hold British passports, and thus are often considered British investors under ZDA's categorization of the origin of investment. However, many of the more established farms are relatively well known throughout Zambia. This report's focus on more recent investments has eliminated many of the older, more established farms from analysis. Nevertheless, the UK still factors greatly in ZDA's pledged agricultural investment list, particularly due to the UK's role as a financial centre. This trend is more evident when one examines the UK's involvement throughout sub-Saharan Africa; although Zambia does not factor highly on the list of sites of British agricultural land acquisitions, the presence of British companies in agricultural FDI in Zambia is notable. ③

There is increasing awareness of the rise of private equity and venture capital in-

---

① See: Action Aid (2013).
② See: Action Aid (2013) for the exception.
③ Ottaviani (2013).

vestments in African agriculture. While not all British investments are private equity based, nor do all private equity and venture capital funds originate in the UK, there does appear to be a role played by London-based funds in African Agriculture. [①] The British Commonwealth Development Corporation (CDC), a traditional investor in African commercial agriculture, has backed several of these newer funds, seeking early stage markets throughout sub-Saharan Africa. [②] However, former CDC investments have demonstrated that they are not necessarily economically sustainable in the long term, nor can the large-scale agricultural developments be seen to provide tangible, long-term benefits such as job creation and agricultural growth for smallholder farmers. [③]

6) Evaluating Agricultural Investment Efforts in Zambia

A. Agricultural Investment Policy

The purpose of this following section is to begin to provide an evaluation of the agricultural investment efforts in Zambia. This has two facets: firstly, it has become clear that ZDA has had success in attracting investment, which has likely contributed to Zambia's current economic growth; however, *what kind* of agricultural investment pledges has been attracted to Zambia, and in what ways do they confirm to the kinds of investments that ZDA have incentivized? Secondly, after reviewing the kinds of investment pledges have been made, what linkages can be made between what is known about agricultural investment trends and their repercussions for rural Zambian communities?

Although investment policy has been successful thus far in *attracting* investment to Zambia, there are still several areas in which there are gaps or shortcomings in

---

① OECD (2010).
② Silici and Locke (2013).
③ Mujenja and Wonani (2012).

Zambia's investment policies. In particular, these surround the regulatory mechanisms that help ensure that Zambia is able to adapt to changing demands from investors, and the needs of the Zambian population. These include better monitoring
mechanisms and data gathering, and better institutional operation and consultative
mechanisms to provide feedback and facilitate changes. For instance, the OECD
points to several key areas：

— *The improvement of the regulatory framework for investment, which includes a strong investment code, harmonized investment legislation, and a comprehensive investment policy*；

— *Further improvements to the functioning of ZDA and the strengthening of ZDA's capabilities for monitoring and evaluation, and aftercare, in order to maximize its ability to evolve*；

— *Improved consultation and dialogue with the private sector and inter - agency coordina-
tion*；

— *The revision of the tax system with regards to the tax incentives offered, with particular
attention to the mining sector*；

— *Attention to the type of investment models, which includes the promotion of public private
partnerships, with attention to infrastructure development sector*；

— *The creation and enforcement of a competitive environment with good corporate conduct*；

— *And the translation of investments into human resource development, through proper attention to education and employment demands.* ①

While the government has outlined a number of priority sectors related to agriculture, through a number of incentives facilitated by ZDA, it does not appear that
there have been any attempts to assess the effectiveness of these priority sectors in a-
chieving agricultural growth. In looking at the ZDA data, particularly of the top 50
investments (see Appendix 2), investments appear to favour crop farming, which is
not a priority sector per se. There appears to be little evidence that these investments

---

① OECD (2012).

are for the export of raw products; instead, such investments may contribute towards the growth of the manufacturing sector, through a model of vertically integrated agribusiness operations. The two largest investments pledged, Chobe Agrivision and Amatheon Agri① are perhaps most indicative of those trends. ②

Across different investors, UK investors and European-based companies appear to continue their dominance in the agricultural sector, by size and number, although the increasing investments from India, South Africa, and China suggests that there will be growth in the SME sector as well (primarily medium-scale enterprises). It is difficult to assess the full extent of the growth of SME-level agricultural investment, as SMEs are less likely to be accounted for and regulated,③ but it is the arrival of large-scale investments that pose an interesting distinction between new trends in investment and traditional investments. Thus, large-scale investments might be considered an anomaly and part of a global 'rush' for land, while the growth in the smaller sectors will have to be assessed separately in order to understand if the effort made by ZDA to attract agricultural investment is able to provide a longer-term, more sustainable overall growth.

ZDA priorities fail to address the linkages between agricultural growth and rural poverty reduction. This includes not only understanding the impacts to smallholder farmers (as discussed in the next section), but in understanding the ways in which smallholders can be incorporated into agricultural investments. With regards to the monitoring of agricultural investments, there may be important lessons learned about how investment trends can support smallholder farmers and SMEs. The disaggregation of investment pledges into further categories would improve the understanding of

---

① Big Concession has formally changed its name to Amatheon Agri Zambia Ltd and is more often referred to by this name.

② For more information on both companies, see: http://www.chaytonafrica.com and http://www.amatheon-agri.com/home.html.

③ Mlachile and Takebe (2011).

the ways in which FDI trends do or do not support the growth of smaller industries.

B. Regulatory Environment for Agricultural Investments

Monitoring and evaluation, and data collection in general, are crucial to the assessment of the effectiveness of ZDA's investment policies. ZDA is making inroads to address capacity issues in monitoring and evaluation, but there are still a number of questions that should be addressed. Although the dataset from ZDA provides interesting insight into agricultural pledges (and thus the effectiveness of ZDA in garnering investment interest), there is little data available on important issues such as： the percentage of investment pledge realization or disbursal, the extent of investment, the barriers faced in the implementation of agricultural pledges, the actual modes of production of investments, production levels, taxation paid, employment created, spillover impacts into other sectors, amongst many other questions. If the government seeks to ensure that the wider Zambian population is to benefit from increased global interest in agricultural investment in Zambia, it must ensure to continue to improve ZDA's capacity and ability to collect data and monitor investments.

Box 3： Agriculture projects in other sectors

There are a number of other agricultural projects and investments that have not been taken into account in this report. While ZDA data captures a large number of primary agricultural investments under the agricultural sector distinction, many other known agricultural production projects can be found in other sectors, in particular, the manufacturing sector.

This holds particularly true for the biofuels sector, sugar, as well as the cotton sector, where investments in primary production is strongly linked with a more integrated value chain approach. Therefore, understandings of FDI in agriculture based on the agricultural sector designation runs a risk of leaving out a number of additional facets, particularly with regards to understanding the overall impacts of the investments. ZDA" s main incentives with agricultural investment is provide a means to diversify the economy away from mining and to find ways to address rural poverty; both of these will require a broader based approach to the agriculture sector.

Therefore, additional studies on this topic may seek to include a wider approach to agriculture to encompass changes to agriculturally related manufacturing, and wider change to agricultural markets through quantities of production, provision of rural employment, and changes to food prices.

In addition to assessing agricultural investment policy, there is a need for greater attention to the regulations that are in place that help ensure that agricultural investments made conform to Zambian laws, and the compliance to and adequacy of such laws. Agriculture projects, unlike other key primary sectors in investment such as mining or tourism, do not require additional licenses for operations. ① This includes regulations for the acquisition and conversion of land, or the regulation or monitoring of crops grown.

Currently, regulation for agricultural projects only occurs in the initial project development stage, which is primarily restricted to the conditions set forth through the Environmental Protection and Pollution Control (Environmental Impact Assessment) Regulations (1997). This requires that new projects must be subjected to an Environmental Project Brief for Environmental Impact Assessment (EIA), or an Environmental Impact Statement (EIS) for pre-existing projects undergoing change. EIAs are specifically required for the following actions with regards to agriculture:

  a) Land clearance for large-scale agriculture

  b) Introduction and use of a new agrochemical in Zambia

  c) Introduction of new crops and animals especially exotic ones new to Zambia

---

① Mining licenses are granted at the ministry level (Ministry of Mines, Energy and Water Development) while tourism projects often have to be approved by the Zambia Wildlife Authority (ZAWA).

d) Irrigation schemes covering an area of 50ha or more

e) Fish farms; production of 100 tonnes or more a year

f) Aerial and ground spraying[1]

EIAs are likely required for most new commercial farming projects, particularly for
new investments, but also for brownfield projects, as they likely involve the clearance of land. [2] However, in practice, EIAs not always conducted for agricultural
projects, particularly for small and medium scale projects. [3] Furthermore, ZEMA has
faced criticism over its capacity to monitor and enforce not only the application of
EIAs, but also in to monitor and enforce environmental and social regulations after
the EIA has been approved and the project has been initiated. Therefore, as one of
the only regulatory mechanisms that apply to agricultural projects, the EIA is unlikely
to be an effective regulatory process from which to assess both social and environmental impacts.

C. Processes of Land Acquisitions

The processes of land acquisition and allocation, displacement, and lands rights de-
serves a special discussion on its own, as restricted access to land remains one the largest barriers for smallholder farmers and rural communities. [4] Acquisitions of large
scales of land by agricultural investors, in both customary and state land, have potentially large impacts to local communities who may not hold security of tenure. The
following section will provide an analysis for the processes in which agricultural investors can acquire land, then follow with a discussion of some of the trends in land ten-

---

[1] GRZ (1997).

[2] Brownfield projects include developments on land, which has previously had use or 'underutilised' land,
     whereas Greenfield denotes projects that occur on undeveloped land.

[3] ZEMA has made available a database of all EIAs submitted to ZEMA for the years of 2003 – 2011. Although
     agriculture projects are present on the list, they appear underrepresented. Anecdotally, ZEMA staff reported
     that they believed that agricultural projects were underrepresented in EIAs.

[4] Hichaambwa and Jayne (2012).

ure that are taking place from agricultural investment.

In Zambia, all land is vested in the President of Zambia, via the Commissioner of Lands, according to the Lands Act of 1995; this system was maintained from the previous land tenure system under the Kaunda government during the Republican era after independence. The Lands Act is the main piece of legislature that dictates the terms and conditions under which land can be allocated, which also includes provisions for land allocations to non-Zambians (non-residents).

After Independence, non-Zambians were denied the right to acquire land; it was only after the Lands Act of 1995 allowed foreign nationals to once again hold land. There are a number of means by which a foreign agricultural investor can hold land according to the Lands Act, which includes if they are permanent residents, if they hold investment permits, if they have consent from the President, if the land is held by a foreign company registered in Zambia, or if land is held under a five – year short lease or tenancy agreement. ① Therefore, the Lands Act provides easy access to land acquisitions by any investor registered by ZDA.

Investors can acquire titled land either through the acquisition of leasehold (state) land through the transfer of a title deed or through the conversion of customary land into statutory land and thus the acquisition of a title deed. Land under leasehold title can be granted for up to 99 years and is also subject to ground rents, payable to the Ministry of Lands. Occasionally, land is offered under 14 year lease to investors, particularly foreigners, as a means to check the development within the allocation of that land; however, such leases are perceived to hold less security, and thus less desirable to investors. ② Titles can then be transferred (or sold) onward by willing sellers, but requires registration through the Ministry of Lands.

In order to acquire customary land, through its conversion to statutory land, there

---

① These are set forth in the Lands Act (GRZ, 1995).

② Adams (2003); ZLDC (2013).

are a number of steps and approvals to be undertaken by the acquirer. Generally, the process includes:

— *The consent of the local village headperson, on behalf of the Chief, through which consultation with communities is assumed.* [1]

— *Approval from the Chief, in the form of a letter, which must be presented to the District Council.*

— *Approval from the District Council, through the form of an application presented to the Ministry of Lands for the titling process. This then requires a further inspection of the land in question, and demarcation from a registered surveyor.*

— *With the submission of the surveys, a title deed is granted from the Ministry of Lands.*

— *Depending on the size of the land conversion, other approvals may be required. The conversion and allocation of land over 250 ha of customary land requires approval from the Commission of Lands.* [2]

Maintenance of the title deed requires the payment of annual ground rent. This process is time consuming and involves various fees, both specified, and unspecified, such as in the form of customary gifts to traditional leaders. In addition, much of the process is centralized, requiring travel and long waits in Lusaka; all of these factors are often barriers to the acquisition of land by smallholder farmers or rural families, but are often facilitated by ZDA for investors.

There are other ways to acquire agricultural land, as a Zambian citizen. One is through the application to a resettlement scheme, operated through the Office of the Vice President, Department of Resettlement. This land has already been demarca-

---

[1] Although consultation is not set forth in the Administrative Circular No. 1 (1985), it is a requirement set out by the Lands Act (1995). However, the nature of the consultation is not specified, allowing for vague definitions as to what may constitute consultation. Often, consultation with communities is assumed to take place before the traditional authority provides approval, although in practice this often does not hold.

[2] This is set forth in the Administrative Circular No. 1 (1985).

ted, surveyed and converted to statutory land by the government. Historically, the resettlement strategy was meant to help control large-scale, speculative acquisition of land, by designating land that can be acquired by commercial farmers, rather than allowing them to negotiate for, or seize, customary land. This was the strategy undertaken by the colonial government, to limit and control settler agriculture, and has resulted in a legacy of farm block schemes and large amounts of 'underused' farmland. While the new resettlement schemes are not of the same magnitude, with regards to the size of plots of land available, this historical process is more similar to the government's current strategy of farm block development, which includes the Nansanga farm block in Serenje district.

Funds, and the ability to navigate through a centralized, cumbersome, and inefficient Lands Registry, are often the advantages that foreign investors have over local investors and smallholder farmers in competing for the acquisition of state land. However, smallholder farmers can sometimes also face land tenure insecurity for the land they already hold, resulting in displacement. In Zambia's dual tenure system,[1] those who hold customary land, such as the majority of smallholder farmers, are facing an increasing amount of land tenure insecurity when others, namely headmen, chiefs, and the government, have the power to re-allocate land to investors.

Although investment plans envisioned that foreign and large-scale investors would acquire land through the ZDA farm block programme,[2] an examination of the top agricultural investment pledges suggests otherwise, as the farm blocks continue to struggle to become operationalised. There appears to a favouring of the acquisition of

---

[1] Zambia's land tenure system is defined as dual tenure, because of the presence of both statutory and customary land holding systems.

[2] Oakland Institute (2011); Nolte (2014).

statutory land by agricultural investors. ① This is likely due to the existence of large areas of historically designated farmland, which is already in close proximity to main roads and other infrastructure, such as electricity, following the colonial-led settlement by European commercial farming populations in the most favourable farming areas. Otherwise, the process of converting customary land to titled land can be cumbersome, time consuming, and expensive with a greater risk of tenure insecurity and land conflict. A brief examination of a few of the known investments suggests a preference for statutory land for these reasons. The historical farm blocks, such as Mkushi farm block and the Big Concession farm block in Mumbwa district have been the targets for Chobe Agrivision and Amatheon Agri, as well as areas around the line of rail in the Copperbelt and Southern Provinces. At least 9 of the top 50 agricultural investments are known to be in statutory areas, ② while the locations listed for a number of others suggests that they are also taking place in areas with large amounts of statutory land. ③

Those living on customary land are not afforded any greater land tenure security if their local traditional authority opts to re-allocate and convert the land, or if the government chooses to compulsorily acquire the land. However, under such circumstances of compulsory acquisition by the government, communities must be

---

① When displacement occurs under these circumstances, the impacts can be particularly devastating. There have been a number of incidences in which communities find themselves living on land that they were not aware is designated state land, through the existence of absentee landlords. When the land is then reclaimed by a title – holder, those living on the land are designated as 'squatters' and all their claims to the land are therefore removed, as Zambia does not hold any 'squatters rights' policies. Underlying the problem are the increasing land pressures faced by smallholder farmers in high-density customary land areas, and the lack of access to land tenure status information. The Zambia Land Alliance has documented a number of these cases.

② These are: Chobe Agrivision, Amatheon Agri, ETC Bioenergy Ltd, Somawhe Estates Ltd, Khal Amazi Ltd, Silverlands Ranching, African Crops Ltd, CBL Agri Zambia Ltd, and Pro Alia Zambia.

③ Investment locations are listed in Appendix 2; while sometimes the location listed is in actually, the location of the main offices, it is frequently also located in the same location as the farm. Therefore, it is thought that those listed either in Southern Province or in the Copperbelt region are likely to be investments in statutory land.

consulted, and are entitled to compensation. ① If agricultural investments continue to follow current trends of acquisition of statutory farmland, then rural communities will face land pressures from two sources: evictions for those who are found living on the edges between customary and statutory land without realization of their 'encroachment', and another kind of encroachment where agricultural investors begin to look to acquire land beyond designated state land in neighbouring customary land areas.

Although customary land does not appear to be widely sought, there is also a danger that agricultural investments are contributing to a wider trend that already taking place, in the rapidly growing conversion of customary land to state land. This has already been occurring, particularly through investments in the mining, and tourism sectors, and through the influence of local elites. If enterprising elites and Chiefs see greater opportunities in attracting investment by converting land to offer to investors, while the investors themselves may not be responsible for the conversion of land, land will still be alienated from rural communities.

Understanding the baseline scenario of land pressures and issues in access to land by smallholder farmers must be part of understanding the impacts of agricultural investors. While land holding size can have a direct impact on agricultural growth and productivity, restrictions in land holding size can be the limiting factor for smallholder growth. Yet, smallholder farmers are not only prevented from accessing land due to land constraints, but also as a result of the lack of adequate information; either with regards to information on land tenure status, or with regards to different means to access land. Existing land pressures can also push smallholder farmers into marginal lands, placing them in precarious land tenure security scenarios, with low productivity land.

---

① This is set forth in the Lands Acquisition Act (1975), and the Land Act (1995). However, this differs from processes of acquisition through private means through the conversion of land through consent of the local traditional authority.

Agricultural models such as crop farming and plantation farming tend to rely on large areas of contiguous and titled land. Many of these investments have been satisfied by the acquisition of colonial – era designated farmland. While further investments in these models may not have the impact of displacing whole communities, who are able to assert land tenure status, they can easily push out vulnerable communities who already live at the margins. Meanwhile, outgrower schemes are often only available to those who can demonstrate tenure security, and who have the ability and means to further invest in their land.

It is clear that women and men face different land access issues. [1] A number the factors identified as land tenure security issues point to a gendered problem; even when they are able to access land, women often not able to exert the same amount of tenure security as men, and hold more marginal and vulnerable pieces of land. They are thus already disadvantaged when land tenure security is threatened, and have less access to means to resolve conflicts or to safety nets.

There are a number of international guidelines that can help governments, investors, civil society, and communities navigate through issues of land acquisitions. With regards to displacement and resettlement, Zambia does not currently have a Resettlement Policy, although the government is currently undergoing efforts to address this. [2] Thus far, there is no coherent mechanism to regulate protection of rural communities from displacement, nor is there a set of minimum guidelines for compensation and resettlement.

The FAO has recently adopted 'Voluntary Guidelines for the Responsible Gov-

---

[1]   FAO (2013a).

[2]   This has primarily been under the guise of the domestication of the African Union's Kampala Convention on Internally – Displaced Peoples. Therefore, issues of displacement and resettlement are being framed under the auspices of forced displacement. These do not quite address the issue of development – induced displacement, which can be addressed using the World Bank's Operation Policy 4. 12 and the International Finance Corporation's Guidance Note 5, which large-scale agricultural investors such as Amatheon Agri and Chobe Agrivision have adopted.

ernance of Tenure of Land, Fisheries and Forests in the Context of National Food Security'. [1] The Voluntary Guidelines, composed for the use of governments, civil society organizations, the private sector, and communities, seeks to improve the governance of land tenure and reinforces the ways in which various actors must actively recognize and respect land use rights. In Zambia, there have not yet been efforts to domesticate such guidelines or to assess agricultural investments against such international standards. However, the movement must come from both host and home country ends, with a call for international investors to also adhere and enforce the guidelines.

D. Agriculture and Livelihoods

Aside from land pressures, agricultural investors can have a large impact, both positive and negative, to smallholder farmers through market connections. Agricultural investors can either act as in competition or collaboration, to smallholder farmers. The question of greatest concern in analyses of FDI in agriculture has been the corollary impacts to local smallholder farmers and poverty levels, whether it is through direct impacts (access to land), or indirect impacts (such as the provision of local employment, or the development of local agricultural livelihoods and markets). Although the understanding and quantifying the impact of agricultural investments to rural communities requires extensive fieldwork and is beyond the scope of this report, instead, this section focuses on understanding the linkages between what has been learned about agricultural investments to two areas of ground-level impacts for exploration: agricultural models and employment, and agricultural livelihoods.

Agricultural labour models and employment

As agricultural investment in rural areas has been promoted as a driver for increased

---

[1] This will be referred to as the 'Voluntary Guidelines' for shorthand.

employment opportunities for rural communities, there must equally be attention to evaluating how different models contribute to the local labour markets. Historically, agricultural models can be divided into three categories: plantations, contract farming, and commercial farming. [1] Plantations typically grow one crop, but rely on large amounts of labour (both resident and migratory) for production. Contract farming can follow a number of different systems, either through a centralized nucleus and peripheral outgrowers, or dispersed smallholders organised via contracts. Lastly, commercial agriculture relies on a contiguous area and can include a number of different crops, but tends to be highly mechanized and relies on a small number of farm labourers, depending on the crop, but to a lesser extent than plantation agriculture.

An analysis of the top 50 Investments indicates that 16 investments are for commercial agriculture operations (12 crop farming and 4 mixed farming – includes the Chobe Agrivision, Amatheon Agri, Somawhe, Pro Alia, and ETC Bioenergy investments). Plantation agriculture is also present on the list, in the form of sugar, rice, and tobacco farms (7 in total, including CBL Investments and African Crops Ltd). Contract farming arrangements, such as outgrower schemes, are not specified under the ZDA categorization. However, poultry, livestock, and fish farming operations remain high in number (11, including Silverlands Ranching), and are not considered in the traditional approaches to agricultural models, despite being of a significant number in Zambia. Lastly, 3 investments are listed under biofuels, 2 investments listed were for horticulture/floriculture (listed separately from commercial farming due to high value nature of crop) and

---

[1] Smalley (2013). Other categorisations of models also exist, such as the one promoted by IIED, which includes the following models: contract farming, management and lease contracts, tenant farming and sharecropping, joint ventures, farmer – owned businesses, and upstream/downstream business links. However, a number of these models are less commonly seen in Zambia, including management and lease contracts, tenant farming and sharecropping, and joint ventures. (Vermeulen and Cotula, 2010).

8 were unspecified.

Nominally, it appears that there are investments being made in low – labour agricultural models, such as crop farming, and livestock and fish farming operations. High-value products and plantation agriculture are both present, and present more labour-intensive models. However, there does not seem to be a discernable trend between the agricultural model proposed and employment pledges, as the production size of the investment is unknown, and is another important variable.

There are a number of investments under agro-processing (3). The trend towards vertical integration and the emphasis towards processing and manufacturing within the country will contribute to providing further employment opportunities for rural communities, if the processing facilities are built in these areas; thus far agricultural processing facilities remain centralized in urban centres such as in the Copperbelt towns or in Lusaka.

Despite the policy emphasis on the promotion of outgrower schemes, agricultural investors do not seem to favour these models, although there are some promising examples under sugar investments not included in Appendix 2. The largest examples of agricultural outgrower schemes in Zambia are in the sugar and cotton sectors. Investments such as the Zambia Sugar/Illovo Sugar operations in Mazabuka, and cotton investments, are notably absent in this ZDA list as they are, instead, listed as investments in the manufacturing sector.

Another factor of employment is not simply the number of jobs created, but the accessibility of jobs to the local community. How meaningful is this job creation to the local community? There is a fine balance between being able to provide jobs to the local community, and finding enough skilled workers to meet the demand within agricultural operations; a market of local skilled workers is not always available. Models such as crop farming and plantation agriculture tend to favour low-skilled employment, which helps create immediate, short-term jobs. It was found on the former ETC farm in Mpongwe, and the Zambia Sugar plantation in Mazabuka that permanent positions favour male employment, while jobs available for women are typically limited to seasonal, part-time, and often non-contract work. ① Outgrower schemes in Zambia have been typically limited to cotton growing, although previously jatropha, and increasingly soya, are two crops that have been considered viable for outgrower schemes. Outgrower schemes can be coupled with the provision of skills and technology transfer, but require the smallholder farmer to take on greater risk.

As indicated above, if employment opportunities are seen as one of the biggest draws for agricultural investment, then there must also be greater attention to the ways in which rural employment can be regulated to ensure that they do indeed provide meaningful benefits to rural communities. Thus far, it does not appear that agricultural investments have contributed to a large base of rural employment, particularly because a large number of the large investments have been made in low labour models.

Other questions that remain concern the ability of agricultural investments to address poor working conditions, such as low (or below minimum) wages, the enforcement of safety and labour laws, and the provision of social security benefits. In addition, as in the case of land tenure insecurity, women are often already face a disadvantage in the labour market, with precarious employment and low job security, primarily in low-skilled jobs, and thus jobs with lower pay. Outgrower opportunities can equally benefit women as men, if women can access the opportunity through having access to land and labour. ②

Although corporate social responsibility programmes put in place by various large – scale investors can play a positive role in local community relations, the IIED have identified that the agricultural business model can have an even greater impact to local

---

① FAO (2013a).
② FAO (2013a).

community. The more that local communities and smallholder farmers are able to take part in an agricultural investment through first, influencing decisions, and secondly, through business models, and the more willing the investment is to use inclusive business models, the more likely an investment will have a positive impact on surrounding communities. [1] Government policy can also play a strong role in influencing and incentivising different agricultural models, although the Zambian government, through ZDA, have yet to succeed in this.

Local agricultural markets and food security

Agricultural productivity and low diversification are typically identified as challenges to smallholder agricultural growth. One such way for agricultural investments to contribute to smallholder productivity is through the transfer of skills and technology, either by providing training programmes, particularly for workers, or though the creation or expansion of local markets for simple and accessible agricultural technology.

The dominance of hybrid maize for smallholder farmers is noticeable throughout rural Zambia. While only a limited understanding of crop selection by investors can be made at this stage, the selection of the type of crops (for instance, staple crop versus cash crops) can have an important distinction, if the crop will compete against smallholder production in local markets. The dominance of commercial crop farming, livestock, and fish farming suggest production for within Zambia or the region, rather than export-led crops such as horticultural products or plantation crops. However, livestock and fish farming, as well as non-maize staples such as wheat and soya, suggest production for urban markets, rather than local rural markets.

Poor integration into local rural markets, both upstream and downstream, will ensure that agricultural investments act as relative enclaves, serving urban centres rather than acting as a positive influence for local communities. Economies of scale

---

① Vermeulen and Cotula (2010).

can be achieved for access to inputs, or processing and storage hubs, if agricultural investments work closely with local communities. Vertically integrated models, such as those intended by Chobe Agrivision and Amatheon Agri, have the potential to contribute to district development if they are allowed to integrate into local value chains.

Increased agricultural investment is meant to contribute not only to the greater food security of a Zambia as a whole, but also within the district of investment itself. Food security can be achieved through the increased availability or introduction of certain crops, in particularly those of high nutritional value, or through the increased accessibility through increased income (through wages, access to markets, and other means). A comprehensive assessment of contributions to food security would require both access to baseline data of conditions prior to investment, as well as analysis of changing household wages and spending patterns, and of local markets and food prices.

7) Conclusions and Recommendations

This report has investigated not only the basic aspects of agricultural FDI in Zambia and their drivers, but also the ways in which such agricultural FDI is played out, in the form of agricultural production. This provides the key foundation from which impacts to the poor of Zambia, both local and throughout the country can be understood. In conjunction to a worldwide increase of interest in developing world agriculture, Zambia has seen a trend of increased agricultural investment. However, while agricultural investments continue to have a relatively small contribution to Zambia's total FDI inflows, as well as GDP, agricultural growth plays a crucial role in contributing to economic diversification and importantly, poverty reduction. However, it is important to note that agricultural investments do not always equate to poverty reduction, and the task is to ensure that the investments encouraged are ones that also translate into benefits for smallholder farmers.

This task is particularly crucial presently, as agricultural investments have been on the rise since 2008. This is taking place both in terms of investments in small and medium sectors, as well as unprecedentedly large investments. Investments have been facilitated by a number of investment policy improvements, notably in the consolidation of investment incentives through ZDA. This, combined with stable political conditions, has made Zambia an attractive site for investment.

The use of ZDA data has allowed for a more comprehensive overview of agricultural investments in Zambia. Data from ZDA shows interest in investments of both large-scale and of the SME level, and investments from traditional investors such as the UK, Zimbabwe, and South Africa, who continue to dominate agricultural investments, as well from a number of new actors including emerging economies (such as China and India), and investments following complex financial chains, facilitated through known financial conduit nations. However, there are also limitations to the data in that there is little data on the rate of realisation of investments, and it is expected that SME level investments are underreported. However, regardless of the origin of agricultural investments, all investments are subject to the same constraints and policy regulations in Zambia.

This report has also identified the policy gaps related to the facilitation of agricultural investment. Transparency of information remains a key area of concern. This applies to both the willingness of government agencies and companies to participate in research, but importantly, it also applies to the availability of information. Even with cooperation, it was often found that data important to the monitoring and evaluation of investment, such as rates of realisation of investments from pledges, was not available. EIAs remain the most important public source of information about investments, but many are not publically available, despite being public documents. The capacity of both ZDA and ZEMA must be strengthened in order to effectively monitor incoming agricultural investments, both with regards to data collection, as well as creating regulatory mechanisms with which to assess investments and their impacts. These mechanisms should look to new international guidelines, such as the FAO's Voluntary Guidelines, as models.

With regards to identifying the impacts of agricultural investments thus far, a few early conclusions can be made. Demand for agricultural land has been high, and if the demand for agricultural land continues, there are very few mechanisms that will ensure the security of customary land tenure of the smallholder farmers. The key area of employment and labour, as well as agricultural markets and food security, have been identified as areas in which investments are able to contribute both positive and negatively. However, there is no one mechanism in which agricultural investments will follow in order to determine impact; much of this depends on the agricultural model of the investment. Thus far, a large number of investment pledges that have proceeded through ZDA appear to favour large-scale commercial and plantation models, with low employment provision and little integration into local communities. Despite policy intentions, there has been little ability for ZDA to thus far, influence the use of pro-poor agricultural models of investments. Agricultural investment policy needs to be reconsidered in order to effectively promote agricultural models that can incorporate smallholder farmers and rural communities into their value chains. While it is likely too early to be able to quantitatively assess such changes, stubborn rural poverty and the desire (and often desperation) for wage income facilitate cheap labour for agricultural investment in more rural areas.

The next step for further research should focus on the systematic gathering of baseline data and the qualification and quantification of change at local district and household levels, in order to comprehensively evaluate the impacts of new forms of agricultural investment by both large – scale commercial farms, and smaller but more competitive SMEs. Such research may choose to focus on several key facets of the impacts of agricultural investment, including:

— *Access to land holdings, the impacts of land consolidation to land markets, land rights and land tenure security, land acquisition and the role of 'free and prior informed consent' (FPIC), displacement and resettlement, and environmental impacts resulting from land use change;*

— *Labour and employment – particularly to do with wage labour and labour conditions, and the translation of wages into household welfare, in particular, in the areas of health, food security, and education, workforce composition and gendered impacts of workforce changes;*

— *Changes to agricultural markets – in particular food prices and the competitiveness of the smallholder farmer and agricultural livelihoods, access to upstream and downstream services (such as inputs, processors) and markets;*

— *Food security and nutritional transitions – access and availability of various agricultural products; changes to food security strategies at the household level.*

References

A. Data Sets Consulted

FAO, FAO Stats (Accessed 1 July 2013).

UNCTAD (2013) 2013 World Investment Report Annex Tables.

UNCTAD, UNCTAD Stats (Accessed 1 July 2013).

World Bank, World Development Indicators (Accessed 1 July 2013).

ZDA (2013) Pledged Investments from 2000 to May, 2013.

ZDA (2013) 2012 Comprehensive Pledged Investments with Employment.

B. Interviews Conducted

— Zambia Development Agency (ZDA)

- Research Unit
- Business Development Manager
- Land Bank Advisor

— Zambia Environmental Management Agency (ZEMA)

— Ministry of Agriculture and Livestock

— Jesuit Centre for Theological Reflection (JCTR)

— Consumer Unity and Trust Society (CUTS) International

— Centre for Trade and Policy Development (CTPD)

— Zambia Land Alliance (ZLA)

— Department for International Development (DFID), Zambia Office

— Professor T. Sinkala

— Professor G. Hampwaye (UNZA)

C. Investment Policy Documents Analysed

Bank of Zambia (2012) Foreign Private Investment and Investor Perceptions in
Zambia – 2012: Fast-tracking Investment and Growth through Accelerated Infrastructure Development, Zambia: Government of the Republic of Zambia.

[OECD] Organization for Economic Development and Cooperation (2011)
OECD Investment Policy Review of Zambia: 2011 *Preliminary Draft.*

SADC (2012) *Zambia Investment Policies, Practices and Incentives*, Available at: http: //investment. sadc. int/ [Accessed 1 July 2013].

ZDA (2011) Agriculture, Livestock and Fisheries: Sector Profile, Zambia:
ZDA. ①

ZDA (2012a) Zambia: Africa's new frontier for investments and profits, 4th edition, Zambia: JICA and ZDA.

ZDA (2012b) Zambia Investor's Guide, April 2012 Edition, Zambia: ZDA.

ZDA (2013a) Cost of Doing Business in Zambia, 3ʳᵈ Edition, Zambia: JICA
and ZDA.

ZDA (2013b) Application Manual for Investors – Certificate of Registration and

---

① In the process of being updated; new version will be released late 2013.

other Licenses, Zambia: JICA and ZDA.

D. Works Cited

Action Aid (2013) Sweet Nothings: The human cost of a British sugar giant avoiding taxes in southern Africa, UK: Action Aid.

Adams, M. (2003) Land tenure policy and practice in Zambia: Issues relating to the development of the agricultural sector. Draft report.

Amatheon Agri Zambia Ltd (under Big Concession Agriculture Ltd) (2012) Proposed Development of an Agricultural Irrigation Scheme for Food Crop Production in the Big Concession Farming Block, Mumbwa District: Environmental Impact Assessment. Finalised June 2012.

Amatheon Agri Zambia Ltd (2013) Proposed Development of a Commercial Irrigated Agricultural Scheme for Food Crops in the Big Concession Area, Mumbwa District: Phase 2. Environmental Impact Statement. Submitted to ZEMA 25 August 2013.

[AfDB] African Development Bank (2011) 'Case Study on Foreign Direct Investments (FDI) in Zambia' *Draft Report*.

Bhinda, N., Leape, L., Martin, M., and Griffith-Jones, S (1999) *Private Capital Flows to Africa: Perception and Reality*, The Hague: FONDAD.

Brautigam, D. and Tang, X. (2009) 'China's Engagement in African Agriculture: 'Down to the Countryside' *The China Quarterly* 199: 686 – 706.

Brautigam, D. and Zhang, H. (2013) 'Green Dreams: Myth and Reality in China's Agricultural Investment in Africa.' *Third World Quarterly* 34 (9): 1676 – 1696

Brautigam, D. (2013) 'Chinese engagement in African agriculture: Fiction and Fact.' in Allen, J. A., Keulertz, M., Sojamo, S. and Warner, J., eds., Handbook of Land and Water Grabs in Africa: Foreign direct investment and food and water security. London: Routledge.

Carmody, P. (2013) The Rise of BRICS in Africa: The geopolitics of South –
South relations. London: Zed Books.

[CSO] Central Statistics Office of Zambia (2013) The *Monthly News Bulletin of
the Central Statistics Office*, Volume 127 November 2013.

Cheru, F. and Obi, C. , eds. , (2010) The Rise of China and India in Africa:
Challenges, opportunities and critical interventions, London: Zed Books.

Cheru, F. and Modi, R. , eds. , (2013) Agricultural Development and Food
Security in Africa: The impact of Chinese, Indian and Brazilian Investments, London: Zed Books.

ChobeAgrivision (2011a) Environmental Impact Assessment for Whispering Hope
II Dam and Beckett Dam: EIS Final Report Submitted to ZEMA. November 2011.

ChobeAgrivision (2011b) Environmental Impact Assessment for Mushiwemba
Dam Project: EIS Final Report Submitted to ZEMA. November 2011.

ChobeAgrivision (2012) Somawhe Estates Mpongwe Draft Environmental Impact
Statement Report (Acquisition Environmental Impact Assessment.

CUTS International (2003) 'Investment Policy in Zambia – Performance and
Perceptions' *CUTS Discussion Paper.*

Deininger, K. and Byerlee, D. (2011) Rising global interest in farmland: can it
yield sustainable and equitable benefits? Washington, DC: World Bank.

FAO (2013a) The Gender and Equity Implications of Land – Related Investments
on Land access, Labour and Income – Generating Opportunities: A case study of selected agricultural investments in Zambia, Rome: Food and Agriculture Organisation
of the United Nations.

FAO (2013b) Trends and Impacts of Foreign Investment in Developing Country
Agriculture: Evidence from case studies, Rome: Food and Agriculture Organisation
of the United Nations.

[GRZ] Government of the Republic of Zambia (1975) *The Lands Acquisition
Act*, Lusaka: Government Printers.

GRZ (1995) *Lands Act*, Lusaka: Government Printers.

GRZ (1997) Environmental Protection and Pollution Control (Environmental Impact Assessment) Regulations, Lusaka: Government Printers.

GRZ (2006) Vision 2030: 'A prosperous Middle – income Nation by 2030, Lusaka: Government Printers.

GRZ (2010) Living Conditions and Monitoring Survey 2006 – 2010, Lusaka: Government Printers.

GRZ (2012) 2011 Annual Progress Report: Sixth National Development Plan (SNDP), Lusaka: Government Printers.

GRZ MACO (2004) *National Agricultural Policy 2004 – 2015*, Lusaka: Government Printers.

German, L., Schoneveld, G., Wertz – Kanounnikoff, S., and Gumbo, D. (2011) 'Chinese trade and investment and its impacts on forests' *CIFOR Working Paper* 84.

German, L., Schoneveld, G., and Mwangi, E. (2013) 'Contemporary Processes of Large – Scale Land Acquisition in Sub – Saharan Africa: Legal deficiency or elite capture of the rule of law? *World Development* 48: 1 – 18.

Goldstein, A., Pinaud, N., Reisen, H. and Chen, X. (2006) *The Rise of China and India: What's in it for Africa?* France: OECD Publishing.

Hall, R. (2012) 'The Next Great Trek? South African commercial farmers move north' *The Journal of Peasant Studies* 39 (3 – 4): 823 – 843.

Hichaambwa, M. and Jayne, T. (2012) 'Smallholder Commercialisation Trends as Affected by Land Constraints in Zambia: What are the Policy Implications?' *IA-PRI Working Paper* 61 (*April* 2012).

Hofman, I. and Ho, P. (2012) 'China's 'Developmental Outsourcing': A critical examination of Chinese global 'land grabs' discourse' *The Journal of Peasant Studies* 39 (1): 1 – 48.

Jayne, T. S., Govereh, J., Chilonda, P., Mason, N., Chapato, A., and

Haantuba, H. (2007) 'Trends in Agricultural and Rural Development Indicators in Zambia' FSPR Working Paper No. 24.

Li, X. , Qi G. , Tang, L. , Zhao, L. , Jin, L. , Guo, Z. and Wu, J. (2012) Agricultural Development in China and Africa: A comparative analysis, Oxford and New York: Earthscan.

Locke, A. and Henley, G. (2012) Scoping Report on Biofuels Projects in Five Countries. Overseas Development Institute.

Lusaka Times (2010) 'Zambia, Brazil sign eight agreements' Lusaka Times, 8 July 2010, Available at: http://www.lusakatimes.com/ [Accessed 1 July 2013].

Mawdsley, E. and McCann, G. , eds (2011) India in Africa: Changing Geographies of Power, Oxford: Pambazuka Press.

McKinsey Global Institute (2010) Lions on the move: The progress and potential of African economies, USA: McKinsey and Company.

Mlachila, M. and Takebe, M. (2011) 'FDI from BRICs to LICs: Emerging Growth Driver? IMF Working Paper WP/11/178.

Mujenja, F. and Wonani, C. (2012) Long – term outcomes of agricultural investments: Lessons from Zambia, London: IIED.

NEPAD OECD (2011) Highlights of the Policy Framework for Investment in Zambia, prepared for 'Accelerating reform in Africa: Mobilising investment in infrastructure and agriculture, Africa Investment Initiative.

Nolte, K. (2014) 'Large – scale agricultural investments under poor land governance in Zambia Land Use Policy 38 (2014): 698 – 706.

O' Neill, J. (2001) 'Building better Global Economic BRICs' Goldman Sachs Global economics paper no. 66.

Oakland Institute (2011) Understanding Land Investment Deals in Africa. Country Report: Zambia Oakland: Oakland Institute.

OECD (2010) 'Private Financial Sector Investment in Farmland and Agricultural Infrastructure' OECD Food, Agriculture and Fisheries Papers No. 33, OECD Publishing.

OECD (2012) *Investment Policy Reviews: Zambia* 2012, OECD Publishing.

Ottaviani, J. (2013) 'How much African land is the UK leasing?' *The Guardian News* 27 November 2013, Available at: http://www. theguardian. com/news/datablog/2013/nov/27/african – land – uk – investment? CMP = twt_ fd (Accessed 1 March 2014).

The Post (2012) 'Sata asks Nawakwi to oversee bio – fuel investment' *The Post*, 30 *October* 2012.

Prizzon, A. (2013) 'The Age of Choice: Zambia in the New Aid Landscape,' *ODI Research Report.*

[RBTH] Russia beyond the Headlines (2013) 'Black Earth founder invests in dairy cows in Chechnya' *Russia Beyond the Headlines*, 15 *October* 2013, Available at: http://rbth. co. uk/business/2013/10/15/black_ earth_ founder_ invests_ in_ dairy_ cows_ in_ chechnya_ 30801. html (Accessed 15 October 2013).

Resnick, D. and Thurlow, J. (2014) 'The Political Economy of Zambia's Recovery: Structural Change without Transformation? *IFPRI Discussion Paper* 01320.

Sautman, B. and Yan, H. (2009) 'Chinese Farms in Zambia: From Socialist to 'Agro – Imperialist' Engagement? *African and Asian Studies* 9 (2010): 307 – 333.

Silici, L. and Locke, A. (2013) 'Private Equity Investments and Agricultural Development in Africa: Opportunities and Challenges' *Future Agricultures Consortium Working Paper* 062.

Sitko, N. and Jayne, T. (2012) 'The Rising Class of Emergent Farmers: An Effective Model for Achieving Agricultural Growth and Poverty Reduction in Africa?' *IAPRI Working Paper* 69 (*October* 2012).

Smaller, C. , Qiu, W. and Liu, Y. (2012) 'Farmland and water: China invests abroad. '*International Institute for Sustainable Development Report.*

Smalley, R. (2013) 'Plantations, Contract Farming, and Commercial Farming Areas in Africa: A comparative review,' *Land and Agricultural Commercialisation in Af-*

rica (*LACA*) *Review Paper*, Future Agricultures Consortium Working Paper 055.

Sun, H. L. (2011) 'Understanding China's Agricultural Investments in Africa' *SAIIA Occasional Paper No.* 102.

Sutton, J. and Longmead, G. (2013) *An Enterprise Map of Zambia*, London: International Growth Centre (IGC).

Times of Zambia (2013) 'Biomas [s] Firm KBZ to Pull Out of Zambia' *The Times of Zambia*, 11 March 2013, Available at: http://www.times.co.zm/ (Accessed 1 July 2013).

UNDP (2013a) 'Zambia: Explanatory note on the 2013 HDR composite indices,' Available at: http://hdrstats.undp.org/images/explanations/ZMB.pdf (Accessed 1 July 2013).

UNDP (2013b) Human Development Report 2013 – The Rise of the South: Human Progress in a Diverse World, New York: UNDP.

UNDP (2013c) Millennium Development Goals Progress Report Zambia 2013, Lusaka: UNDP and GRZ.

UNIDO (2008) 'Foreign Direct Investment in Sub – Saharan Africa: Determinants and Location Decisions' *Research and Statistics Branch Working Paper* 08/2008.

Vermeulen, S and Cotula, L (2010) *Making the most of agricultural investment: A survey of business models that provide opportunities for smallholders*, London: IIED.

Wiggins, S. and Keats, S. (2013) 'Looking back, peering forward: What ahs been learned from the food – price spike of 2007 – 2008' *ODI Briefing*, 81.

Wood, A. P. (1990) "Agricultural Policy since Independence." In A. P. Wood, S. A. Kean, J. T. Milimo, and D. M. Warren, eds. *The Dynamics of Agricultural Policy and Reform in Zambia*, Ames: Iowa State University Press.

World Bank (2005) *Zambia Diagnostic Trade Integration Study (Trade Component of Private Sector Development Program for Zambia)*, Washington, DC: World Bank.

World Bank (2007) World Development Report 2008: Agriculture for Development, Washington, DC: World Bank.

World Bank (2009) *Awakening Africa's Sleeping Giant: Prospects for Commercial Agriculture in the Guinea Savannah Zone and Beyond*, Washington, DC: World Bank.

World Bank (2013) *Doing Business* 2013: *Economy Profile Zambia*, Washington, DC: World Bank.

[ZLDC] Zambia Law Development Commission (2013) *Addressing Challenges in the Administration of Customary Land in Zambia*, Draft Report, May 2013.

Appendices

Appendix 1: General income tax and value added tax (VAT) incentives offered by ZDA

Income Tax Incentives

a) Income earned by companies in the first year of listing on the Lusaka Stock Exchange (LuSE) qualifies for a 2 percent discount on the applicable company tax rate in the particular sector; however, companies with more than one third of their shareholding in the hands of Zambians qualify for a 7 percent discount;

b) Implements, machinery and plant used for farming, manufacturing or tourism qualify for wear and tear allowance of 50 percent of the cost per year in the first two years;

c) Building used for manufacturing, mining, or hotel qualify for wear and tear allowance of 10 percent of cost in first year and 5 percent of cost in subsequent years;

d) Duty free importation of most capital equipment for the mining and agricultural sectors;

e) Corporation tax at 15 percent on income from farming, fertiliser production, and non-traditional exports (all exports other than copper and cobalt)

f) Farm works allowance of 100 percent of expenditure on stumping, clearing, prevention of soil erosion, bore holes, aerial and geophysical surveys and water conservation;

g) Development allowance of 10 percent of the cost of capital expenditure on growing of coffee, banana plants, citrus fruits or similar plants

h) Farming improvement allowance – capital expenditure incurred on farm improvement is allowable in the year of incurring the expenditure;

i) Dividends paid out of farming profits are exempt for the first five years the distributing company commences business;

j) Initial allowance of 10 percent on capital expenditure incurred on the construction or improvement of an industrial building is deductible;

k) Foreign exchange losses of a capital nature incurred on borrowings used for the building and construction of an industrial or commercial building are tax deductible;

l) Dividends declared by companies assembling motor vehicles, motor cycles and bicycles are exempt from the first five years of initial declaration of dividends;

m) Carry forward of Losses for: Copper and Cobalt mining: 10 years; Other mining: 5 years; Non-mining: 5 years; Farming and non-traditional exports: 5 years

Value Added Tax Incentives

a) Relief for VAT registered enterprises on imports of eligible capital goods. (VAT deferment);

b) Zero rate on export of taxable products;

c) Relief of VAT on transfer of business as a going concern;

d) Equal treatment of services for vat-reverse VAT;

e) Cash accounting for specialized associations e. g. association of building and civil engineering contractors;

f) VAT relief on input tax paid for purchases made by registered suppliers.

g) Input tax claim for three months prior to vat registration for businesses that have already commenced trading;

h) Reduction of VAT rate for investors in tax free zones.

i) The sector specific VAT incentives are as follows;

a. Agriculture: Input tax claim for three months prior to vat registration for businesses that have already commenced trading; Reduction of VAT rate for investors in tax free zones.

b. Manufacturing: Refund of Zambian VAT on purchase and export of Zambian products by non-resident businesses under the commercial exporters scheme; Input tax claim for three months prior to registration for businesses that have already commenced trading; Input tax claim for two years prior to commencement of production.

c. Mining: Input tax claim for five years on pre-production expenditure for exploration companies in the mining sector; Zero rate on mining products for export.

d. Tourism: Zero rate – tour packages; Zero rate – other tourist services; Refund to non-resident tourists and visitors; No import vat on all goods temporarily imported into the country by foreign tourists.

Source: ZDA (2013a).

B. Appendix 2: Top 50 agricultural investment pledges, by amount, as reported to ZDA (1998 –2012)

Year	Company	Sub – sector	Town	Nationality of Investor	Employment Pledged	Amount (USD) Pledged
2009	Chobe Agrivision Company Limited	Crop Farming	Lusaka	British	1630	$ 250000000
2012	Big Concession Agriculture Limited	Crop Farming	Mumbwa	British	92	$ 243434722
2011	Equator Farms (Z) Ltd	Crop Farming	n/a	South African	358	$ 164724256
2011	Aman Trade Limited	Agricultural Activities	n/a	Malawian	1992	$ 112000000
2007	ETC Bio Energy Ltd	Crop Farming and Biofuels	Mpongwe	Indian	0	$ 59648687
2011	NehaAgri Zambia Ltd	Crop Farming – Rice	n/a	Singaporean	78	$ 35000000
2012	Blackstar Agricultural Limited	n/a	n/a	South African	100	$ 24000000
1999	Zamita Farms	Crop Farming	Lusaka	Zambian	72	$ 20000000
2011	Terra Gold (Z) Ltd	Crop Farming – Rice	n/a	Mauritian	20	$ 20000000
2011	Crown Millers Limited	Agro – Processing	n/a	Indian	79	$ 17800000
2005	Zambezi Leaf Limited	Crop Farming – Tobacco	Lusaka	British	233	$ 16109155
2009	Multi – Trex Agro – Alled Processing Limited	Crop Farming	Lusaka	Nigerian	565	$ 15506000
1998	KalonjeHolidng Company	n/a	Mpika	Zimbabwean	1110	$ 15413003
2010	Earthstone Resources (Z) Ltd	Crop Farming	Lusaka	Indian	1000	$ 15000000
2012	The Purpose Driven Foundation Ltd	n/a	n/a	South African	1100	$ 15000000
2012	Ross Breeders Zambia Ltd	Poultry	n/a	Seychelles	450	$ 14520000

续表

Year	Company	Sub – sector	Town	Nationality of Investor	Employment Pledged	Amount（USD） Pledged
2003	Zambia Leaf Tobacco Company Ltd	Crop Farming	Lusaka	Zimbabwean	1200	$ 14083500
2006	Somawhe Estates Ltd	Crop Farming	Ndola	Danish	70	$ 14060000
2011	Zeta Farms Zambia Limited	n/a	n/a	British	60	$ 13650000
2008	Innscor Gold Agriculture Ltd	Poultry	Chongwe	British	178	$ 12579808
2009	Khal – Amazi Limited	Horticulture	Chongwe	British	170	$ 12500000
2010	Giant Logistics Ltd	Crop Farming	Ndola	South African	46	$ 12450000
2012	Eureka Chickens Limited	Poultry	n/a	Zambian	15	$ 12000000
2012	Silverlands Ranching	Mixed Farming	Zimba	Ireland	62	$ 11914792
2011	Mpende Fisheries Ltd	Fish Farming	n/a	Zambian	37	$ 11572000
1998	Flamingo Farm Limited	Poultry	Luanshya	Zambian	145	$ 11050000
2001	Kamwayasunka Farms Limited	Floriculture	Chibombo	Zambian	938	$ 10801027
2001	Soilmaster	Crop Farming	Lusaka	Zimbabwean	154	$ 10520165
2011	Sterling Agricultural Enterprises Ltd	Agro – Processing, Sugar	n/a	Mauritian	870	$ 10300000
2011	Agriculture Science & Technology Co Ltd.	Agro – Processing	n/a	Chinese	104	$ 10001042
2006	D1 Oils Zambia Ltd	Crop Farming – Biofuels	Lusaka	South African	77	$ 10000000
2008	African Crops Limited	Crop Farming	Choma	Zambian	0	$ 10000000
2008	Progressive Poultry Ltd	Poultry	Lusaka	South African	64	$ 10000000

续表

Year	Company	Sub – sector	Town	Nationality of Investor	Employment Pledged	Amount (USD) Pledged
2012	Silverlands Zambia Limited	Mixed Farming	Zimba	Ireland	114	$9776600
2011	Kariba Harvest Ltd	Fish Farming	n/a	Mauritian	320	$9642000
2006	IACZ Farming Ltd	Crop Farming/Poultry	Ndola	German	506	$9395000
2006	Golden Lay Ltd	Poultry	Luanshya	Australian	22	$8738371
2012	Verino Agro Industries Limited	n/a	n/a	British	45	$8000000
2011	Joko Commodities and Contractors	Mixed Farming	n/a	South African	5	$7700000
2012	Yalelo Limited	Fish Farming	Siavonga	Cayman Islands	82	$6640000
2009	Lundazi Tobacco Limited	Crop Farming – Tobacco	Lundazi	Zimbabwean	2	$6506169
2009	CBL Agric Zambia Limited	Crop Farming – Sugar	Mazabuka	South African	n/a	$5900000
2010	Pro Alia Zambia	Mixed Farming	Lusaka	British	187	$5900000
2006	Cool Amarula Ltd	n/a	Lusaka	Cypriot	154	$5831940
2009	M and M's Company Limited	Crop Farming	Luanshya	Greek	27	$5765301
2011	Billis Farm Limited	n/a	n/a	British Virgin Islands	0	$5402631
2005	Mikata Agricultural Company Ltd	Poultry	Ndola	Irish	73	$5070000
1998	Decloet (Africa) Limited	Crop Farming	Chongwe	Canadian	308	$5070000
2008	Environmental Biofuels Ltd	Biofuels (seed production)	Lusaka	British	254	$5000000
2012	Savenda Management Services Ltd	n/a	n/a	Zambian	248	$5000000

Abbreviations and Acronyms

AGOA   African Growth and Opportunity Act

AU   The African Union

BRICS   Brazil, Russia, India, China, and South Africa

CAADP   Comprehensive Africa Agricultural Development Programme

CDC   Commonwealth Development Corporation

COMESA   Common Market for East and Southern Africa

CSO   Central Statistics Office (GRZ)

DAC   Development Assistance Committee

DRC   The Democratic Republic of Congo

EIA   Environmental Impact Assessment

EIS   Environmental Impact Statement

FAO   Food and Agriculture Organisation of the United Nations

FDI   Foreign Direct Investment

GDP   Gross Domestic Product

GRZ   Government of the Republic of Zambia

HDI   Human Development Index (UNDP)

IFC   International Finance Corporation (World Bank)

LMIC   Lower Middle Income Country

MDG   Millennium Development Goal

MFEZ   Multi – Facility Economic Zone

NAIP   National Agricultural Investment Policy

NAP   National Agricultural Policy

NTDA   Non – Traditional Development Assistance

PACRA   Patents and Company Registration Agency

ODA   Official Development Assistance

OECD   Organisation for Economic Cooperation and Development

SADC   Southern Africa Development Community

SME   Small and Medium Enterprise

SNDP   Sixth National Development Plan

UK   United Kingdom

UNCTAD   United Nations Conference on Trade and Development

UNDP   United Nations Development Programme

UNIDO   United Nations Industrial Development Organisation

VAT   Value Added Tax

ZDA   Zambia Development Agency

ZEMA   Zambia Environmental Management Agency

Report Two

Indian Private Agro-Investments in Zambia

a case study

Aparajita Biswas & Ajay Dubey *

1   Introduction to the Study

Indian scholars are researching various facets of Indian engagement in Africa at present. Most of these studies tend to examine issues at a pan-Africa level, often addressing broad questions. This is primarily due to two reasons: one, African studies as an important geopolitical subject is beginning to gain traction; and two, the amount of data available to conduct an issue or country-specific research is negligible. This could be attributed to the lack of funding to carry out focused studies. In such circumstances, the opportunity provided by Oxfam to analyse the role of Indian private players in Zambia's agriculture sector is significant and well timed.

The purpose of this study is to not only assess India's growing footprint in Zambia as an increasingly significant investor, trading partner and donor, but also to analyse the nature and sustainability of foreign direct investment (FDI) in Zambia's agriculture sector. The study is pertinent from the point of view of India's larger Africa poli-

* Aparajita Biswas, Professor, Policy Research Institute of the African Studies Association and Prof. Ajay Dubey, Policy Research Institute of the African Studies Association. Acknowledgment: Dr. Sachin Chaturvedi, Research and Information System for Developing Countries, for his valuable feedback on the draft of this report. April, 2014.

cy, given that India's approach to Africa has changed considerably since 2000. Instead of relying on historical goodwill alone to further relations, economic rationale has also been given pre-eminence. Government of India's (GoI) reinvigorated policy toward Africa emphasises on a sustainable and organic development model. This means New Delhi's relations with Zambian capital Lusaka will involve helping the country steer away from excessive economic dependence on the extractive sector and focus on the development and promotion of other economic activities such as agriculture.

This does not, however, ignore the fact that the post-globalised society in India saw immense potential for its own entrepreneurs in Zambia. The focus on the agriculture sector in Zambia becomes significant not only because it has presented Indian corporate entities with an untapped investment opportunity but also due to the issue of food insecurity in India. GoI has gone on record to state that it is effectively considering private purchases of farm land overseas to ensure food security for India (*The Economic Times*, 2012).

India's Ministry of Agriculture has asked its domestic farmers' associations and agri – business organisations to examine proposals it has received from several countries to farm on leased land in their countries. Countries that have invited India, through the ministry, include Egypt, Ethiopia, Mongolia, Senegal, Sudan, Trinidad and Tobago and Tunisia, among others. "This department is receiving a number of proposals from several countries offering opportunities for acquisition of land for farming by companies, for meeting their commercial objectives, as well as Indian farmers or their conglomeration for taking up smallholdings for agriculture," states a letter issued in late December 2009 by the joint secretary of the Department of Agriculture and Cooperation, Ministry of Agriculture. The objective of such offers is to increase agricultural production in the respective countries to result in reduced dependence on foodgrain import as well as surplus foodgrain export to third world countries (Goswami, 2010).

While analysing India's involvement in Zambia's agriculture sector, the study covered various aspects. At the outset the Indian players in Zambia's agriculture sector and the quantum of their holdings were identified. The stakeholders in the sector in Zambia were listed and their role established. Additionally, the impact of FDI on the livelihoods of smallholder farmers, especially rural women, and communities in Zambia, was looked into. The repercussions of inflow of FDI into the agriculture sector in Zambia including the various rewards such as agricultural development and poverty reduction and risks such as forced evictions and increasing conflicts over land and water were examined closely, and other technical aspects of FDI such as the nature, scope, drivers and modalities, assessed. The various administrative and governance structures present in Zambia and India to facilitate these investments were also analysed.

This literature review is a first step towards addressing the knowledge gaps present in this domain. This report is divided into four sections. Section 2 provides an overview of India – Africa relations and India's FDI policy. The overview of India – Africa relations provides a summary of the evolution of India – Africa relations from historical times to contemporary times and the latter provides a synoptic view of the Indian FDI policies pre-and post-liberalisation. The overview lays the foundation for the report. Section 3, titled "India in Africa's agricultural sector", comprises a summary of GoI's initiatives such as treaties and conventions, lines of credit etc on the one hand, and Indian private investments and FDI in agriculture on the other. Section 4, "India – Zambia Engagement", has two sub sections. The first sub section reviews the literature available on some of the Zambian policies, incentives, regulations, tax incentives etc. to encourage Indian private investments, particularly in the agriculture sector; the second focuses on Indian investments in agriculture in Zambia.

Most literature used in this review is from secondary non-Indian sources since there is a dearth of studies conducted on this topic in India. It is also pertinent to highlight that the analysis provided in this literature review is limited, due to lack of specific information available to answer the questions posed by this research. The study relies heavily on primary data collected during the field visit to gain a more comprehensive understanding of ground realities.

Section 2   Overview

2. 1   India – Africa relations

India's involvement with Africa goes back a long way—to the country's early days of independence movement in the 1960s and before. The current level and intent of India's involvement is on a different plane though. In the early days, India looked towards African countries in the context of an emerging Afro-Asian solidarity among the Third World countries. India's presence was notable in infrastructure projects, with finance and building of railroads in East African countries, besides its assistance in setting up small scale industries in Tanzania and Kenya, joint ventures in textiles, etc. In the subsequent decades, India provided technical expertise, doctors, educational scholarships and various other forms of aid under the Indian Technical and E-conomic Co-operation programme.

Over the first decade of the 21st century, the scope of India – Africa cooperation has expanded significantly, especially with India's emergence as an important player in the world economy and India's own important need for oil and other natural re-sources. This is evident given that in India – Africa Forum summits India offers signifi-cant loans, grants and development assistance to woo African countries. The most im-portant initiative that India has taken to advance its relationship with African countries is its Focus Africa Programme. Ministry of Commerce and Industry, GoI, launched the programme under the Export Import (EXIM) Policy in 2002 to help Indian companies do business in Africa. The primary objective of the programme is to in-crease interaction among the two, by identifying potential areas of bilateral trade and investment. Effective April 1, 2003, the "Focus Africa" programme was extended to cover the entire African continent (Ministry of Commerce and Industry). Through this programme, GoI provides financial assistance to various trade promotion organi-sations, export promotion councils and apex chambers and Indian missions (Ministry of Commerce and Industry).

India is increasingly courting the continent for a number of reasons. At the fore-front of India's foreign policy priorities is energy security. Second, Africa has e-merged as an important market for Indian goods and services, as well as a vital ele-ment in India's quest for strategic minerals and other natural resources needed to feed its burgeoning economy (Mawdsely and Gerard, 2011). Similarly, African coun-tries have been interested in acquiring cost effective and intermediate technology from India in the areas of information technology, agriculture, health and pharmacy. Third, as its economic prowess grows, India has decided to project its military power in the Indian Ocean region, which it has long considered to be with-in its sphere of influence. Given the existence of extremist organisations and criminal syndicates that traffic drugs, arms and people, as well as pirates in the Indian Ocean region, India has begun to dramatically expand its military presence in the Horn of Africa and Indian Ocean, reportedly to include the establishment of listening posts in the Seychelles, Madagascar and Mauritius; in late 2009, it successfully co-opted The Republic of Maldives as part of its southern naval command. Furthermore, India im-ports about 70 percent of its oil through the Indian Ocean to its various ports (Mawdsely and Gerard, 2011).

Africa therefore is crucial and strategic for India's priorities and needs, and these have ensured growth in relationship between India and Africa.

2.2   Indian FDI Policies

FDI is a natural extension of globalisation, which often begins with exports. In the process, countries try to access markets or resources and gradually reduce the cost of production and transaction, by expanding overseas manufacturing operations in coun-tries where certain ownership – specific advantages can help them to compete globally. Adoption of such strategies helps them catch up with competing economies (H. R. Khan, Speech, 2012). A significant uptrend in outward FDI has also been observed in the case of India in recent years. Since globalisation is a two – way process, integration of the Indian economy with the rest of the world is evident not only in terms of higher level of FDI inflows but also in terms of increasing level of FDI inflows and outflows. In 2005 – 07 the total FDI inflow to India was $ 17,766 million while the FDI outflow from India was $ 11,501 million. The same trend continued in 2011 due to an increase in the inflow of $ 36,190 million. Similarly, in 2012 the FDI inflow was $ 25543 with the outflow at $ 8,583 (UNCTAD, 2013). The overseas investment of domestic corporate sector through FDI has provided them better access to global networks and markets, transfer of technology and skills and also enables them to share research and development efforts and outcomes. It can also be seen as a corporate strategy to promote the brand image and utilisation of raw materials available in the host country. In the Indian context, overseas investments have been primarily driven by either resource seeking or market seeking or technology seeking motives. Of late, there has been a surge in resource seeking overseas investments by Indian companies, especially to acquire energy resources in Australia, Indonesia and more importantly Africa (Reserve Bank of India, 2012).

However, this is not to suggest that overseas investment by Indian companies is a phenomenon of 1990s. Indian firms began to invest overseas in the 1960s, but India's restrictive policies for overseas investment limited them to small, minority joint ventures in developing economies. The first major overseas Indian venture was a textile mill set up in Ethiopia in 1959 by the Birla Group of companies (Authkorala, 2009). Overseas investment operations were primarily concentrated in West and East Africa, Middle East and South and East Asia with which India shared a colonial heritage and historical linkages.

Change in policy environment across economies has greatly influenced the outward investment pattern in the global economy. Nonetheless, recognising the concerns of capital outflows, governments in different countries, particularly emerging and developing economies, have been relatively more circumspect on undertaking policy liberalisation of outward investment. Therefore, it is important to highlight how the Indian policy in this regard has evolved over time.

In the Indian context, entrepreneurs recognise overseas investments in joint ventures and wholly owned subsidiaries as important channels to promote global business. The broad approach has been to facilitate outward FDI through joint ventures and wholly owned subsidiaries and provision of financial support to promote exports, including project exports from India. With a steady rise in capital inflows, particularly in the second half of 2000s, the overall foreign exchange reserve position provided comfort to progressive relaxation of the capital controls
and simplification of the procedures for outbound investments from India. Three distinct overlapping phases can be discerned in the evolution of the Indian outward FDI policies (H. R. Khan, 2012):

Phase 1 (1992 – 1995): Period of liberalisation of Indian economy

Phase 2 (1995 – 2000): Creation of Fast Track Route leading up to the creation of the Foreign Exchange Management Act (FEMA)

Phase 3 (2000 – present): Liberalised framework under FEMA

Outward FDI from India has mainly been by way of equities and loans. According to UNCTAD's World Investment Report 2011, based on the magnitude of FDI outflows, India was placed 21st in the world. In terms of value of net purchases i. e. cross border acquisition deals by Indian companies in 2010, India was placed fifth in the world after USA, Canada, Japan and China. Importantly, the scale of overseas investment by domestic companies has also expanded as India was placed second in 2010 only after China in terms of average size of net purchase deals— $ 190 million in India as compared to $ 197 million in China (UNCTAD, 2011).

India also figures among the top five emerging and developing economies whose state owned enterprises are increasingly becoming transnational corporations. It is not surprising that in recent years, India's public sector units (PSUs), viz. National Thermal Power Corporation (NTPC), Gas authority (of) India Limited (GAIL), Oil and Natural Gas Corporation Limited (ONGC) and National Alumin-ium Company Limited (NALCO), have undertaken significant overseas green – field investments (H. R. Khan, 2012).

Even though policy changes with respect to overseas investments have facilitated the growing cross-border acquisitions by the Indian corporate sector, other structural reforms undertaken since 1992, such as industrial deregulation, trade liberalisation and relaxation of regulations governing inward FDI led to major restructuring in the Indian industry. A trend analysis shows that the level of outward FDI from India has increased manifold since 1999 – 2000. The level of net outward FDI flows recorded a sharp upswing at $ 74. 3 billion during the second half of 2000s (2005 – 06 to 2009 – 10) compared to $ 8. 2 billion in the first half of 2000s (2000 – 01 to 2004 – 05). Even though India's outward FDI was moderately affected during 2009 – 10, a sharp rebound was seen in 2010 – 11.

Table 1   Year – wise position of actual outflows in respect of
outward FDI and guarantees issued (Figures in US $ Millions)

Period	Equity	Loan	Guarantee Invoked	Total	Guarantee Issued
2000 – 2001	602. 12	70. 58	4. 97	677. 67	112. 55
2001 – 2002	878. 83	120. 82	0. 42	1000. 07	155. 86
2002 – 2003	1746. 28	102. 10	0. 00	1848. 38	139. 63
2003 – 2004	1250. 01	316. 57	0. 00	1566. 58	440. 53
2004 – 2005	1481. 97	513. 19	0. 00	1995. 16	315. 96
2005 – 2006	6657. 82	1195. 33	3. 34	7856. 49	546. 78
2006 – 2007	12062. 92	1246. 98	0. 00	13309. 90	2260. 96
2007 – 2008	15431. 51	3074. 97	0. 00	18506. 48	6553. 47

续表

Period	Equity	Loan	Guarantee Invoked	Total	Guarantee Issued
2008 – 2009	12477. 14	6101. 56	0. 00	18578. 70	3322. 45
2009 – 2010	9392. 98	4296. 91	24. 18	13714. 07	7603. 04
2010 – 2011	9234. 58	7556. 30	52. 49	16843. 37	27059. 02
2011 – 2012 *	4031. 45	4830. 01	0. 00	8861. 46	14993. 80
Total	75247. 61	29425. 32	85. 40	104758. 30	63504. 05

* April 2011 to February 22, 2012

Table 2   Sector wise Indian investments abroad
between 2000 and 2010: (Figures in US $ Millions)

Year	Manufacturing	Financial Services	Nonfinancial Services	Trading	Others	Total
2000 – 01	169 (23. 84)	6 (00. 85)	470 (66. 29)	52 (07. 33)	12 (01. 69)	709 (100)
2001 – 02	528 (53. 82)	4 (00. 41)	350 (35. 68)	79 (08. 05)	20 (02. 04)	981 (100)
2002 – 03	1271 (70. 69)	3 (00. 17)	404 (22. 47)	82 (04. 56)	38 (02. 11)	1798 (100)
2003 – 04	893 (59. 77)	1 (00. 07)	456 (30. 52)	113 (07. 56)	31 (02. 07)	1494 (100)
2004 – 05	1170 (65. 88)	7 (00. 39)	304 (17. 12)	192 (10. 81)	100 (05. 63)	1776 (100)
2005 – 06	3407 (67. 46)	160 (03. 17)	895 (17. 72)	377 (07. 46)	207 (04. 10)	5050 (100)
2006 – 07	3545 (26. 34)	28 (00. 21)	7486 (55. 62)	1739 (12. 92)	656 (04. 87)	13459 (100)
2007 – 08	6240 (34. 84)	26 (00. 14)	1635 (09. 13)	8993 (50. 21)	1010 (05. 64)	17910 (100)
2008 – 09	6817. 0 (42. 74)	174. 9 (01. 97)	1068. 0 (06. 70)	640. 1 (04. 01)	7247. 8 (45. 44)	15947. 8 (100)
2009 – 10	4443 (43. 11)	—	2895 (28. 09)	1174 (11. 39)	1794 (17. 41)	10306 (100)

Source: RBI Annual Reports at www. rbi. org. in/Publications

In recent years, outward FDI continued to be mainly financed through equity and loans. Although guarantees issued have been rising, their invocation has been negligible during 2009 – 10 and 2010 – 11. It has been observed that the number of outward FDI proposals under the Automatic Route during 2000s was on the rise, indicating the growing appetite of the Indian companies to establish their footprint abroad under a liberal regulatory regime.

The sectoral distribution of India's outward FDI reveals that during the period 2000 – 01 to 2009 – 10, the manufacturing sector accounted for most of India's outward FDI, barring 2000 – 01 and 2006 – 07. The share of manufacturing sector increased from 23. 84 per cent to 43. 11 percent during the period 2000 – 01 to 2009 – 10. The share of non – financial services, which was as high as 66. 29 per cent in 2000 – 01, registered a steep decline in subsequent years, but improved considerably in 2009 – 10 (28. 09 per cent). The share of financial services was negligible throughout the period.

Sectoral pattern also suggests that greater outward investment by the Indian corporate sector seems to have been motivated by long-term strategic considerations rather than short-term profitability. For instance, ONGC Videsh Ltd. , a fully-owned subsidiary of ONGC, has overseas assets in 33 projects in 14 countries of Middle East, Africa, Commonwealth of Independent States and Far East and Latin America at present. Oil India Limited has exploration blocks in eight countries—Libya, Gabon, Iran, Nigeria and Sudan. Similarly, Coal India Limited has formed a subsidiary Coal Videsh Ltd. to acquire coal abroad and also set up a joint venture called International Coal Ventures Ltd with other companies to acquire metallurgical and thermal coal assets outside India. Overseas investment by Indian companies in extractive industries assumes importance as it is required to support rapid economic growth, industrialisation and urbanisation in the domestic sector and guarantee long-term and stable supply of natural resources to the country against a background of rising commodity prices (H. R. Khan, 2012).

Substantive research has gone into tracking the evolution of Indian corporate in the globalised world order, their increasing influence and the role of outward FDI in enhancing India – Africa relations. Singh, Lakhwinder and Jain Varinder's, "Emerging Pattern of India's Outward Foreign Direct Investment under Influence of State Policy: a Macro-view", states that the emerging growth dynamism of Indian economy in a rapidly globalising world is well recognised and critiqued by several researchers. In fact, India has long made a concerted effort to develop strategic and competitive capabilities in the agents of production. These capabilities have started paying of late. Such trends became more lucid with the strengthening of Indian capital, especially abroad, as the Indian capital has initiated collaborations and mergers with global players. The study provides insights into such achievements of the Indian economy. Besides providing a review of theory and practice of emerging multinationals from developing countries, the paper examines India's outward FDI in an evolutionary perspective. In its endeavour, the study, besides tracing the emerging pattern of India's outward FDI, hints at the facilitating role of state policy to encourage the outflow of FDI (Singh Lakhwinder, Jain Varinder, 2010).

Table 3　Sector wise overseas investments by Indian companies 2008 – 2012 (in billion US $)

Period	2008 – 09	2009 – 10	2010 – 11	2011 – 12*	Total
Manufacturing	10. 18	5. 35	5. 04	2. 74	23. 31
Financial Insurance, Real Estate Business & Business Services	3. 55	4. 41	6. 53	2. 53	17. 03
Wholesale & Retail Trade, Restaurants & Hotels	1. 17	1. 13	1. 89	1. 00	5. 19
Agriculture & Allied Activities	2. 38	0. 95	1. 21	0. 41	4. 94
Transport, Communication & Storage Services	0. 31	0. 38	0. 82	1. 34	2. 85
Construction	0. 35	0. 36	0. 38	0. 37	1. 46
Community, Social & Personal Services	0. 39	0. 18	0. 70	0. 18	1. 45
Electricity, Gas & Water	0. 14	0. 84	0. 10	0. 04	1. 19
Miscellaneous	0. 12	0. 11	0. 18	0. 10	0. 51
Total	18. 58	13. 71	16. 84	8. 73	57. 86

* April 2011 to February 22, 2012

Pattanaik, R. K. and Bhargavi, J. in "Outward Foreign Direct Investment: An Indian Perspective", explain that India's outward FDI is one of the key outcomes of globalisation and has been contributing significantly to the economic growth and development in recent years. Although the vast flow of outward FDI from developing countries at an international level is relatively a new phenomenon, a few large Indian conglomerates, namely the Tata and the Birla, have been investing overseas from the early 1960s. However, the full scale emergence of outward FDI from India was limited until the mid 1990s as India followed a more restrictive foreign trade and investment policy regime since independence in 1947. Nevertheless, outward FDI from India gained momentum after the gradual liberalisation of trade and investment regime from the early 1990s. The surge in Indian outward FDI since the 1990s, and its various new features, appears to be a result of the interactions among changes in national policy, corporate behaviour and international developments in trade and investment. The removal of the restrictive measures on the growth of firms (like FERA), removal of the licensing regime, dismantling of product reservation systems for public-owned and small-and medium-sized enterprises, facilitative measures for foreign firms, and a massive reduction in import duties led to intense competition in Indian markets (Pattanaik, R. K. and Bhargavi, 2011).

Consequently, the past decade has experienced a marked increase in outward FDI, mergers and acquisitions in terms of both quality and magnitude. According to Pattanaik and Bhargavi, India became the seventh largest outward foreign direct investor among emerging Asian nations and 21st globally in 2008. Outward FDI from India increased to over \$79 billion in 2010 from a mere \$0. 2 billion in 1990. The growth of outward FDI is spectacular (more than 2, 000 times, as per UNCTAD OFDI data) over the past decade and ranked third after United Arab Emirates and Egypt during 2000 and 2008 (Chowdhury, 2011).

Investments have increased phenomenally in select sectors, viz. , chemicals and oil and gas industries contributing around half of the total flows during 2000 – 07. Indian state owned oil companies are wielding an increased presence in natural resource based industries and becoming an established trend in African countries. In fact, the authors of another study perceive African region as an increasingly contested economic battleground due to its resource richness and improved growth prospects (Sauvant K., Pradhan J., 2010). Jorgrn Dige Pedersen's article, "The Second Wave of Indian Investments Abroad", assesses the recent international expansion of Indian companies by contrasting it to the earlier—much more modest—wave of investments abroad. It also traces the evolution of the Indian government's policy towards outward investments and claims that an important reason for the rise of investments abroad is the gradual relaxation of the Indian government's restrictions on capital outflow after the economic reforms of the 1990s. The new Indian investments abroad are characterised by being dispersed over a very large number of countries and economic sectors and—most remarkable—Indian companies are now also targeting markets in Africa along with Europe and USA through acquisitions of local companies. At the same time, Indian companies have continued to expand their presence in other developing countries, where their activities may contribute to both economic progress and reduction of economic dependence on relations with developed countries (Pedersen J., 2008).

Jaya Prakash Pradhan in his article, "Trends and Patterns of Overseas Acquisition by Indian Multinational", wrote overseas acquisitions by Indian firms can also be seen as their response to a globalised competition since 1990s. With liberalisation and changes in trade, industry, foreign investment and technology policy regime, previously protected Indian companies got exposed to global competition at once. Indian firms increasingly realised their existing technological and other capabilities accumulated with predominant dependence on protected home markets and the import substitution policy regime of the past were clearly inadequate to cope with this new competition unleashed by a more liberalised business environment. They were forced to improve their competitive strength immediately and enlarge their position in the world markets. Indian companies realised that adopting long-term competencies with large investment in R&D, advertising, etc was relatively more risky and costly than pursuing the route of overseas acquisitions (Pradhan, Jaya Prakash, 2007).

Ravi Ramamurti and Jitendra V. Singh's edited book, *Emerging Multinationals in Emerging Markets*, makes an outstanding contribution to understanding the new configuration of world markets and its new competitive structure. As the different country studies show, multinationals from emerging economies share a number of common structural features, as well as the imprinting of specific local experiences. For managers and business practitioners, the book offers valuable tips on how to shape the new international order (Ramamurti, R., Singh, J., 2010).

Kinfu Adisu, Thomas Sharkey, Sam Okoroafo in their paper, "Analyzing Indian Policies and Firm Strategies in Africa", investigate India's policy and Indian firms' strategic presence in Africa. Recognising the historical link between the two entities, they say foreign investment outlays to Africa are sustainable. Further examination using FDI and Porter's Competitive Advantage theories[1]suggest some advantages enjoyed by Indian firms there. Three Indian companies, Tata Group, Bharti Enterprises and Reliance, have made extensive use of strategic alliances to penetrate and quickly accelerate activities (Kinfu, A., Sharkey, T. and Okoroafo, S., 2013).

---

[1] Michael Porter's famous Five Forces of Competitive Position model provides a simple perspective for assessing and analysing the competitive strength and position of a corporation or business organization. The five forces are Existing competitive rivalry between suppliers, Threat of new market entrants, Bargaining power of buyers, Power of suppliers and Threat of substitute products (including technology change). Porter's Five Forces model provides suggested points under each main heading, by which you can develop a broad and sophisticated analysis of competitive position, as might be used when creating strategy, plans, or making investment decisions about a business or organization.

Section 3　India in Africa's Agriculture Sector

3.1　Development Cooperation and Agriculture

Cooperation in the field of agriculture between India and Africa, which dates back four decades, is one of the pillars that support the India – Africa relationship. This cooperation has been strengthened and furthered with the impetus given by the two consecutive India – Africa Forum Summits held in New Delhi in 2008 and Addis Ababa in 2011. Both summits prioritised cooperation in the agriculture sector which, according to Indian and African leaders, has great potential in the backdrop of the strong complementarities between India and Africa. Leaders of both Indian and African countries were enthusiastic about developing the agriculture sector in Africa to ensure food security (Ministry of External Affairs).

India's cooperation in Africa's agriculture sector is noteworthy, for the purpose of building Africa's long-term trade and production capacity. At the India – Africa Forum Summit 2008, India committed to ensure greater cooperation in these sectors. Moreover, India's move towards economic and technical cooperation in African agriculture over the past decade must be seen against the backdrop of declining support from traditional donors such as Canada, Germany, Japan, Netherlands and the United States to this sector (DFID, 2004).

In fact, there has been a substantial drop in the share of agriculture expenditure in the total government spending in most African countries. In the *Africa India Framework for Cooperation*, which was adopted during the India – Africa Forum Summit 2008, Africa and India agreed that development of agriculture was an effective approach to ensure food security, eradicating poverty and improving people's livelihood, and agreed to strengthen cooperation in this sector to improve food security in Africa and increase its exports to world markets. It was also decided that cooperation would be extended to land development, water management, agricultural plan-

tation, breeding technologies, food security, agro-processing machinery, combating agro-base diseases, experimental and demonstrative projects and training (African Union – Africa India Framework for Cooperation, 2008).

India – Africa cooperation in agriculture is on multiple levels. At one level, it is an
effort to boost diplomatic ties and facilitate South – South cooperation based on mu-
tual benefits. India has offered aid, set up agricultural institutions, and provided
scholarships to African students in various agricultural universities in India. As a result
of decisions taken during the first India Africa Forum Summit 2008, it was decided
that 300 special agriculture scholarships would be offered to African scholars (Indian
Embassy, Addis Ababa). As part of the Indo – African programme, 49 students of
African origin are at present studying in different agriculture universities in India
(Stein Sunstol Eriksen, Aparajita Biswas and Ajay Dubey).

At another level there is a new collaboration focused on agriculture between India
and USA in Liberia, Malawi and Kenya to enhance food security. The three – year
India – US – Africa triangular partnership programme is expected to share proven innovations from India's private and public sectors to address food insecurity, malnutrition and poverty in the target countries. India has emerged as a hub for low-cost, effective local innovations to deal with challenges arising from factors like climate
change, shrinking natural resources, decline in cultivable land and rising demand for
food. The US Agency for International Development's (USAID) food security office director Bahiru Duguma launched the programme, which is being supported by
the US government's global hunger and food security initiative "Feed the Future".
This partnership aims to improve agricultural productivity and support market institutions in Kenya, Liberia and Malawi. The programme plans to train 180 agriculture
professionals from the three African countries by providing marketing and extension
management training at the Chaudhury Charan Singh National Institute of Agricultural Marketing (NIAM) in Jaipur and National Institute of Agricultural Extension
Management (MANAGE) in Hyderabad. The initiative is led by USAID and NI-

AM. The first triangular partnership in agricultural training was inaugurated at MAN-AGE in January 2013 for 30 trainees from Africa (*Business Standard*, 2013). Japan and other countries are also seeking similar partnerships with India to work in the agriculture sector.

India also made a commitment to raise Lines of Credit (LoC) facilities to the African agriculture sector. According to the EXIM bank report, the largest single LoC approved by the bank so far is the one to Ethiopia (\$640 million) for its Tindaho Sugar Project, which is expected to facilitate Indian investments. This LoC is not only for Tendaho project but also for revival of Wonji/Shoa, Fincha sugar unit. The EXIM bank also extended an LoC of \$27 million to Senegal for export of equipment for irrigation projects in 2006. Moreover, at the Second India – Africa Summit, Prime Minister Manmohan Singh announced a grant of 75 billion CFA (\$160 million) to Senegal for the second phase of the programme of mechanisation of agriculture (Second Africa – India Forum Summit, 2011). According to the EXIM bank report, there are 140 LoC currently being made available to foreign governments or financial entities with nearly 100 in Africa, mostly in the agriculture sector. In 2013, the EXIM bank opened a \$217 million credit line to finance infrastructure projects in Mozambique (All Africa, 2013).

At the Second Africa – India Forum Summit 2011, Africa and India reaffirmed their commitment to cooperate to increase agricultural output and achieve the Millennium Development Goal of reducing by half the proportion of people suffering from hunger and malnutrition by 2015. Leaders at the summit also focused on the need to develop scientific research for raising agricultural productivity on the one hand, and conservation of land and environment on the other. The aim is to "ensure food security for their people and to bring down the currently rising cost of food prices so as to make food for the implementation of the Comprehensive Africa Agricultural Development Programme (CAADP)" (Second Africa – India Forum Summit, 2011).

One of the main features of India – Africa cooperation in agriculture is India has actively pursued capacity building and sharing its experiences to help develop the African agriculture sector. Particular attention has been given to research and knowledge sharing methods on various agricultural practices. According to the document titled, "India & Africa Partners in Development: Capacity Building Programmes & Lines of Credit", in 2011, India sent teams of farm experts from the Indian Council of Agricultural Research (ICAR) to Zambia, Ethiopia and South Africa and several African countries to get firsthand knowledge of how African countries explore ways of improving their agricultural practices (MEA).

Moreover, Platform for India – Africa Partnership in Agriculture (PIAPA) has been set up by The International Crops Research Institute for the Semi – Arid Tropics (ICRISAT), the International Agriculture Consulting Group (IACG) and Indian Council of Agricultural Research (ICAR) to bring various stakeholders on board as consortium partners to create better policies, more effective institutions, improved infrastructure and better access to markets and higher quality inputs, particularly for dry land farmers in India and Africa.

Then, ICRISAT has set up ICRISAT South – South Initiative (IS-SI) to provide a systematic and effective cooperation between India and Africa in the agriculture sector. It has already established strong and successful India – Africa partnerships to scale up its role as a driver of prosperity and economic opportunities in the dryland tropics (ICRISAT, 2013). According to the report published by ICAR in December 2011, an MoU for cooperation in the field of agricultural research and education was signed between the Department of Agricultural and Research (DAER) and ICAR and the Director General of Ethiopian Institute of Agricultural Research (EIAR), Ethiopia. The priority areas of cooperation include agricultural research in horticulture, crop science, fisheries, animal science, agricultural engineering and natural resource management, agricultural extension and agricultural education. Both countries agreed to extend cooperation through exchange of scientists, scholars, technologies, literature, information and germplasm, as well as pursue collaborative research projects. Precise areas of collaboration were also discussed and a draft biennial work plan was developed and shared (ICAR, 2011).

To further develop human resources, the Prime Minister of India proposed to establish new institutions in the areas of agriculture and rural development. He stressed on the need to form an India – Africa integrated textile cluster, to support the cotton industry, an Africa – India food processing cluster to contribute to value addition and creation of regional and export markets, and an India – Africa centre for medium range weather forecasting to harness satellite technology for agriculture and fisheries.

The document titled 'Key Assertions and Documentations', by EXIM bank and Confederation of Indian Industry (CII), pointed out that five key areas received special attention during the course of deliberations at the conclave: bilateral trade expansion, Indian investments in Africa, capacity building, food security and energy security. The document states that delegates from both the regions deliberated on the need for greater cooperation in agriculture and agro-processing, which would have a great bearing on the food security situation in Africa and India. Africa's farm sector is expected to grow to the tune of $ 1 trillion by 2030, although this growth will depend largely on adequate technology infusion (EXIM bank and CII). The delegates also spoke about how Africa could learn from India's Green Revolution, White Revolution and expansion of its agri-processing industries. Tractorisation of African farm sectors was cited as an important area to be addressed. While some parts of northern and southern Africa have increasingly inducted tractors for agriculture, farmers in most parts of Africa still depend on hand-held implements for farming.

The experts suggested that Indian companies could help Africa's agriculture sector in the following ways: farm mechanisation, agro-processing and storage, investments in training and development of human resources for the farm sector, and employment generation, greenfield investments, local vendor development and agriculture exports to neighbouring countries, setting up agro parks in Africa, setting up horticulture industries and floriculture units and contract farming (CII – EXIM Bank Conclave on India – Africa, 2013).

3. 2   India's Investment in Agriculture in Africa

The past few years have seen rapid increase in the demand for land suitable for agriculture by foreign investors in Africa. Although foreign investments in agriculture and land are not a new phenomenon, the issue of growing edible food crops primarily for the purpose of shipping back home to domestic markets as part of a food security strategy have provoked debate in various international forums. A World Bank report points out that majority of the foreign investments in agricultural land have taken place in Sub-Saharan Africa. Sudan, Ethiopia, Ghana, Nigeria and Mozambique alone covered 23 per cent of the global land investment projects during 2002 – 2009 (World Bank, 2010).

According to Food and Agriculture Organization (FAO) of the United Nations, the main form of recent investments is acquisition mostly through long term leasing of up to 99 years of agricultural land. The land investments can be large scale with many involving more than 10,000 hectares and some more than 500,000 hectares. A particular pattern of bilateral investment flows also emerged following established cultural, political and business ties and geographical restrictions on investment funds. For example, Gulf countries prefer investments in Sudan and other, mainly African, OIC member states, while Asian countries prefer Zambia, Angola and Mozambique. However, the pattern is becoming more diffused (Hallam, 2009).

A recent database on land deals reports that almost 5 per cent of Africa's agricultural land has been bought or leased by investors since 2000. Researchers estimate that more than 200m hectares of land—roughly eight times the size of the UK—were sold or leased between 2000 and 2010. New international land deals database reveals rush to buy Africa (*The Guardian*, 2012).

The disquieting factor is there is as yet no detailed data on the extent, nature and impact of these investments. Available FDI data lack sufficient details and are too ag-gregated to determine just how much investment in agriculture there has been and what form it takes. It is therefore difficult to say with any precision whether the re-cent investments are a totally new development or a continuation of existing trends (FAO, David Hallam, 2009).

A study conducted by the FAO titled, 'Resource – seeking Foreign Direct In-vestment in African Agriculture', reviews the main findings of eight case studies in select African countries: Uganda, Mali, Madagascar, Sudan, Morocco, Ghana, Senegal and Egypt. It shows a mixed picture, as the impacts vary significantly across countries and locations within a given country. They depend on many factors, in-cluding the contents of the investment contract, the type of business model imple-mented and the institutional framework in place in the host country. The main ben-efits that can be expected for the host country are economic benefits such as em-ployment creation, higher productivity, improved access to finance and markets for smallholders, technology transfer and enforcement of production standards. How-ever, some studies found that FDI had not generated the expected benefits and two studies even observed that investment projects removed income opportunities for lo-cal farmers. The studies also found that the legal framework and procedures gover-ning land acquisition, land registration, land – use and the rights of smallholders are generally unclear and not transparent. The granting of land without undertaking the relevant studies and public consultations to ensure the social, environmental and e-conomic feasibility of an investment project was seen as a critical problem likely to have adverse effects on local communities. To maximise the positive impacts of in-ternational investment while minimising the risks, governments should verify that the existing policies, regulations and institutions are adequate and that preliminary studies and consultations are conducted with all stakeholders (Christin Gerlach and Pascal Liu, 2010).

Indian companies have leased or acquired significant portions of land in Africa,

South America and South East Asia to grow foodgrain, pulses and edible oils. A major underlying concern of the recent upturn in Indian investments in agricultural land abroad is its concern for food security. Its foodgrain production is unable to match its growing population. The import of edible oils is the second largest drain on India's foreign exchange after crude oil. The situation is even more critical in the case of pulses (lentils), which provide most Indians the protein component in their food.

The situation has become so critical that India's prime minister constituted three high-powered committees of chief ministers and central ministers to recommend ways of containing inflation and boosting agricultural production. The working group on agricultural production was chaired by Haryana chief minister B. S. Hooda, with chief ministers of West Bengal, Punjab and Bihar as members. The Hooda Committee suggested that, like many other countries that have "shopped for land abroad for growing crops to meet consumption needs", Indian companies could also be encouraged to buy land in other countries for producing pulses and edible oils. "We should seriously consider these options," the committee recommended, "for at least 2 million tons of pulses and 5 million tons of edible oil for 15 – 20 years" (*The Times of India*, Biraj Patnaik, "The new shifting agriculture: Shopping for fields overseas", July 9, 2010).

The Indian government facilitates the process of outsourcing food production overseas by Indian firms in a number of ways. The government has led many trade missions of its farmers to various countries and regions, and supported efforts to facilitate the entry of Indian foreign agricultural investors at major regional trade and business summits. The Indian government has supported a host of various initiatives to facilitate Indian agricultural companies in their overseas investments in Africa and elsewhere, including thorough support for conventional new greenfield FDI; merger and acquisition (M&A); purchases of existing firms; public-private partnerships (PPPs); specific tariff reductions on agricultural goods imported to India; negotiation of regional bilateral trade and investment treaties (BITs); and double taxation (avoidance) agreements (DTAs).

Another major way in which the Indian government has financially facilitated the process is by giving concessional Lines of Credit (LoC) to various developing country governments, banks and financial institutions, as well as regional financial institutions, through the Indian EXIM bank. Often such LoC are for the purpose of national development projects, and where these projects involve agricultural development, Indian foreign investors stand ready to win concessions and contracts for agricultural development in the form of their FDI.

The EXIM bank also gives soft loans and LoC directly to Indian companies, although it is difficult for the public to obtain details on this activity for specific companies. For example, India has allotted $ 75 million LoC to Zambia for its development project; and a grant of $ 5 million for projects on health, education and social sectors and a loan agreement between EXIM bank and the Zambian Ministry of Finance and National Planning was signed to extend to Zambia's $ 50 million LoC for Itezhi Tezhi hydropower project in which TATA and Zesco are joint venture partners (High Commission of India, Lusaka).

Then, Tata group has been given a land lease in Uganda to run a pilot agricultural project, while the Jaipurias of RJ Corp have a lease of a 50-acre model dairy farm. Construction major Shapoorji Pallonji & Co has acquired the lease for 50,000 hectares of land in Ethiopia and may look at agricultural projects in future. And it's not just large Indian companies, small and medium enterprises in sectors ranging from spices and tea to chemicals are looking at entering the commercial agriculture space in Africa.

Indian companies entering into contracts to work in Africa stand to benefit because they are being given all support, but they do little in return to ensure African farmers benefit or safeguard the environment. There are virtually no limits on groundwater use or environmental pollution, or obligations related to labour, wages or working conditions, transfers of technology or purchases of local goods or services (Rowden, 2011).

Table 4   A Sample of Indian Companies Investing in Agricultural Land in Africa

Sl No.	Company	Country	Details
1	Karuturi Ago Products Plc.	Ethiopia	Acquired 100, 000 ha in the Jikao and Itang districts of the Gambela region for growing palm, cereal and pulses, with conditional option to acquire another 200, 000 ha. Karuturi Ago Products is a subsidiary ofKaruturi Global Ltd.
2	Ruchi Soya	Ethiopia	Acquired a 25 – year lease for soyabean and processing unit on 152, 649 ha in Gambela and Benishangul Gumaz states
3	Verdanta Harvests Plc.	Ethiopia	Acquired a 50 – year lease for 5, 000 ha in the Gambela region for a tea and spice plantation
4	Chadha Agro Plc	Ethiopia	Acquired up to 100, 000 ha in Guji Zone in Oromia regional state for a sugar development project
5	Varun International	Madagascar	Subsidiary Varun Agriculture Sarl leased or purchased 232000 ha to grow rice, corn and pulses
6	Uttam Sucrotech	Ethiopia	Won a $ 100 – million contract to expand the Wonji – Shoa sugar factory
7	McLeod Russel India	Uganda	Purchased tea plantations worth $ 25 million, including Uganda's Rwenzori Tea Investments; McLeod Russel India is owned by BM Khaitan
8	ACIL Cotton Industries	Brazil, Congo and Ethiopia	Plans to invest nearly $ 15 million (Rs 68 crore) for land leases to start contract farming pulses and coffee in Brazil, Congo and Ethiopia

续表

Sl No.	Company	Country	Details
10	Sannati Agro Farm Enterprise Pvt. Ltd.	Ethiopia	Acquired a 25 – year lease on 10, 000 ha in Dimi District, Gambela region, for cultivation of rice, pulses and cereals
9	Adani Group	Africa, Brazil, Argentina, Indonesia and Malaysia	Plans to (as of October 2010) set up farms to cultivate edible oil and pulses
11	Jay Shree Tea & Industries	Rwanda, Uganda	Acquired two tea plantations in Rwanda and one in Uganda; Jay Shree Tea & Industries is controlled by BK Birla
12	ACIL Cotton Industries	Brazil, Congo and Ethiopia.	Announced plans in January 2011 to invest nearly $ 15 million (Rs 68 crore) to start contract farming of crops like pulses and coffee in Brazil, Congo and Ethiopia.
13	BHO Bio Products Plc.	Ethiopia	Acquired 27, 000 ha to grow cereal, pulses and edible oil crops
14	MMTC Ltd (state – owned)	Kenya and Tanzania	Plans to (as of October 2010) grow pulses

Source: Rowden, R. Grain and Economics Research Foundation

Indian perspective on such investments

During the course of this study the team contacted several Indian company heads for their inputs on this issue. The team contacted Ms. Indrayani Mulay from the Confederation of Indian Industry (CII) and Ms. Shiela Sudhakaran from the Federation of Indian Chambers of Commerce and Industry (FICCI). Ms. Mulay provided details regarding the ninth CII – EXIM Bank Conclave on India Africa Project Partnership held from March 17 – 19, 2013 in New Delhi, which presented a different dimension to the India Africa relations in the economic sector. The event witnessed the presence of various dignitaries from India and various African nations, especially Zambia, Burundi and Cameroon. A few sessions were dedicated to the agriculture sector. Ms. Mulay mentioned that the organisation creates a platform to bring various delegates and investors onto a common table through conferences and conclaves in which CII acts as a mediator and highlights the opportunities.

Ms. Sudhakaran highlighted that Zambia holds huge potential for Indian investment as the country has a stable political and emerging economic environment. She further apprised that FICCI has been actively associated with the energy auditing team of Vedanta Group, a major Indian investor in Konkola Copper Mines. The organisation is working towards contributing to promote India – Africa investment in agriculture. In this regard, FICCI organised India – Africa Agribusiness Forum in February this year, which saw several African nations participating in it, including Zambia.

In addition to this the team also contacted Mr. Wilfred at the Indian Social Action Forum (INSAF), Mr. Ashish Kothari at Kalpavriksh and Mr. Anil Chowdhary at PEACE. They apprised the author regarding the land grabbing issue in Africa. Mr. Kothari furnished a few reports regarding land grabbing in Africa but since most of their work has been on Ethiopia, they regretted not being able to provide anything in particular on Zambia. Mr. Chowdhary provided various reports and research findings on land grabbing in Africa. The team contacted Mr. R. Sreedhar at Mines, Minerals and People too. He is a legal petitioner against Vedanta resources. He told the author that investors sought tie ups with the local governor and tribal chiefs offering them incentives who in turn do not seek consensus from local people. Investors are seeking soft targets like Ethiopia and Mozambique, he said. He further stated that under the name of empowerment there is a "resource curse". He foresees a bleak future as companies are destroying natural resources to raise their own investments and profits.

The team also held meetings with Ms. Kavery Ganguly at Food and Agriculture

Centre of Excellence, Mr. Abhilash Puljal at Avignam Group and Mr. Sriram Sub-ramaniam at the EXIM bank. Mr. Puljal spoke about the China factor. African countries like Ethiopia preferred Indian investors to investors from China and western countries. The reason is Indian firms work with locals and they believe in capacity building, while China imports its population. In fact they bring their prisoners for intensive labour work. He agreed that there is certain kind of land grab but the picture presented in media was extreme and a bit far from the real picture.

Section 4   India – Zambia Engagement

4.1   Zambian Agriculture policies

In Zambia, agriculture plays a key role in the economy and could be a major driver of growth and poverty reduction. The sector is characterised by a dual struc-ture, where a small number of large commercial farms, concentrated along the rail-way line, co-exist with scattered subsistence smallholders and a few small commer-cial farmers who face severe difficulties accessing input and output markets. It is esti-mated that about 40 percent of rural households are engaged solely in subsistence ag-riculture. While the agriculture sector has long been neglected by the government's urban bias and single-minded emphasis on maize for food self-sufficiency, the country's infrastructure, extension services and agricultural research and develop-ment remain underdeveloped, especially in remote rural areas (Bonaglia, 2008).

Since the early 1990s, Zambian agricultural policy has undergone a major change, shifting from heavy government intervention to a liberalised system aimed at bolstering private sector participation in various aspects of agricultural production including input supply, processing, marketing and extension service provision. As part of the government disengagement, the Ministry of Agriculture, Fisheries and Forestry ventured into public-private partnerships by creating agricultural trusts with the mandate to manage public assets on a commercial basis and provide research, advisory and training services (Bonaglia, 2008). However, the 1996 – 2001 Agricultural Sector Investment Program (ASIP) designed by the Government of Zambia and donors to facilitate the transition to a market economy in agriculture did not produce the desired outcome. A series of droughts coupled with an unsupportive and unpredictable business environment contributed to reducing the incentives for the private sector to fill the void left by public intervention (Katharina Felgenhauer, 2007).

The new National Agricultural Policy (NAP) 2004 – 2015 provides the overall vision and policy framework for the agriculture sector and assigns a pivotal role to the private sector, which is expected to engage increasingly in service provision. The Ministry of Agriculture and Co-operatives (MACO) is expected to focus on its core functions (policy formulation, enforcement of legislation and regulation) while developing partnerships with other stakeholders in the sector to ensure extension services, agricultural research, and monitoring and evaluation. Donors are encouraged to provide financial, technical and other support in the implementation of agricultural policies and programmes and capacity building for stakeholders (Bonaglia, 2008). MACO uses its staff from the national level down to the field level to implement extension programmes. At the national level, Zambia public extension comprises 742 staff members and is managed by a team of 308 senior staff according to the MEA's report (2011). Seven of the senior staff members have a PhD and 31 were trained at the Master of Science level. Women account for 13 per cent of senior management staff. There are 64 subject matter specialists, 323 field-level extension staff and 26 ICT staff. The report indicated that the public sector does not employ in-service training staff.

There are several Zambian government sources that showcase Zambia as a viable investment opportunity. The office of the Minister of Commerce, Trade and Industry and organisations such as the Zambian Development Agency (ZDA) and Zambian International Trade and Investment Centre publish various reports and studies that highlight the great investment potential of the country. The United Nations came out with a comprehensive study titled, "Investment Guide to Zambia-Opportunities and Conditions", in 2011 that provides in depth information on various variables. The report suggests that three good reasons to invest in Zambia are investment friendly environment, market access and resources and opportunities. There are different arguments on how Zambia can work towards wealth creation and distribution, economic growth, employment creation and improve the livelihood of Zambian people. One common thread that runs through them all is the understanding that foreign investment is a crucial component. With India increasing its engagement in most parts of Africa, various official bodies in Zambia have made available data and information that will aid potential investors.

A comprehensive report put together by NEPAD and OECD titled, "Accelerating reform in Africa: Mobilising investment in infrastructure and agriculture—Highlights of the Policy Framework for Investment in Zambia", covers a wide range of topics related to Zambia. It discusses the various reforms put in place by the Zambian government in its transition from a state dominated to a private sector driven economy. The reforms were designed to introduce a market-based and private sector-driven economy, rather than the state-dominated economic system that prevailed. Various pieces of legislation were enacted and statutory institutions created to implement the reforms. Among these institutions were the Zambia Investment Centre (ZIC), the Export Board of Zambia (EBZ), the Zambia Privatization Agency (ZPA), the Zambia Export Processing Zone Authority (ZEPZA) and the Small Enterprises Development Board, each with specific mandates focused on promoting trade and investment in the country. Additionally, it also details the various agreements made to protect investors, various strategies made to promote investment, steps taken to ensure the basis for a corporate governance framework that promotes overall economic performance and transparent and efficient markets and so forth (OECD, 2011).

A report prepared by Steven Haggblade for Food Security Research Project—Zambia titled, "Returns to Investment in Agriculture", begins by emphasising the significance of investment in agriculture as it is necessary to ensure rapid economic growth and poverty reduction in Zambia. He explains in great detail the various policy measures in place since the NEPAD initiative and the structural flaws that hold back development. For instance, in allocating these funds, Zambia spends majority of its discretionary agricultural budget on recurrent subsidies for private farm inputs, primarily fertiliser, while spending far less on rural infrastructure and technology development (Haggblade S. J. , 2007).

Organisations such as the Oakland Institute provide in depth analyses of the various facets of investment deals in Africa. Its country report on Zambia focuses on under – researched aspects such as the nature of land acquisition by various actors and the economic, social and environmental impact on Zambian society among others (The Oakland Institute, 2013).

Correspondingly, the working paper published by the German Institute of Global and Area Studies (GIGA) authored by Kerstin Nolte titled, "Large-Scale Agricultural Investments under Poor Land Governance System: Actors and Institutions in the Case of Zambia", also provides interesting insights. The report scrutinised the Zambian land governance system and its evolution, the process that an investor has to go through to acquire land and the actors responsible for shaping the process. The study highlights that enforcement of formal rules is weak when it comes to the processes involved in acquiring land. This study also conducted power analyses of all the stakeholders including the investors, local authorities, government and contends that the local land users play an increasingly negligible role. The report also stresses that there is a great development opportunity with these land deals and that to categorise them as "land grabs" by affluent "powerful actors" would be o-versimplification (German Institute of Global and Area Studies, GIGA, 2013).

Mujenja, Fison and Wonani, Charlott in their paper, "Long-term outcomes of agricultural investments: Lessons from Zambia", discuss two agricultural investments in Zambia: Kaleya Smallholders Company Ltd (KASCOL) and Mpongwe Develop-ment Company Ltd (MDC) and its successors ETC Bio Energy and Zambeef. The two projects started in the 1970s and early 1980s as joint ventures between the gov-ernment of Zambia and the Commonwealth Development Corporation (CDC), and were privatised recently. The involvement of CDC reflected the development o-rientation of both projects at their inception. Given this circumstance and the signifi-cant implementation time behind these two experiences, the case studies can provide valuable insights on the longer-term development outcomes of best-practice invest-ments in agriculture. These insights may be a useful contribution to today's interna-tional debates about agricultural investment (Mujenja Fison, Wonani Charlott, 2012).

The government of Zambia has provided the following general investment incen-tives and allowances for the agricultural sector (Zambia Development Agency, 2011):

- *Corporation tax at* 15 *per cent on income from farming and non-traditional exports*

- *Farm works allowance of* 100 *per cent for expenditure on stumping, clearing, prevention of soil erosion, bore holes, aerial and geophysical surveys and water conservation*

- *Development allowance of* 10 *per cent of the cost of capital expenditure on growing coffee, banana plants, citrus fruits or similar plants*

- *Farm improvement allowance, which includes capital expenditure incurred on farm im-provement, is allowable in the year of incurring the expenditure*

- *Dividends paid out of farming profits are exempt for the first five years the distributing company commences business*

- *Carry forward losses for five years*

Furthermore the Zambia Development Act provides additional incentives for investors investing not less than $ 500,000 in the following agricultural related priority subsectors—floriculture, horticulture, processed foods, beverages and stimulants, production and the processing of the following products in the textiles sector: cotton, cotton yarn, fabric, agro processing, production and processing of the following products in the leather sector: cattle hide, crust leather, leather products and garments.

The priority sector incentives provided for under the ZDA are:

- *A corporate tax of 0 per cent for an initial period of five years from the first year profits are made*

- *For years six to eight, corporate tax will be paid on 50 per cent of profits and in year nine to 10 on 75 per cent of the profits*

- *Dividends shall be exempt from tax for five years from the year of first declaration*

- *Capital expenditure on improvement or for the upgrading of infrastructure shall qualify for improvement allowance of 100 per cent of such expenditure*

- *Suspended customs duty to zero for five years on machinery and equipment*

4.2   Indian Agricultural Investments in Zambia

Zambia possesses huge potential in the agriculture sector. Gifted with good soil and an area of 60 million hectares of arable land, out of which only 15 per cent is in use, ample amount of surface and underground water, climate conditions are appropriate for cultivating a wide variety of crops like wheat, soyabean, coffee, cotton, tobacco, sugar, paprika etc. The Zambian government is also contributing to the enhancement of this sector by allocating vast tracts of land near the rail and road networks for prospective investors and electrification of these blocks is underway. Agro-processing of wheat, soyabean, cotton, tobacco, spices, sugar

and vegetables is encouraged to add value to local produce. Special incentives are offered to commercial and small-holder farmers. Zambia has rich forestry reserves con-
sisting of pine and eucalyptus, but logging is threatening the natural resources. In
terms of fisheries, commercial fish production is about 70, 000 tonnes per
year. Both government and the private sector are involved in the fisheries industry
and are working to implement programmes of sustainable fishing practice (Government of India, Focus Africa).

The government of India has categorised Zambia as one of the important countries
in the 'Focus Africa' programme. One of the major platforms that has facilitated the
creation of various new policies is the India Africa Forum Summit. Detailed reports
that list out the various inducements for trade are easily available. For instance, India
Africa Forum summit increased existing credit lines to Africa from $ 2. 15 billion to
$ 5. 4 billion till 2012. The funds are disbursed through India's EXIM
bank. Additional measures include duty free access to 85 percent of India's total tariff
lines; duty access to 9 percent of India's total tariff lines by Africa's 33 LDCs; Zambian Minister for Commerce, Trade and Industry signing the letter of intent to utilise
India's Duty Free Tariff Preference Scheme (DFTP) in May 2010. With the signing of this letter and on completion of documentation, Zambian products gained
access up to 94 percent of the Indian market. Moreover, three institutions are proposed to be established in Zambia: Human Settlement Centre, Entrepreneurship
Development Institute and Cluster of Biomass Gasifier Systems (High Commission
of India, Lusaka).

Both nations have a consistent flow of high level political and business delegations
visiting each other. Such meetings result in new policies to attract entrepreneurs. For
instance, on August 17, 2007, India and Zambia successfully concluded review of
the convention between India and Zambia for avoidance of double taxation. Another case in point is when the Zambian delegation visited India from July
29-August 5, 2010 with the objective of attracting investments from India through

public private partnerships (PPP). The delegation included Deputy Minister of Finance and National Planning David Phiri and Deputy Minister of Commerce Trade and Industry Lwipa Puma. They visited Delhi and Mumbai. Around 30 Indian companies took advantage of the PPP model and entered into various investment portfolios.

According to Commerce, Trade and Industry Minister Felix Mutati, Zambia has benefited from Indian investment worth over $ 3 billion over the past three years. For instance, an Indian company, Shree Renuka, is to invest about $ 200 billion on a turn – key sugarcane plantation and factory to be sited in the southern province of Zambia, which suffers chronic sugar shortage. The company has granted the Mazabuka council an undertaking that it will create 6, 000 new jobs in the rural district and build a sugar factory that will also produce ethanol from sugarcane residues as well as generate power.

4. 3   Field visit in Zambia

During the field visit, the author of this report spoke to several companies that have invested in Zambia. Danma Corporation Ltd, a horticulture enterprise, started operations in January 2011. The owners were earlier in the construction business. They hold 25 acres of land which includes four greenhouse facilities, land, packaging and cold storage. They plant tomatoes, peppers, strawberries, cabbage, carrots, cauliflower and broccoli. The profitable crops are red and yellow bell peppers and strawberries. The seeds used are imported from Korea and South Africa. They have not conducted social or environmental impact assessments to date nor invested in any major infrastructure. Various aspects of the supply chain were: four greenhouses and irrigation facilities were imported from South Korea; coco – peat imported from India and Sri Lanka; red cabbage seeds sourced from Israel; tomato seeds from South Africa; and strawberry plants from local suppliers under a patents related agreement with the University of California. They sought consultancy services from an Israeli agronomist. Their produce is supplied to local markets especially Shoprite, Spar and Pick and Pay and second grade produce goes to the Soweto market. Their plan is to increase the volume of production and export to Angola at higher prices. With regard to labour, they employ 80 people of which 70 per cent are women. One-fourth of them are permanent and they pay labourers 16 kwa a day plus one meal, which works out to about 400 kwa per month. They are members of Zambian National Farmers Union.

The next company the team approached was the Export Trading Group (ETG). Over the past 40 years, ETG has studied agriculture in Ethiopia, Kenya, Tanzania, Uganda, Malawi, Mozambique and Zambia. Founded in 1967 and purchased by its current directors in 1986, ETG owns and manages a vertically integrated agriculture supply chain in Africa, with operations in procurement, processing, warehousing, distribution and merchandising. ETG is based in 45 countries in the world with its group headquarters in Dal-e-Salaam and financial headquarter in Mauritius. ETG has 6, 500 employees in total, with 73 in Zambia. The company is also involved in mid and downstream agriculture processing, cleaning and packaging businesses. ETG currently has 26 such plants operating in Africa and Asia, transforming maize, rice, cashew nuts, wheat, pulses, soybean, sesame seeds, coffee and fertiliser into marketable products for regional and international distribution.

The company's production is over 25 million tonnes a year. It is primarily an agro trading corporation, which imports fertilisers and facilitates crop diversification. ETG focuses on procurement and movement of agricultural goods as well as supply of agricultural inputs and best farming practice support.

In 2002, the group substantially increased investment in agricultural processing. Currently, ETG has 21 processing centres in Zambia, Malawi, Tanzania, Uganda, Ethiopia, India and Mozambique. The agro-processing plants help create jobs for the local communities, earn foreign currency for the countries in which the group operates.

This agro trading firm utilises contract farming: maize procured from small holder farmers, stored in warehouses and then exported to South Africa and Malawi. Seeds and fertilisers at subsidised and fixed rates are provided to small holder agriculture farmers. They are looking to establish a sugar factory soon where they plan to procure sugar from the small holder agriculture farmers. They own a sugar plantation which is about 12,000 ha, of which only 4,000 ha is farmable. Of the 12,000 ha, only 100 ha is being used for production.

Motherson was another firm the team met with. They initially started in the cement manufacturing industry but are now looking to produce wheat and maize. They got involved in agriculture last year. They own 234 ha on a 99-year lease. They produce maize and soya. The owners are planning to bring machinery from India while seed is imported from Thailand and India. To facilitate land acquisition, customary land had to be converted into privately owned state land (Mumbwa, Zambia). More than 200 ha (234 ha) were leased at $500 per ha. They had to negotiate with the headman as well as the chief and paid about $600 per ha. They are unclear about the role of the ZDA in this negotiation. They also pointed out that equipment is more expensive in Zambia because it is a land locked country.

Another company the team approached was Olam. It claims to be a global leader in the supply chain management of agricultural products and food ingredients. Olam has a direct sourcing and processing presence in most major producing countries catering to 13600 customers across the world. The company's team comprises 23,000 people and deals in cocoa, coffee, cashew, sesame, rice, cotton and wood products, says the company's website.

Olam is a multinational company, headquartered in Singapore, but it was started in Nigeria by people of Indian origin. It has presence in 66 countries, of which 24 are in Africa. It employs 1200 workers at any point in time; of which 200 are permanent. Its turnover is $5.5 billion. They have strong links, including a cashew processing factory in Tanzania. Environmental and social impact assessments are conducted and IFC requirements are followed because there are no local laws in Zambia to safeguard rights. CSR activities include 'license from communities', alternate employment opportunities, work on education and health by partnering with NGOs (Solidaridad and others).

Table 5 Stakeholders in Zambia's Agriculture Sector

Indian Companies in Zambia	Government and Public Research and Educational Institutions	Farmer Based organisations
Neha International Ltd.	ASTI Agricultural Research and Development	Zambia Export Growers Association (ZEGA)
Sterling Agriculture Enterprise Zambia limited (SAEL) – a subsidiary company of SP Group of India	Zambia Development Agency (ZDA)	Zambia National Farmers Union (ZNFU)
	Zambia Agricultural Commodities Exchange (ZAMACE)	Organic Producers and Processors Association of Zambia (OPPAZ)
	Ministry of Agriculture and Cooperatives (MACO)	Grain Traders Association of Zambia (GTAZ)
Vedanta Resources	Zambia Land Alliance	Zambia Cotton Ginners Association (ZCGA)
	Zambia Agricultural Research Institute (ZARI)	Zambia Seed Traders Association (ZSTA)
Mohan Exports	National Institute for Scientific and Industrial Research (NISIR)	Conservation Farming Unit (CFU)
	Department of National Agricultural Information Services (NAIS)	Farmer Organisation Support Program (FOSUP)
	University of Zambia, School of Agricultural Sciences Department of Agricultural Economics and Extension	National Peasants and Small – Scale Farmers Association
		Large – Scale Commercial Representative

Section 5   Outline of India Team Research Findings

5. 1   Methodology

For the purpose of this study the research team elaborated the definition of an "Indian company". The team approached companies that are owned and managed by Indians or members of the Indian Diaspora in Zambia. These companies are not necessarily based in India, with most of them headquartered overseas and their activities extending to various parts of the world including India. For instance, Danma Corporation Ltd started operations in January 2011 in Lusaka. Similarly, ETG is headquartered in Dar-e-Salaam, with its financial headquarters in Mauritius.

For the purpose of critical assessment of the larger impacts of these companies, it was decided not to use the yardsticks provided in the NVGs (National Voluntary Guidelines) of the Ministry of Corporate Affairs, Government of India, 2011. These Guidelines are inappropriate as they were expressly designed for the Indian context, taking into consideration mandatory Indian laws related to land acquisition, labour, minimum wage, environment etc. The same Guidelines have been extended to cover the activities of companies operating outside India, where such laws are either entirely absent, weak or different. Besides, these Guidelines were primarily framed by corporate India, in consultation with (and not in agreement with) other stake holders and notified as such by Government of India. In terms of enforcement, even within India, they are required to operate on "apply or explain" basis. Therefore, the imperatives for their compliance overseas are either nonexistent or very weak. As a result, the methodology to understand the impacts of private sector investment in agriculture was to examine them within the statutory, legal and local regulations as given and monitored by bodies like Zambia Land Development Agency and others.

Table 6　Information on the companies interviewed

Company	Danma Corporation Limited	ETG Trading Company Limited	Motherson Enterprises Limited	Olam International Limited
Back ground	Company started operations in January 2011; Earlier involved in construction business 25 acres of land; First sale/yield in September 2011; Four greenhouses facilities, land, packaging and cold storage; Horticulture: tomatoes, peppers, strawberries, cabbage, carrots, cauliflower, broccoli; Profitable crops: red and yellow bell peppers, strawberries; Plans for agro-processing soon (tomato sauce), providing salad packs Seeds are imported from Korea, South Africa; 25 acres purchased at USD 8,000/acre; Sub-leased land, state land: 76 years left (original title holder local Zambian farmer. Unclear who holds the title)	East African company Group HQ – Dar – e – Salaam, Financial Headquarters – Mauritius; Based in 45 countries in the world – 30 in Africa; 6,500 employees in total: 73 in Zambia – ETG increases local employment and adds value to local economies by investing in mid – and downstream agriculture processing, cleaning and packaging businesses. ETG currently has 26 such plants operating in Africa and Asia, transforming maize, rice, cashew nuts, wheat, pulses, soybean, sesame seeds, coffee and fertiliser into marketable products for regional and international distribution. Production over 25 million tonnes/year; Agro trading – Import fertilizers – They facilitate crop diversification – 12,000 hectares of land, cultivate sugar cane and pigeon peas; No agreements with ZDA They facilitate crop diversification. They are actively following up various CSR activities	Initially started in the cement manufacturing industry Looking to produce wheat and maize Got involved in agriculture last year 234 hectares of land – 99 year lease Produce: Maize, soya; The firm is planning to bring machinery from India; Seed is imported from Thailand and India	Multinational company (HQ: Singapore) but Indian management and PIOs Started in Nigeria by people of Indian origin; Based in 66 countries, 24 in Africa; 1200 workers at any point in time; 200 are permanent Supply chain managers/ contract farming model – link between SHA farmers and raw material consumers (Nestle, Kraft and Mars) Turnover $5.5 billion – Present in 66 countries – 26 African – Strong forward linkages – They have a cashew processing factory in Tanzania; In Zambia: maize, wheat, sugar and cotton produced locally, inputs provided by Olam; Services provided to SHA farmers: inputs, training, knowledge in best practice; Agro – processing: cotton, cashews; Own coffee plantation near Kasama – 2000 ha. Brownfield site but without infrastructure; Environmental and social impact assessments conducted, followed IFC requirements, requirements as per national law are weak; CSR activities – 'license from communities': alternate employment opportunities, education, health through NGO partnerships (Solidaridad and others)

Company	Danma Corporation Limited	ETG Trading Company Limited	Motherson Enterprises Limited	Olam International Limited
Supply chains	Four greenhouses and irrigation facilities imported from South Korea; Coco – peat imported from India and Sri Lanka; Red cabbage seeds sourced from Israel, tomato seeds from South Africa; Strawberry plants: agreement with local suppliers (who have an agreement with University of California) Consultancy services sought from an Israeli agronomist; Produce is supplied to local markets; Major: Shoprite, Spar and Pick and Pay Also second grade produce goes to the Soweto market; Future plans: to increase volume of production and export to Angola (higher prices)	It owns and manages the most vertically integrated agriculture supply chain on the African subcontinent with operations spanning in procurement, processing, warehousing, distribution and merchandising.		It has included small scale farmers within their supply chain. This is aimed to improve farmers' income, transfer agriculture and business skill to farmers, developing thriving communities through improvement in local infrastructure and providing practical solutions to issues such as food security, water constrains etc. They work with large – scale farmers to embed sustainable agricultural practice specialty in the areas of water, carbon and energy. The goal is to increase yield so as to maximise agricultural land utilisation. These yield increases a need to be achieved without increasing the use of fertiliser and water. Trageted drip irrigation facilities are used to ensure " more crop per drop"
Labour	80 people employed, 70% women20/80 (one fourth): permanent; Member of Zambian National Farmers Union; Pay labourers 16 kwa/ day plus one meal (works out to about 400 kwa per month)	120 Zambian labourers –80 permanent; They pay casual labourer 30 Kwacha/per diem		

续表

Company	Danma Corporation Limited	ETG Trading Company Limited	Motherson Enterprises Limited	Olam International Limited
Production Model	Agro – trading: maize, sugar, soya, groundnut Contract farming: (upto 10000 hectares; there is no regulation) Maize procured from small holder farmers, stored in warehouses and then exported to South Africa, Malawi Seeds and fertilisers at subsidised and fixed rates provided to SHA farmers; Looking to establish a sugar factory (agro – processing) soon (procuring sugar from the small holder agriculture) Owns a sugar plantation which is about 12000 ha of which only 4000 ha is farmable Of the 12000 ha only 100 ha is being used for production ZDA's role in facilitating investments – limited in success In the future – crop diversification as a means to reduce fertiliser use (partnering with local NGO) and promote production of pigeon – peas; Four crucial steps to ensure sustainable growth in the future: Providing Bigger Markets for Existing Small Growers New Products and Regions Adding Value via Vertical Integration	Agro – processing and packaging are its specialisation. They also facilitate crop diversification and import fertilisers. They buy seed and produce it locally but it is made for international consumption. Therefore a large chunk of the produce is exported; They engage small scale farmers	Phasing out production – 40 ha (ready for cultivation) out of 234 ha; Anticipated volume: $2,500 per yield of maize; Plans to import equipment from India; seeds from Thailand and India; For the 40 ha, looking to invest $40000; expecting to earn 2.5 times as much, recoup in four months (maize); Maize to be supplied to local chains	One of the leading players in the global rice trade, OLAM is involved across the entire value chain from origination to distribution; has several innovative ideas. For example, its Nigerian operation, Olam Nigeria Limited, recently adopted a production model endorsed by the Rockefeller Foundation which is poised to deliver 16,000 tonnes of rice annually by 2018

续表

Company	Danma Corporation Limited	ETG Trading Company Limited	Motherson Enterprises Limited	Olam International Limited
Land acquisition			Customary land had to be converted into privately owned — state land (Mumbwa) 234 ha leased at 500 $/ha Had to negotiate with the headman as well as the chief, paid approx. $600/ha; Unclear about the role of the ZDA in this negotiation; Displacement of people — has promised electricity, construction of schools, outgrowing schemes Equipment more expensive in Zambia because it is a land locked country	

5.2　Zambia Development Agency

The Zambia Development Agency (ZDA) was established in 2006 by an act of Parliament and became operational in January 2007 after the amalgamation of five statutory bodies that hitherto operated independently to foster economic growth and development by promoting trade and investment through an efficient, effective and coordinated private sector led economic development strategy. These institutions were the Zambia Investment Centre (ZIC), Zambia Privatisation Agency (ZPA), Export Board of Zambia (EBZ), Small Enterprise Development Board (SEDB) and Zambia Export Processing Zones Authority

(ZEPZA). Their mandate is to monitor pre-and pro-investment facilities, bring investors and train and pursue them. They are active in diversification of economic resources and looking at developing other sectors besides copper. They are also keen on building PPPs.

The act gives powers to the ZDA in key areas of trade development, investment promotion, enterprise restructuring, development of green fields' projects, small and enterprise development, trade and industry fund management, and contributing to skills training development.

The amalgamated agency is therefore a semi autonomous institution with its board of directors appointed by the Minister of Commerce Trade and Industry. The board comprises members of the public and private sector as well as civil society organisations, while both the chairperson and the vice chairperson are appointed from the private sector. The organisation has its head office in Lusaka and regional offices in Chipata, Kitwe, Kasama, Livingstone, Mansa, Solwezi and Mongu. The functions of ZDA are as follows.

- *The ZDA is responsible for fostering economic growth and development in Zambia by promoting trade and investment and an efficient, effective and coordinated private sector led economic development strategy.*
- *The agency also has the challenge to develop an internationally competitive Zambian economy through innovations that promote high skills, productive investment and increased trade.*
- *The ZDA principally furthers the economic development by promoting efficiency, investment and competitiveness in businesses, as well as promoting exports. It also addresses the high cost of doing business in the country by simplifying the processing of various business formalities, such as licensing.*
- *It builds and enhances the country's investment profile for increased capital inflows, capital formation and employment creation. It also promotes the growth of the SME sector by providing incentives that can propel long – term sustainable domestic growth.*

- *ZDA is a one stop shop for all investors and it is evident that Zambia is open for all to do business.*

During the team's interactions with various company heads it was pointed out that ZDA has assisted and facilitated several investors. They also facilitate and make a-vailable work permits. One of the functions of ZDA is to convert customary land to statutory land. In the district level there are two committees that carry out random survey of land. According to an official in the ZDA, the chiefs can give only 250 ha and the rest is up to the state. They also encourage integrated farming, involving growing, processing and marketing. They have introduced farming blocs in 10 provinces. Government facilitates infrastructure building for farm blocs.

5. 3   Zambia Land Alliance

Zambia Land Alliance is a network of seven NGOs working for just land policies and laws that take into account the interests of the poor in Zambia. The NGOs have branches in different districts. It was formed in 1997 primarily in response to the government land law. NGOs wanted to protect customary land. They did not want multinational companies to invest in these lands. Although under customary law an individual has no right to buy or sell land, it was found that certain chiefs were selling land to private companies.

The natives of the customary land believed they had a right over their land. However, the customary system is informal and the government is seeking to systematise the process and bring it under state control. The alliance promotes secured access, ownership and control over land through lobbying and advocacy, research and community participation. According to the organisation's website, the overall objectives include lobbying and advocating for inclusive policies, laws and administrative systems; conducting research on land related issues; stepping up awareness on land rights, gender etc; and networking and collaborating with a range of organisations to share experiences on land issues.

5. 4   Observations and Findings from the Field Visit

- *The share of India' s investment in agriculture sector in Zambia is very small. It is not backed by Indian government. These are mainly individual investments.*

- *One has to differentiate between India' s investment and investment by Indian diaspora population in Zambia.*

- *South African and Zimbabwean farmers are main competitors of Indian farms.*

- *Indian farmers suffer losses because of fluctuation of market price for agricultural produce and lack of forward linkages.*

- *Only 6 per cent of Zambia' s land belongs to the State. The remaining is customary. The government of Zambia is looking to reformulate land policies to facilitate privatisation of customary land rights. In 1995, Zambian government enacted a pro – investment law to attract foreign investment. Consequently, large tracts of customary land were converted to private tenure because of increasing foreign investments.*

- *Investors access land by acquiring leasehold title in the form of provisional certificate which is valid not exceeding 14 years. After six years upon submission of the boundary survey in accordance with the procedure stipulated in the 1971 survey procedure investors may apply for 99 years' certificate title which is non – contestable.*

- *While land act recognises existing rights to land in customary areas, it also enables foreign investors to convert land in customary areas to leasehold and to acquire title.*

- *For acquiring land, investors either seek consent directly from the chief with consultation of the village headman or a lands working group with the ministry of lands and ZDA negotiates land transfer on behalf of the investors. If acquisition is approved, the chief issues an approval letter. The investors then carry out physical demarcation of the area with a sketch map in the presence of village headman. Both are submitted to the district council. The council issues a letter of recommendation to the commissioner of lands, who either recommends or sends it to the president for approval.*

- *In recent years the government has embarked on a number of initiatives to encourage foreign investors under Private Sector Development Reform Programme. These include*:

— *A land working group comprising ZDA and Ministry of Land*

— *Supporting farm block development programme*

- *No protests have been recorded arising from re – allotment or displacement of land so far.*

Section 6   Interviews in Delhi

As part of the field visit in Delhi the research team interviewed government officials, private agencies and NGOs. Observations after interacting with them have been thematically arranged in this section. The respondents provided insights on Indian investments in Africa and Zambia. While CII and FICCI were optimistic about the Indian government's engagement in Africa and have taken several initiatives to promote this, the NGOs views were quite the contrary. Officials from the Ministry of External Affairs were difficult to reach even after repeated attempts of getting in touch with them. The Zambian consulate in Mumbai and the embassy in Delhi were not cooperative either. No documents were available at the consulate in Mumbai on this topic.

6. 1   Promoting India – Africa Economic Cooperation

According to Ms. Indrayani Mulay, Deputy Director, CII, it is one of the most important organisations that provides a platform for cooperation between India and Africa. Ms. Mulay provided details regarding the 9th CII – EXIM Bank Conclave on India Africa Project Partnership held from March 17 – 19, 2013 in New Delhi which presented a different dimension to the India Africa Relations in the economic sector. The outcomes of the sessions on agriculture included:

- *A session on ' Building Partnerships for Infrastructure and Agricultural Projects ' headed by Mr. Naresh Kumar Sharma, Head Marketing Communications, Tata Projects Ltd. and Mr. Amit Sridharan, GM and Business Head – Pulses, Tata Chemicals.*

- *A plenary session, moderated by Mr. Sanjay Kirloskar, Chairman and Managing Director, Kirloskar Brothers Ltd. , on the theme "Achieving Food Sufficiency in Africa – Opportunity for Collaboration", focused on food security as a common concern for both India and Africa.*

- *Discussions took place on the various steps needed to boost Indian investments in Africa's agriculture sector.*

- *Questions such as: Are Indian farm technologies suited for making Africa a global food basket and in what ways can India and African countries step up cooperation in agriculture R&D, were raised.*

- *A session on Zambia was held which focused on how the bilateral trade and investment could be enhanced.*

- *Officials of Zambia from different ministries including Dr. Guy Scott, Vice President, Republic of Zambia attended the conclave.*

- *Dr Guy Scott, Vice President, Republic of Zambia, said in his address that African economies should look to emulate India's industrial growth experience. He urged Indian companies to invest in Africa and in particular Zambia, by adding that Africa offers the highest returns.*

- *Day three of the conclave witnessed a session on "Developing Partnership in Mobility, Power and Farm Tech Prosperity".*

- *The conclave was declared a success since at the end of the conference since there were 475 projects worth $64 billion on the table, compared to the 8th edition where projects worth $30 billion were declared.*

CII though could not provide concrete figures of the post conclave events and follow ups because the delegates did not come back to them to confirm their partnership. Ms. Mulay further stated that Indian aid to African countries especially in agriculture sector is not properly channelled. Alongside investments, India should also empower and train locals, especially rural women as this would add a social element and create a positive India branding if India is considering long term business opportunities. She also spoke of CII's Mission Africa, where CII Regional Business Delegation visited Zambia, South Africa and Kenya from June 22 – July 2, 2013. In an attempt to make a strong case for India, particularly the eastern region, and to facilitate regular exchanges of dialogues, promote deeper understanding and forge strategic partnerships, a 14 – member delegation, led by Mr Sandipan Chakravortty, former chairman, CII eastern region, went on a business mission. During the 11 – day visit, the delegation interacted with local industry leaders, chambers of commerce, government officials and diplomats. The aim of the mission was to enhance bilateral trade and business, interact with local industry leaders, chambers of commerce, government officials in South Africa, Zambia and Kenya, and also explore investment opportunities for Indian companies. The focus was on getting the African countries to engage more deeply with India.

The CII delegation rounded off its visit to Zambia with an MoU with the Lusaka Chamber of Commerce & Industry (LCCI). On behalf of CII, Mission Leader Mr Sandipan Chakravortty and Mr G Rossi, President, LCCI, signed the MoU. CII and LCCI agreed that as part of their common commitment to developing bilateral trade and commerce and promoting investments, they would assist each other in promotion and development of business opportunities. They would exchange information on all economic, commercial, industrial and agricultural matters and promote investment.

According to Ms. Kaveri Ganguly from CII – FACE, with technical partner as US-AID, they endeavour to build capacity while leveraging technology and innovation to improve productivity and the environmental footprint of agriculture. Ms. Ganguly gave a brief of their present venture which is working towards capacity building measures in collaboration with Tata Motors in agriculture sector of Kenya, Malawi and Liberia. But they would pursue their future ventures in Zambia, Kenya and Ethiopia as well.

6. 2　Beyond Food Security

On February 6, 2013 the Indian Social Action Forum (INSAF), Kalpavriksh, PEACE, and The Oakland Institute convened a day-long civil society summit at the India International Centre, New Delhi, bringing together activists re-
sisting land grab across India and Ethiopia. According to the aforementioned institutions the meeting provided a groundbreaking opportunity for dialogue among
Ethiopian small farmers and land rights activists and their Indian counterparts,
providing space for those directly affected by landgrab to share their experiences,
suffering and collectively strategise to challenge institutional and corporate land
grabbers.

Mr. Chowdhary divulged that they have been working on the issue of land
grabbing extensively and the purpose of the meeting was to provide a platform to
the affected countries to voice their opinions. He also put in the picture of various
factors that are driving the India foreign investments in agriculture. These include
India's food security concerns, mounting water shortage in India and profit mo-
tive.

6. 3　Indian Investment in Zambian Agriculture

Food security is not the only driving factor of India outsourcing food production. Indian companies are attracted to Africa because of low cost of farming
there. Developing countries like Zambia are also inviting foreign firms to invest in the
country. Zambia's move towards economic diversification is important to reduce reliance on a single commodity (copper). Other stated reasons for investment in agriculture focus include: to improve food security (at national and household level);
to increase exports earnings; and to continue economic reforms required under
World Bank's Structural Adjustment Programme.

Zambia has created an attractive investment climate through numerous incentives, including low levels of taxation. The relative low cost of land (particularly if obtained directly from chiefs) in the absence of a well – established land market, as well as the lack of limitations on water, perceived abundance of land and water with favourable growing conditions, central location to Southern African markets and political stability are also cited as reasons that make Zambia attractive to investors.

Numerous incentives are available to investors in the agriculture sector:

- *No tax on profits for a period of five years from the first year the profits are made. From years six to eight, only 50 per cent of the profits will be taxed, and from years nine to 10, 75 per cent of the profits will be taxed*
- *No tax on dividends for a period of five years from the first year dividends are declared*
- *Customs duty exemption on capital equipment and machinery*
- *Reduced or free duty on imports of certain raw materials including organic and inorganic fertilisers and pesticides*
- *Numerous other tax incentives including wear and tear allowance of 50 per cent per year on machinery used for farming; capital expenditure allowance of 20 per cent per year for the first five years on farming improvement; capital expenditure allowance on the growing of coffee, tea, bananas, citrus fruits or similar plants qualify for a development allowance of 10 per cent per year up to the second year of production; and farm work allowance of 100 per cent for expenditure on farm land such as stumping, clearing prevention of soil erosion, boreholes, wells water conservation and aerial or geophysical survey.*
- *Fifty percent depreciation allowance per year for the first two years on machinery used for farming.*
- *Twenty percent capital expenditure allowance per year for the first five years on farm improvements.*
- *Ten percent development allowance per year, up to the first year of production, on capital expenditure incurred for the purpose of growing coffee, tea, bananas, citrus fruits or similar*

plants.

These are only a handful of packages provided to the investors according to the ZDA Act.

Mr. Chowdhary said according to the work done by their NGO, Indian government has supported a host of various initiatives to facilitate Indian agriculture companies in their overseas investments in Africa through support for conventional new greenfield foreign direct investment, mergers and acquisitions, purchase of existing firms, tariff reductions on import of agriculture products, public private partnership, double taxation avoidance agreements and lines of credit where foreign investors win concessions and contracts.

The brunt of land acquisitions have been borne by the local people. As reported by different sources the daily labourers complain of inhuman behaviour and low wages, issues created due to highly mechanised technologies with limited employment creation, the environment is depleting due to chemical contamination and adverse effects on land and water due to poor production practices.

6.4　The Other Side of the Engagement

Mr. R. Sreedhar said the corporate sector is looking for countries in which government structures are fragile and weak. In 2007 Vedanta Resources bought stakes in Konkola Copper Mines in Zambia for $ 48. 3 million and paid $ 25. 3 million and signed a contract in which every year $ 5 million has to be paid. In 2008, the company earned a profit worth $ 208 million. Since the past few years Indian companies have not been very eagerly investing in Zambia as the mining Industry in India is also going through a bad phase. "India should not advance aggressively through corporate sector as India has the capacity of global stewardship for it possesses the potential to work on organic and skill development," he concluded.

Mr Puljal enlightened that the reason African countries are lacking in land investments is due to non-mapping of land before making it available for lease. He added that small land acquisitions are more successful than large acquisitions. He even named some companies which have acquired 100, 000 hectares of land are not being able to fully capitalise the potential thus proving a farce deal for the host country. In addition, the pessimistic milieu created under the name of land grabbing to an extent has been due to projection of technology and investment of seed capital followed by raising funds and eventually not investing them in projects.

Mr. Puljal believes there are some lacunae in policies that should be addressed urgently. He suggested that the government should help and promote SMEs more in land investment. Another point he referred was that the Banda regime in Zambia was pro-China due to which the influx of Chinese investors in land and agriculture was prominent but the present regime is open to all investors especially India which was apparent in the recent CII-EXIM bank conclave.

6.5   India, a crucial player

India holds 4. 5 million hectares of African land and is perceived to be a significant player in farmland acquisitions. Its investments in Zambia though are still in a nascent stage. Nevertheless it would seem that there is growing investor interest due to a number of incentives offered by the Zambian government. Also, Indian investments in Zambia appear to be less controversial, relative to Ethiopia or Madagascar, where large-scale land acquisitions by foreign countries have led to visible cases of land related displacements. Zambia has the gift of large tracts of agricultural land on offer and the opportunity to acquire land is enormous. Add to that the fact that the Zambian government has created an attractive investment climate through numerous incentives, including low levels of taxation. The National Agricultural Policy too has facilitated an increase of FDI in the country's agricultural sector. Consequently, foreign companies are investing in large numbers. In the case of India, organisations such as FICCI and CII as well as government programmes such as Focus Africa have furthered Indian industry's interests in Zambia. Zambia has a comparatively more stable political and economic environment, which serves an important incentive for industry.

Indian agriculture companies are in various stages of operation in Zambia. Some, such as Champions Food Limited, are not fully functional, while others, such as Danma Corporation Ltd., have only recently begun their operations in Zambia. Whilst this study offers a preliminary, conceptual framework to better understand the nature and modalities of Indian agro-investments in Zambia, there is a need to conduct further analytical and detailed socio-economic impact assessments of these investments. Anecdotal evidence collected during field visits suggests that negative impacts such as displacements may have been limited in Zambia so far. However, systematic evidence is lacking, making it difficult to assess whether and how these investments have reduced rural poverty and improved the livelihoods of small holder farmers. Furthermore, in the absence of both a coherent land acquisition-related displacement and resettlement policy in Zambian law, and binding mechanisms within the Indian context that regulates Indian corporate activity overseas, the risk of 'land grabbing' in the future remains quite high. Whilst not an immediate threat, it may well become one if current investment trends continue and Indian corporates are not held accountable for compliance with social, economic and environmental safeguards.

References

African Union, *Africa India Framework for Cooperation*, 2008, http: //summits. au. int/en/sites/default/files/AFRICA - INDIA% 20 FRAMEWORK% 20FOR% 20COOPERATION% 20 ENGLISH% 20 - % 20FINAL% 20VERSION. doc (Accessed: 6 June 2013).

Address by Shri H R Khan, Deputy Governor of the Reserve Bank of India, at the Bombay Chamber of Commerce & Industry, Mumbai, 2 March 2012. http: //

rbidocs. rbi. org. in/rdocs/Speeches/PDFs/OV27022012. pdf （ Accessed: 6 June 2013）.

African nations offering land for free to Indian farmers, 11 July 2010, Moneylife （online news）, See http: //www. moneylife. in/article/african - nations - offering - land - for - free - to - indian - farmers/8105. html （Accessed on Aug 10 2013）

African Manager, Indian firm invests US $ 200 billion on sugar in Zambia, See http: //www. africanmanager. com/site_ eng/detail_ article. php? art_ id = 11866 （Accessed on Aug 10 2013）

Business Standard, "India and US partner to help improve agriculture in Africa", July 30 2013.

Christin Gerlach and Pascal Liu, Resource - Seeking Foreign Direct Investment In African Agriculture: A Review Of Country Case Studies, Fao Commodity And Trade Policy Research Working Paper No. 31, See

http: //www. fao. org/fileadmin/templates/est/PUBLICATIONS/Comm _ Working_ Papers/EST - WP31. pdf （Accessed: 6 June 2013）.

CII - EXIM Bank Conclave on India - Africa, 2013. 9 th CII - EXIM Bank Conclave on India - Africa Project Partnership. （ online ） Available at: http: // www. ciiafricaconclave. com/images/Report% 20% 20 - % 209th% 20CII - EXIM% 20Bank% 20India - Africa% 20Conclave% 202013. pdf （Accessed: 16 Jul 2013）.

Ecumenical Service for Advocacy work on Southern Africa （KASA）. 2011. Land Grabbing - A " Shopping tour" through Africa. （online） Available at: http: // www. woek. de/web/cms/upload/pdf/kasa/publikationen/kramer_ 2011_ land_ grabbing_ en. pdf （Accessed: 16 Jul 2013）.

Dheeraj Tiwari & Rituraj Tiwari, "Food Security: Govt Mulls Private Purchase of Farm Land Abroad ", The Economic Times, 5 March 2012. See http: // articles. economictimes. indiatimes. com/2012 - 03 - 05/news/31124242_ 1_ farm - land - food - processing - pulses （Accessed on May 1 2013）

Emma Mawdsely and Gerard (eds.), *India in Africa: Changing Geographies of Power* (Pambazuka Press: Nairobi, 2011) .

German Institute of Global and Area Studies (GIGA). 2013. Large – Scale Agricultural Investments under Poor Land Governance Systems: Actors and Institutions in the Case of Zambia. GIGA Research Programme: Socio – Economic Challenges in the Context of Globalisation, Working paper No. 221. (report) Germany: GIGA. Available at: http: //www. giga – hamburg. de/dl/download. php? d =/ content/publikationen/pdf/wp221_ knolte. pdf (Accessed: 8 Jul 2013) .

Government of India, Focus Africa, Investment oppertunties: Zambia, See http: //focusafrica. gov. in/Investment_ Opportunities_ in_ Zambia. html (Accessed on May 1 2013) .

Goswami, R. (2010) "African landrush", Infochange News & Features, 5 April.

High Commission of India, Lusaka, India – Zambia Bilateral Relations, Available at: http: //www. hcizambia. com/india – zambia% 20bilateral% 20relations. htm, (Accessed: 6th July, 2013).

Haralambous, S. , Liversage, H. and Romano, M. , ' The Growing Demand for Land Risks and Opportunities for Smallholder Farmers ' , IFAD, Discussion Paper prepared for the Round Table 2 organized during the Thirty – second session of IFAD's Governing Council, 18 February 2009, Available at: http: // www. ifad. org/events/gc/32/roundtables/2. pdf, (Accessed: 1 July, 2013).

High Commission of India, Lusaka, See http: //www. hcizambia. com/india – zambia% 20bilateral% 20relations. htm (Accessed: 1 July, 2013).

Harun R. Khan, Deputy Governor, Reserve Bank of India at the Bombay Chamber of Commerce & Industry, Mumbai on March 2, 2012. (Speech)

Haggblade J. , Steven Joe, "Food Security Collaborative Policy Briefs. 2013. Returns to Investment in Agriculture", (online) Available at: http: //econpapers. repec. org/paper/agsmidcpb/54625. htm (Accessed: 8 Jul 2013) .

Indo – African Chamber of Commerce & Industries, 'Business Opportunities & Challenges In African Agri – Food Sector' See http：//www. indoafrican. org/iacci – agro2. html（Accessed：6 June 2013）.

India and US partner to help improve agriculture in Africa, Business Standard, July 30 2013, See http：//www. business – standard. com/article/news – ians/india – and – us – partner – to – help – improve – agriculture – in – africa – 113073000690_ 1. html（Accessed on May 1 2013）

ICRISAT. 2013. *Platform for India – Africa Partnership in Agriculture announced.*（online）Available at：http：//www. icrisat. org/newsroom/latest – news/happenings/ happenings1577. htm（Accessed：18 Jul 2013）.

ICAR, *ICAR signed MoU with the Ethiopian Institute for Agricultural Research*, See http：//www. icar. org. in/node/4151（Accessed：6 June 2013）.

Indian Embassy, Addis Ababa, 'Agricultural Scholarships', See http：// www. indianembassy. gov. et/? q = agricultural（Accessed：16 August 2013）.

Kinfu, A. , Sharkey, T. and Okoroafo, S. 2013. Analyzing Indian Policies and Firm Strategies in Africa. Journal of Management Research, 5（3）, pp. 17 – 27.

K. R. Balasubramanyam, An ambition pricked：Ram Karuturi mulls taking his rose – to – maize company private as its stock shows no signs of bouncing back, Business Today, Edition：April 14, 2013（Accessed：6 June 2013）.

Ministry of Commerce and Industry. Trade Promotion Programme – Focus：Africa, Government of India, Available from < http：//commerce. nic. in/trade/international_ tpp_ africa_ 1. asp > ,（Accessed：16 July 2013）.

Mamta B Chowdhury, 'India's Outward Foreign Direct Investment：Closed Doors to Open Souk', See http：//mpra. ub. uni – muenchen. de/32828/Ministry of External Affairs, *Philosophy of the Forum Sum*mit, Government of India, Available from：< http：//meaindia. nic. in/indiaafricasummit/ > ,（Accessed：16 July 2013）

MEA, India & Africa Partners in Development ：Capacity Building Programmes & Lines of Credit

Mozambique: *Exim Bank of India Opens* $217 *Million Credit Line*, http: //allafri-ca. com/stories/201307090302. html (Accessed: 6 June 2013).

Mhlanga, Nomathemba, Private Sector agribusiness investment in sub – Saharan Africa , Agricultural Management, Marketing and Finance Working Docu-ment. Available at www. fao. org/docrep/016/k7443e/k7443e. pdf (Accessed: 16th July, 2013.)

Mujenja, Fison and Wonani, Charlott (2012), "Long – term outcomes of agri-cultural investments: Lessons from Zambia", International Institute for Environment and Development. Available at: http: //pubs. iied. org/pdfs/12571IIED. pdf (Ac-cessed: 6th July, 2013).

Ministry of External Affairs, India – Zambia Relations, Government of India, A-vailable at: http: //mea. gov. in/Portal/ForeignRelation/India – Zambia _ Rela-tions. pdf, (Accessed: 6th July, 2013).

Ministry of Commerce Trade and Industry (MCTI), An Investment Guide to Zambia Opportunities and Conditions 2011, Government of Zambia, Available at: www. mcti. gov. zm (Accessed: 1 July, 2013).

Organisation for Economic Co-operation and Development (OECD), Zambia's Policy Framework for Investment – OECD. Available at: www. oecd. org/daf/inv/investmentfordevelopment/47662751. pdf (Accessed: 1 July, 2013).

Pradhan, Jaya Prakash (2007), Trends and Patterns of Overseas Acquisition by Indian Multinational. Available at http: //isidev. nic. in/pdf/WP0710. pdf accessed on 16th July, 2013 (Accessed: 16 July 2013).

Pattanaik, R. K. and Bhargavi, 2011. "Outward Foreign Direct Investment: An Indian Perspective. Maharashtra Economic Development council", *Monthly Economic Digest*, pp. 5 – 13.

Parul Mittal, Sandeep Aggarwal, "Analysis Of Fdi Inflows And Outflows In Indi-a", *ZENITH International Journal of Business Economics & Management Research* 2 (7), July 2012, See http: //zenithresearch. org. in/images/stories/pdf/2012/JULY/ZI-

BEMR/20 _ ZIBEMR _ vol2 _ issue7 _ july2012. pdf (Accessed: 26 August 2013).

Parthapratim Pal, 'The Surge of Indian Outbound Foreign Direct Investment to Africa: A new Form of South – South Cooperation?' in Karl P. Sauvant, Jaya Prakash Pradhan, Ayesha Chatterjee, Brian Harley (eds.), *The Rise of Indian Multi-nationals: Perspectives on Indian Outward Foreign Direct Investment* (London: Palgrave Macmillan, 2010) .

Ramchandani, R, 1900. *India Africa Relations: Issues and policy option*, New Delhi: Kalinga. Ajay, D, 2010. *Trends in Indo – African relations. New Delhi:* ASA and Manas, Biswas, Aparajita, 2013, *India – Africa Enduring Partnership: Emerging Areas of Cooperation*, New Delhi: Gyan. . Taylor, I. 2012. *India's Rise in Africa.* International Affairs, 88 (4), pp. 779 – 798. , Alden, C and Maxi, S. 2013. *South Africa in the company of giants: the search for leadership in a transforming global order*, International affairs, 89 (1), pp. 111 – 129. , Eriksen, S, Biswas, A, Dubey, A, Eggen, O and Qobo, M. (2012). *India in Africa Implications for Norwegian Foreign and Development Policies.* Available from: http: //english. nupi. no/Publications/ Books – and – reports/2012/India – in – Africa (Accessed: 16 July 2013)

Rowden, R. 2011, *India's role in the New Global Farmland Grab.* (report) New Delhi: GRAIN and Economics Reserach Foundation.

Ramamurti, R. and Singh, J. 2010. *Emerging Multi Nationals In Emerging Markets.* Cambridge: Cambridge University.

Sauvant, K. and Pradhan, J. 2010. *The Rise of Indian Multinationals: Perspectives On Indian Outward Foreign Direct Investment.* New York: Palgrave Macmillan.

18 Pedersen, J. 2008. "The Second Wave of Indian Investments Abroad", *Journal of Contemporary Asia*, 38 (4), pp. 613 – 637.

Singh, Lakhwinder, and Jain Varinder (2010), 'Emerging Pattern of India's Outward Foreign Direct Investment under Influence of State Policy: A Macro – view', MPRA (Munich Personal re – PEC Archive) Paper No. 13439, Available at: http://mpra. ub. uni - muenchen. de/13439/1/MPRA_ paper_ 13439. pdf (Accessed: 16th July, 2013).

Second Africa - India Forum Summit 2011, Addis Ababa, Africa - India Framework for Enhanced Cooperation. http://indiaafricasummit. nic. in/staticfile/framework - en. pdf, Plan of Action of The Framework For Cooperation of The India - Africa Forum Summit 2008, Delhi, India www. indianembassy. gov. et/.../Joint% 20Plan% 20of% 20Action. doc (Accessed: 6 June 2013).

"The Growing Demand for Land Risks and Opportunities for Smallholder Farmers", Discussion Paper prepared for the Round Table organized during The Thirty - second session of IFAD's Governing Council, 18 February 2009.

The Oakland Institute. 2013. Understanding Land Investment Deals in Africa: Country Report - Zambia. (online) Available at: http://www. oaklandinstitute. org/sites/oaklandinstitute. org/files/OI_ country_ report_ zambia. pdf (Accessed: 8 Jul 2013).

The Guardian, Claire Provost, "New international land deals database reveals rush to buy up Africa", 2012. See http://www. theguardian. com/global - development/2012/apr/27/international - land - deals - database - africa? guni = Article: in% 20body% 20link (Accessed: 10 February 2014).

UNCTAD, World Investment Report 2013, See http://unctad. org/sections/dite_ dir/docs/wir2013/wir13_ fs_ in_ en. pdf (Accessed: 10 February 2014)

UK Department for International Development (DFID), Jamie Morrision, Dirk Bezemer and Catherine Arnold, Official development assistance to agriculture, November 2004, See http://dfid - agriculture - consultation. nri. org/summaries/wp9. pdf (Accessed on May 1 2013).

Stein Sunstol Eriksen, Aparajita Biswas and Ajay Dubey, "India in Africa: Implications for Norwegian Foreign and Development Policies", NUPI Report.

Zambia Development Agency, Zambia Agriculture Sector Profile, 2011, See http://www. zda. org. zm/sites/default/files/Sector% 20Profile% 20 -% 20Agriculture.

pdf （Accessed on May 1 2013）

Zambia seeks Indian investment in agriculture. Lusaka Times, （online） 5 August. Available at: http: //www. lusakatimes. com/2010/08/05/zambia − seeks − indian − investment − agriculture/ （Accessed: 6 June 2013）.

Annexure

Annexe 1   What research was done and how

Dates and details of contacts and meetings （farm visits, and others etc. ）; name of contact and contact information （email, phone number etc）.

Company	Action and Response	Name of contact/Position	Contact information
Danma Corporation Limited	16 September 2013/Formal meeting/ Farm Visit	Dhruv Singh/Managing Director	+260 973 310 738 Dhruv. danmacorp@ gmail. com
Olam International Limited	19 September 2013/Formal meeting/Visited their office	Varun Mahajan/Country Head	+260 974 770631 varun. mahajan@ olamnet. com
Astro Holdings Ltd	17 September/Formal Meeting/Visited their office	SM Arora/Executive Director	+260 211 229939 arora@ astroholdings. co. zm
ETG	17 September/Formal Meeting/Visited their office	Mahesh Patel	
Indian Business Council of Zambia	17 September 2013/Formal Meeting/Visited their office	Teza Sikasula and Binod P. Menon/Administration Manager/Executive Secretary	+260 977 781168 ibczsecretariat@ gmail. com
Indian High Commission	18 September 2013/Formal Meeting/Visited their office	Mr. J. S. Variaah/Acting High Commissioner	info. lusaka@ mea. gov. in

续表

Company	Action and Response	Name of contact/Position	Contact information
Motherson Enterprises Limited	16 September 2013/Formal Meeting/Visited their office	Gunasingh Prabahar/Managing Director	+260 0967 204173 mothersonenterprises @ yahoo. com
Zambia Development Agency (ZDA)	19 September 2013/Formal Meeting/Visited their office	Moses K. Mwanakatwe/Manager Business Development	+260 9778 77683 mmwanakatwe@ zda. org. zm
Zambia Land Alliance (ZLA)	18 September 2013/Formal Meeting/Visited their office	Henry Machina/Dimuna Phiri/Executive Director/Re-search	+260 977 240823 henrymachina@ gmail. com
University of Zambia	17 September 2013/Formal Meeting/Visited their office	Kamini Krishna J. B. Phiri	Kaminik04@ yahoo. com +260977804459 Jube56@ yahoo. com

Annexe 2　Log of those who responded

A. Companies

Danma Corporation Limited

ETG Trading Company Limited

Motherson Enterprises Limited

Olam International Limited

Astro Holdings (Ex – director of Tata Zambia)

B. Government/public bodies

Zambian Development Agency

India Business Council of Zambia

Indian High Commission

University of Zambia

Confederation of Indian Industry (CII)

Federation of Indian Chambers of Commerce

and Industry （FICCI）

Indian Social Action Forum （INSAF）

PEACE

Kalpavriksh

Zambia Embassy

National Foundation for India （NFI），

Ministry of External Affairs

Mines，Minerals and People

Food and Agriculture Centre of Excellence

Avignam Group

EXIM Bank – India

C. Civil society organisation

Zambia Land Alliance

D. Parameters used for selecting companies：

Indian origin

Involvement in agriculture sector in Zambia

Registered in the Patents and Companies

Registration Agency

Good and quick response to enquiry

E. Some companies were omitted because they：

Did not respond to calls and e – mails

Are not registered in India

F. In Zambia，the research team contacted the

following：

i）Companies

Danma Corporation Limited

ETG Trading Company Limited

Motherson Enterprises Limited

Olam International Limited

ii) Government/public bodies

Zambian Development Agency

India Business Council of Zambia

Indian High Commission

University of Zambia

iii) Civil society organisation

Zambia Land Alliance

iv) Information was collected through the

following sources:

Patents and Companies Registration

Agency (PACRA), Government of Zambia

Indian Business Council of Zambia (IBCZ)

Internet Search

Information also received from other

sources such as university and academia

The research team could not reach the

following:

Export Trading Group

S. P. Group

Continental Ginery

Savanna Streams

Crown Millers Ltd

Zambian National Farmers Union

Satkar Limited

Earthstone Limited

Induszam Limited

Champions Limited

Annexe 3   List of experts contacted in Delhi

Institution/ Company	Response	Name of contact/ Position	Contact information
Confederation of Indian Industry (CII)	Positive	Ms. Indrayani Mulay, Deputy Director, International Division	Confederation of Indian Industry (CII), The Mantosh Sondhi Centre 23 Institutional Area, Lodi Road, New Delhi – 110003 Tel: 91 11 24629994 – 7 Extn 368/24653092 (D) Fax: 91 11 24601298 Mob: 91 9810750611 Email: indrayani. mulay@ cii. in Website – www. cii. in
Federation of Indian Chambers of Commerce and Industry (FICCI)	Positive	Ms. Shiela Sudhakaran. Assistant Secretary General FICCI Africa Desk	FICCI, Federation House, Tansen Marg, New Delhi – 110001 Phone: +91 11 23738760 – 70 Ext. : 380, 23322564 (D) Fax: +91 11 23765316 (D), 23320714 Email: shiela. jbc@ ficci. com
Indian Social Action Forum (INSAF)	Positive	Mr. Wilfred	A 124/6 Katwaria Sarai, New Delhi 110016 Phone: +91 11 26517814 Fax: +91 11 26517814 Email: insafdelhi@ gmail. com
PEACE	Positive	Mr. Anil Chowdhary	F – 93, Katwaria Sarai New Delhi 110016 Mobile: 9811119347 Email: anilpeace@ gmail. com
Kalpavriksh	Positive	Mr. Ashish Kothari	Flat no 5, 2nd Floor, Shri Dutta Krupa, 908, Deccan Gymkhana, Pune 411004, Maharashtra, India Phone: +91 – 20 – 25670979, 25675450 Fax: +91 – 20 – 25654239 Email: kalpavriksh. info@ gmail. com kalpavriksh. delhi@ gmail. com chikikothari@ gmail. com

续表

Institution/Company	Response	Name of contact/Position	Contact information
Zambia Embassy	Unresponsive		Address Zambian High Commission in New Delhi, India D/54, Vasant Vihar New Delhi India Telephone (+91) 11 –2615 0271 (+91) 11 –26150270 E – mail: zambiand@ sify. com
National Foundation for India (NFI)	Does not have the requisite information pertaining to this study	Mr. Amitabh Behar, Executive Director	amitabh. behar@ gmail. com
Ministry of External Affairs	Follow up underway	Mr. Alok Ranjan Jha, Deputy Secretary (E&SA)	Ministry of External Affairs Room 67 – C, South Block New Delhi – 110 011 Phone: 011 – 23010364 Email: dsesa@ mea. gov. in
Mines, Minerals and People	Positive	Mr. R. Sreedhar	
Food and Agriculture Centre of Excellence	Positive	Ms. Kavery Ganguly	India Habitat Centre, Core 4A, 4th Floor, Lodi Road, New Delhi – 110003 Phone: 2468 2230 – 35 Fax: 24682226 Email: face@ face – cii. in/info@ face – cii. in Website: www. face – cii. in By mail: kavery. ganguly@ cii. in
Avignam Group	Positive	Mr. Abhilash Puljal, Managing Director	Mr. Abhilash Puljal, Managing Director Avignam group Address: First Floor, 8 School Lane, Bengali Market, New Delhi – 110001, India Phone: +91 8800969966 Facsimile: +91 9873109966 Mobile: +91 9871133726 Email: abhilash. puljal@ avignam. com Website: www. avignam. com twitter: @ avignamgroup ǀ facebook: www. facebook. com/avignamgroup

续表

Institution/ Company	Response	Name of contact/ Position	Contact information
EXIM Bank		Mr. Sriram Subra-maniam	Phone: 91 - 11 - 23326375 E - mail: eximndro@ eximbankindia. in Fax: 91 - 11 - 23322758

Annexe 4　Agencies unreachable

Embassies

The research team contacted Mr. Alok Ranjan Jha, Deputy Secretary (E& SA) via email. He suggested contacting Mr. Mahaveer Singhvi, Director (E&SA) and Mr. Srikant Chaterjee, Under Secretary (SAF) who heads Zambia division. The team contacted both but due to their schedules they were unable to give an appointment.

Several attempts were also made to establish contact, telephonically, via email and even by a personal visit, but without success. They were not receptive about scheduling a meeting.

EXIM Bank

Officials were contacted via email but there was no response.

图书在版编目（CIP）数据

赞比亚农业外国直接投资：减贫和发展的机会与挑
战 / 刘海方，刘均主编． -- 北京：社会科学文献出版
社，2017.4

ISBN 978 - 7 - 5097 - 9820 - 1

Ⅰ. ①赞…　Ⅱ. ①刘…　②刘…　Ⅲ. ①农业投资 - 外
商直接投资 - 研究 - 赞比亚　Ⅳ. ①F347.35

中国版本图书馆 CIP 数据核字（2016）第 245719 号

赞比亚农业外国直接投资
——减贫和发展的机会与挑战

主　　编／刘海方　刘　均

出 版 人／谢寿光
项目统筹／高明秀
责任编辑／王晓卿　何晋东

出　　版／社会科学文献出版社·当代世界出版分社（010）59367004
　　　　　　地址：北京市北三环中路甲 29 号院华龙大厦　邮编：100029
　　　　　　网址：www. ssap. com. cn
发　　行／市场营销中心（010）59367081　　59367018
印　　装／北京季蜂印刷有限公司

规　　格／开 本：787mm × 1092mm　1/16
　　　　　　印 张：17.75　字 数：273 千字
版　　次／2017 年 4 月第 1 版　2017 年 4 月第 1 次印刷
书　　号／ISBN 978 - 7 - 5097 - 9820 - 1
定　　价／79.00 元

本书如有印装质量问题，请与读者服务中心（010 - 59367028）联系